ORGANISATION TODT

ORGANISATION TODT

FROM AUTOBAHNS TO THE ATLANTIC WALL

Edited by John Christopher

Based on the official British Report MIRS/MR-OT/5/45,
THE ORGANISATION TODT HANDBOOK
published in London, March 1945.

AMBERLEY

First published 2014

Amberley Publishing
The Hill, Stroud
Gloucestershire, GL5 4EP

www.amberley-books.com

British Library Cataloguing in Publication Data.
A catalogue record for this book is available from the British Library.

ISBN 978 1 4456 3856 0
eBook 978 1 4456 3873 7

Typeset in 10pt on 12pt Sabon.
Typesetting and Origination by Amberley Publishing.
Printed in the UK.

Contents

The Organisation Todt was responsible for all major civil and military construction projects, both pre-war within Germany and during the war throughout the occupied territories from France to Russia. These included the construction of the Reichsautobahn, the Westwall – otherwise known as the 'Siegfried Line' – which ran along Germany's border with France, and the extensive Atlantikwall which was intended to deter an Allied landing on the Continent. Above, construction work is underway for a U-boat base on the French Atlantic coast.

Introduction

From the Autobahns to the Atlantikwall fortifications strung along the west coast of France, mainland Europe is littered with the relics of the Third Reich and, unlike the Reich itself, many are so massive and so solidly built that they will last for a thousand years to come. From bunkers to bridges, from the V-1 and V-2 weapon sites to the submarine bases and subterranean factories, these remarkable structures were built by the Organisation Todt, the OT, which was founded by the charismatic engineer Fritz Todt and, after his death in February 1942, run by Albert Speer, Hitler's architect and the Reich Minister of Armaments and War Production. Although not a military organization as such, let there be no doubt that through its construction work the OT literally underpinned the Nazis' stranglehold on the occupied territories. Not only through the fortifications but also through the systematic and highly controversial use of enforced labour drawn from the populations of the vanquished countries.

At its peak the OT consisted of a force of almost two million men and women, and as the foreword to this publication reminds us, it carried out, in the space of a little over five years, the most impressive building programme since Roman times. So it is all the more surprising to discover that so little has been published about the OT in the English language. Yes there are many books about the structures themselves, but these mostly approach the subject from an engineering, architectural or, mostly, a military point of view. This is understandable; putting aside their antecedence they are impressive structures on any level and the fortifications, the casements, bunkers and observation towers of the Atlantikwall are not only impressive by virtue of their scale, but their clean, sometimes geometrical lines, sliced with slots or apertures can beguile the observer in the same way as a piece of abstract sculpture or the stark lines of the Brutalist architectural movement. That, however, must the subject for another day. Instead of the physical remnants of its work, this book focusses on the lesser known side of the Organisation Todt, the nitty-gritty of its inner workings, administration and day-to-day operation.

The main text is drawn from an official wartime report by the Military Intelligence Research Section (MIRS) – *Handbook of the Organisation Todt (OT)* – which was published in March 1945, only a couple of months before the Second World War in Europe came to an end. This publication date seems remarkably late in the course of the war to be of much use, but there were several very good reasons why the Allies needed this information on the OT. Firstly, there was an urgent requirement to understand every aspect of the defences that they might encounter on the advance into Germany. An understanding of the OT, especially of the way its personnel functioned, would expedite intelligence gathering, including the interrogation of prisoners, in the field. The second stemmed from a genuine concern about the scale of planned German resistance to be expected, not only during the closing stages of the war but also in the immediate aftermath. Rumours of a fanatical guerilla organization – known as Werwolf (the German spelling of Werewolf) – had begun to surface after the Allied landings at Normandy. This threat had been nurtured by the Nazi Minister of Propaganda, Joseph Goebbels, primarily through radio broadcasts. In a series of broadcasts, including the infamous 'Werwolf speech' of 23 March 1945, he urged every German to fight to the death, 'to do or die against the Allied armies, who are preparing to enslave Germans'. The members of the Werwolf group were mostly recruited from the SS and the Hitler Jugend, or Hitler Youth, but given their in-depth knowledge of construction and engineering, Allied Intelligence also feared that members of the OT might also be prime and highly useful candidates as saboteurs:

> OT is indispensable in any protracted resistance the Nazis may intend to offer. Their experience in making the most of terrain in the building of field fortifications, in the building of underground tunnels, depots of all kinds, hide-outs, shelters, in fact, of regular subterranean living an operating quarters of vast proportions, is unique. OT personnel left behind in Allied-occupied territory are ideally fitted for sabotage on vital plants and factories. It is, however, as a post-war political organization that OT presents the greatest potential danger. Its officials are, with few exceptions, not only early and ardent Nazis belonging to either the SS or SA, but have been leaders of men for many years. They have extensive foreign collaborationist connections in practically every country of Europe, besides being in touch with those who were evacuated by OT into Germany. They know through liaison the methods of SD, Kripo, Gestapo and Geheime Feldpolizei. Their connections with high officials of the SS and SA are both intimate and of long standing. Above all, their standing in the Party, combined with their technical qualifications, will earn them the confidence of Nazi leaders in any plans for a last-ditch resistance.

Clearly Goebbels had been masterful in sowing the seeds of fear in the minds of the Allies, but he had seriously misread the mood of the Germans population and their desire to put the long and humiliating war behind them. Resistance proved to be minimal and the individual members of the OT, who had been regarded with so much suspicion, did their part in the reconstruction of war-torn Germany.

About this book
The Handbook of the Organisation Todt (OT), or to give its official designation MIRS/MR-OT/5/45, was published in London in March 1945 and has since been declassified. It contains information gathered by the intelligence agencies, mostly through their activities in the newly-liberated regions of Europe following the D-Day landings at Normandy in June 1944. By the spring of 1945 they had had ample opportunity to interrogate a great many former OT personnel and large quantities of documents had come into their possession. Accordingly the report goes into great detail, for example we learn of the numbers of pairs of socks that an NCO was issued – three pairs as it happens – and the various rates that the personnel were paid (pretty well by general standards). However, it is the human story that is the most compelling and amid the minutiae, every now and again a detail really hits home. For example, in the section on the rates of pay for the labourers it states:

> 15% of the gross wages of Jewish workers are retained for the so-called Judenabgabe (special tax on Jews).

More than anything else, this single, almost-casual, detail tells of the very real toll of misery and suffering that went into the construction of these concrete monuments to tyranny.

On a practical note, the original handbook is a very thick document and accordingly some information has been edited or excluded, such as the extensive Anexes consisting of long lists of names and addresses of known OT personalities, OT-Firms and a long list of abbreviations, has not been included. In addition some of the tables were not clear enough for reproduction in this edition. Minor changes have also been made to smooth the text for the modern reader. Every effort has been made to be truthful to the original document, but the reader should always bear in mind that the information it contains, and the phraseology used, is that of those times.

Only a few photographs were included in the original, specifically the uniforms and insignia, and the remaining images have been added for this new edition. Sources are acknowledged at the back of the book.

Foreword to
the 1945 Handbook

Just as an OT construction unit completed a specific mission somewhere in Europe, permission to begin work on it promptly arrived from Berlin.

The above incident is cited not so much in a spirit of facetiousness, but to illustrate, in a striking manner, the administrative complexities inherent in a paramilitary organisation of the size and extent of OT, as it has evolved over a period of five years. Up to only about six months ago, the Organisation Todt was active in every country of Continental Europe except Sweden, Switzerland, Spain, Portugal and Turkey.

A basic reason for the ponderousness of OT administrative machinery was the fact that the Nazis intended to use the Organisation as a wedge in the regimentation of labour as part of the 'New Order' in a post-war Europe. Long-range plans of this type require stabilisation, and stabilisation involves administration.

In this connection the OT trained and harboured a small army of collaborationists, who, already employed as leaders of foreign labour units within the OT, were groomed for political leadership of European labour with the advent of the 'final Nazi victory'. A considerable number of these men have evacuated with OT into Germany.

As to OT's post-war tasks in the reconstruction of Europe, grandiose plans were made for it; captured German documents reveal visions of express highways radiating from Berlin to the Persian Gulf through Baghdad, and along the Baltic coast to link up with a highway through Finland and to run the length of Norway. A system of canals was to link the Mediterranean and the Atlantic through southern France, as part of a communications scheme connecting Bordeaux with the Black Sea. Part of this programme had already been put into execution, notably in Norway and the Balkans.

OT's comparatively high wages, bonuses, allowances, allotments, and the relative safety it offers, in contrast to combat service in the armed forces, were, and still are,

Adolf Hitler inaugurates a newly completed section of the Reichsautobahn. The building of the modern motorway network achieved many things. Not only did it create thousands of jobs within the construction industry, it also represented a tangible symbol of progress under the Nazi regime, and, not insignificantly, put in place the infrastructure needed for the large scale military projects of the war. Below: The massive scale of the submarine pens under construction in occupied France is evident in this photograph from *Fritz Todt – Der Mensch, Der Ingenieur, Der Nationalsozialist,* a tribute published after his death in 1942.

very attractive to the German male faced with the alternate choice. In fact supervisory assignments in OT were generally reserved for Old Party Fighters, Party members with influential connections, and more recently for older SS members in rapidly increasing numbers. High officials especially, are, with few exceptions, members of the original staff or Nazi technicians which the Party formed as soon as it came into power, and which is represented at the present time by Hauptamt Technik of the NSDAP, headed by Fritz Todt until his death, and now headed by Speer. The result is that while OT is administratively a Ministry agency and not Party formation, in proportion it harbours, at least in its permanent administrative staff, possibly more ardent Nazis than a regular formation of the Party.

If the picture as outlined above has given the impression that nepotism and administrative lag vitally impaired OT's operational efficiency, its record of past performances should serve to dispel the notion. It has carried out, in the space of a little over five years, the most impressive building programme since Roman times. It has developed methods of standardisation and rationalisation in construction to an extent and on a scale heretofore unattempted. The speed with which it effects air raid damage repairs on vital communication systems is indeed impressive.

Today OT is indispensable in any protracted resistance the Nazis may intend to offer. Their experience in making the most of terrain in the building of field fortifications, in the building of underground tunnels, depots of all kinds, hide-outs, shelters, in fact, of regular subterranean living and operating quarters of vast proportions, is unique. OT personnel left behind in Allied-occupied territory are ideally fitted for sabotage on vital plants and factories.

It is, however, as a post-war political organisation that OT presents the greatest potential danger. Its officials are, with few exceptions, not only early and ardent Nazis belonging to either the SS or SA, but have been leaders of men for many years. They have extensive foreign collaborationist connections in practically every country of Europe, besides being in touch with those who were evacuated by OT into Germany. They know through liaison the methods of SD, Kripo, Gestapo, and Geheime Feldpolizei. Their connections with high officials of the SS and SA are both intimate and of long standing. Above all, their standing in the Party, combined with their technical qualifications, will earn them the confidence of Nazi leaders in any plans for a last-ditch resistance.

In regard to this handbook itself, its contents attempt to give as comprehensive a description of the administration and operation of OT as a study of available documentary material would allow. It is as up-to-date as can reasonably be expected of a basic reference book, especially in view of the rapidity with which the current situation is changing. Finally the book should prove equally useful either in the event of a decision to employ OT's capabilities in some form or another for the reconstruction of the devastated parts of Europe, or in the event of a decision to demobilise the Organisation in its entirety.

Basic Facts about
the Organisation Todt

1. OT is not a Nazi Party organisation. It is a Reichsbehörde (a Government agency). The exercise of its administrative and executive authority, therefore, is a governmental (ministry) function.

2. OT personnel are classified by the German Government as militia; its German personnel and some of its foreign volunteers have the right to bear arms and resist enemy action. They have furthermore rendered the same oath of lifelong personal loyalty to Hitler as the regular army soldier.

3. OT's war assignment may be defined as the Construction Arm of the Wehrmacht; as such its activities were, until very recently, spread over all of German-occupied Europe. At the present day it exercises functional control over Army, Air Force and Navy construction agencies and facilities including equipment.

4. In addition to the above assignment, the OT had working agreements with the governments of Rumania, Bulgaria and Hungary.

5. OT's chief is the Reichminister for Armament and War Production Dr Albert Speer. In his capacity as head of the OT, he is responsible directly to Hitler. On 24 August 1944, he also took over the building administration inside Greater Germany. Since this date OT has assumed control over all phases of construction inside Greater Germany.

6. OT's central administrative headquarters and highest echelon is the Amt Bau-OT Zentrale in Berlin. Its chief is Ministerial Direktor Dipl. Ing. Xaver Dorsch. He is responsible only to Speer.

7. OT's fundamental characteristic is the co-operation between the German building industry and the German Government. The building industry furnishes the technical part in the form of individual building firms, with their staffs and equipment. The government furnishes the manpower and material. These two elements, government and industry, are fused under OT control.

8. The above arrangement was evolved by Prof. Fritz Todt for the specific task of completing the 'Siegfried Line', in May 1938. It was so successful that the personnel remained as a permanent construction organisation for the German Armed Forces.

9. The executive of an OT-Firm has a dual function; as the contractor he takes care of his own interests; as a fully paid officer in the OT he takes care of OT's interests.

10. Germany at present is divided into an operational area comprising eight Einsatzgruppen (Area Control Staffs, Army Group level) sub-divided into twenty-two Einsätze (Area Control Staffs, Army level).

11. OT authorities claim to have directly employed a force of a million and a half of both German and non-German personnel at its period of greatest expansion, May 1942 to May 1943. Indirectly OT may have benefited from the labour of over two million men and women. At the present time it is estimated that the OT controls personnel numbering approximately 1,000,000 inside Greater Germany.

12. The German personnel of OT never exceeded 350,000. Due to manpower shortage, the increasing demands of the Wehrmacht and industry, the estimate before D-Day was not over 75,000 and probably less. At the present time it is estimated at approximately 200,000.

13. The two basic types of operation are: (1) mobile (mobiler Einsatz), (2) static (stationärer Einsatz).

14. The Oberbauleitung (abbreviated OBL) is the basic administrative HQ for the operational sector of the static type of operation.

15. The entire trend at the present is to give a high potential mobility to all OT construction units (firms and personnel), thus ensuring a transformation of static to mobile type of operation on short notice.

16. OT's forward echelon (OT-Front) normally does not go beyond the area immediately behind the front lines. Usually it operates in the zone of communications.

17. The number of foreign workers in OT construction units may not be larger than can be controlled by an irreducible minimum of German supervisory personnel (firm engineers, foremen, etc.). This minimum is about 10% of the total personnel in rear areas, and 25% in the forward areas.

18. The transport facilities for OT are provided by three originally separate organisations; the NSKK-Transportbrigade Speer, NSKK-Transportbrigade Todt and the Legion Speer, unified in 1942 under the Term NSKK-Transportgruppe Todt, now known as Transportkorps Speer.

19. Although not a Nazi Party organisation OT is under the political control of the Allgemeine SS with an SS Liaison Officer in every echelon. Since May 1944, this control has been tightened by the inclusion of additional SS personnel in key positions throughout the OT.

PART I

History of the OT

A. 1938 to D-Day

Definition

The OT has been variously defined by the enemy. Hitler called it 'an organisation entrusted with the execution of construction tasks playing a decisive role in the war effort'. Fritz Todt, its founder, proudly referring to it as 'a task force', and deprecating the gradual increase of administrative routine, said on one occasion: 'We are called Organisation Todt without ever having organised.' The German Supreme Command, as early as 1940, stated officially that members of the OT were to be regarded as 'Miliz' (militia). The Organisation in one of its circulars termed itself 'a body charged with military construction for defensive purposes'.

Fritz Todt's Career to 1938

In May 1938, the Army Fortress Engineers had been working on the Siegfried Line, or 'Westwall' as it is now called by the Germans, for two years without any prospect of completing it in time to fit into the Nazi military schedule. The General Inspektor für das Deutsche Strassenwesen (Inspector General of German Roadways), Dr Todt, was the man picked to take over the job from the Army.

Fritz Todt was born on 4 September 1891, in Pforzheim, Baden. He obtained the decree of Dr Ing. (Doctor of Engineering) from the Munich Technical Institute and entered the Imperial Army in 1914, as Lieutenant of the Reserve. He transferred to the Air Force, was wounded in August 1918 in air combat, received the Iron Cross and the Order of the House of Hohenzollern, but still held the rank of Lieutenant at the conclusion of the First World War. Shortly after, he entered the employ of the construction firm, Sager & Woerner at Munich, a concern specialising in road and tunnel construction, and became its manager. He joined the Nazi Party as early as 1922, soon won Hitler's friendship and confidence, and was one of the founders of the Nationalsozialistischer Bund

23.9.1933 Erſter Spatenſtich
23.9.1936 1000 km Autobahn fertig

Above left: Leutenant Fritz Todt in 1917, wearing the Iron Cross awarded during his time as a reconnaissance observer in the Luftstreitkrafte. Above right: Todt is shown standing behind Hitler who is getting his hands dirty in this 1936 propaganda postcard. Below: Dr Todt the family man, pictured on a skiing trip with his son, also called Fritz, and his wife, Ilsebill.

deutscher Technik (Nazi League of German Technicians) which then used the SS training school at Flassenburg near Klumbach as a training and research institute. (The school has since been appropriated by the OT as an indoctrination centre for its ranking personnel.) The League was especially concerned with opening new industrial fields including those of the armament industry, leading to the economic independence of the Reich and to the solution of the unemployment problem. Todt, for instance, wrote a paper in about 1930 entitled, 'Proposals and Financial Plans for the Employment of One Million Men'.

The project as outlined in substance was a plan for a Reich highway system, incidentally, said to have been based on a similar study issued by the German Ministry of Economics as early as 1923. On 28 June 1933, a state-owned public corporation was established by Cabinet decree under the title of Reichsautobahnen (Reich Highway System) and a permanent administrative office with the title of Generalinspektor für das Deutsche Strassenwesen (Inspectorate General of German Roadways) was established simultaneously and put under the direction of Todt. The corporation was set up as a subsidiary of the Reichsbahn (State Railways) which exercised parental control over it. The German Armed Forces, however, retained general powers of control over its plans, which were exercised through Fritz Todt as the Generalinspektor für das Deutsche Strassenwesen. The above arrangement allowed the railway authorities to see to it that the projected highway system would not compete with railway traffic and left control over decisions of strategy to the Supreme Command. The Reichsautobahnen became operative in August 1933 with an initial capital of 50,000,000 Reichsmarks (RM). Its staff was composed of a small number of administrative officials and engineers. In June 1933, it ceased to be a corporation and became a government department, with a staff mainly provided by the Reichsbahn. Later, in June 1941, the Reichsbahn relinquished the greater measure of the administrative control over the Reichsautobahnen, and the latter became independent as far as internal organisation was concerned. The original programme was completed in December 1938, with the building of a super-highway network of some 2,500 miles.

Westwall (Siegfried Line)
Todt took over the construction of the Siegfried Line on 28 May 1938. He used the same technical staff that had directed the construction of the by then practically completed highway system: a combination of personnel of the Inspectorate General of German Roadways and technical representatives of building firms. He established OT's headquarters at Wiesbaden, leaving the Organisation administratively, however, under the Inspectorate General. Most of the manpower working on the highway system was likewise gradually transferred to the Siegfried Line. In fact OT began life as the successor to

Adolf Hitler, with Todt standing beside him, inspecting progress on the Reichsautobahnen in Austria, April 1938. The Führer had promised the German people a bright future with modern, open roads and an affordable KdF-Wagen – later to become the VW Beetle – within the reach of every family through a stamp-savings scheme. In the event no consumer ever got their hands on the car as the factory was coverted to production of the military Kubelwagen.

The Nazis didn't invent the Autobahn. There had been previous plans for controlled-access highways under the Weimar Republic, but when the Nazis seized power they also laid claim to the autobahns, presenting them afresh as the Fuhrer's idea and labelling them as 'Adolf Hitler's Roads'. Work commenced in the spring of 1934 and the first stretch, between Frankfurt and Darmstadt, opened on 19 May 1935. When work ceased, in 1941, the combined German/Austrian network ran for 2,373 miles (3,820 km). The architecture of the Reichsautobahen is undeniably striking with its incredibly modern, clean lines and the bold mix of materials. Opposite: 'Concrete and steel in harmony', a viaduct in central Germany. Right: A masonry bridge in western Germany. Below: Rest-house and petrol station, in other words, motorway services.

Fritz Todt, in uniform on the far right, heads a column of labourers to commence work on the Frankfurt section of the Rechsautobahnen, September 1933.

A scene of animated activity in this staged photo of OT personnel working on the Westwall. Some are in uniform by this time, and most wear the 'Org. Todt' armband. The photograph appeared in an article entitled 'The Men of the OT', published in *Signal*, the German propaganda magazine that was distributed throughout occupied Europe in twenty languages including Dutch and French, plus an English edition which was aimed at a USA readership. See also, pages 80–81.

the Reichsautobahn project. In view of the urgency of the political situation, operational methods were greatly intensified, and co-operation between the construction industry and the government, close as it had been in the case of the Autobahn, became even closer in the case of the OT. Todt himself enjoyed the confidence of the OT construction industry because of his official position and undoubted executive abilities; moreover, he had an extensive acquaintance among its leading executives and was personally well liked. When, therefore, he proposed a programme which, in the space of a little over two months, would provide a twenty-four-hour working schedule for over a half-million men and one-third of the entire German construction industry, the reaction of the latter was extremely favorable. The prospect of gainful employment and the patriotic aspects of the task were at least equally effective as persuasive factors. In addition to what was invested by the construction industry in the form of technical and clerical staffs, and skilled mechanical labour and equipment, the government provided rolling stock such as freight cars and lorries lent to the OT by the State Railways and the Postal Ministry. Of the half-million manpower, about 100,000 consisted of the Army Fortress OT Engineer personnel which had been working on the 'Wall' when Todt took over, assisted by about an equal number of RAD (Reich Labor Service) personnel. The other 300,000 was drawn for the most part from the civilian manpower that had constructed the super-highway system. Thus the OT was operationally launched. Apparently Hitler himself gave the organisation its present name when, in a speech on the Nazi 1938 anniversary celebration (6 September) in Nuremberg, he referred to the gigantic construction enterprise as the 'Organisation Todt'.

The bulk of the work on the Siegfried Line was considered completed early in 1940 – just before the Campaign in the West. OT's methods of construction, which even then depended a good deal on standardisation, had been an unqualified success. Over 14,000 bunkers were built and 189,000,000 cubic feet of concrete were poured into the 'Wall' in a little over a year and a half. The work had been carried out during a period of political turmoil: it began practically on the day of the signing of the Munich Pact, not quite three months after the annexation of Austria, and it drew to completion in September 1939, when Poland was attacked.

Fritz Todt 1939–1941
Todt was appointed General Bevollmächtigter für die Regelung der Bauwirtschaft (Plenipotentiary General for the Regulation of the Construction Industry) by Göring on 9 December 1938. Hitler appointed him a Generalmajor in the Luftwaffe on 19 October 1939. Other appointments followed: in recognition of his uncommon ability to adapt adequate technical methods to meet the problems involved in co-ordinating war production – and of his Party standing – he was

appointed Generalinspektor für Sonderaufgaben des Vierjahresplanes (Inspector General for Special Tasks of the Four Year Plan) in February 1940. A few weeks later he was given the post of Reichsminister für Bewaffnung und Munition (Reich Minister for Armament and Munitions). In the summer of 1941 he was appointed Generalinspektor für Wasser und Energie (Inspector General for Water and Power) putting him in charge of the programme projected for waterways, installations, bridges, hydroelectrical power and water supply systems (a field in which Todt himself had previously shown considerable interest). His standing in the Party had already been acknowledged by his appointments, to the rank of SA-Obergruppenführer, to the post of Leiter des Hauptamts für Technik (Chief of the Technical Department of the Nazi Party), and to the office of Reichswalter des NSBT (National Chairman of the Nazi League of German Technicians). Finally Todt became a Reichsleiter (Member of Nazi Party Supreme Directorate). In the field of learning he had been awarded the honorary degree of Professor Extraordinarius.

War Employment of OT

It is not at all unlikely that OT's role as a paramilitary organisation performing the tasks of a self-contained, heavy-duty and highly mobile Engineer Corps was foreseen by the Nazis in their preparation of military plans. Very probably Dr Todt had been charged with the formulation of such plans for some time. At any rate, the OT was promptly put on a war footing in September 1939 on the outbreak of war and the Organisation was officially declared to be a Wehrmachtsgefolge (Army Auxiliary Body). There were, accordingly, two basic organisational changes. One was the establishment of the administrative OT Frontführung (Front Area Personnel Section) which took over the billeting and messing of personnel, tasks formerly performed by the DAF (Deutsche Arbeitsfront – German Labour Front) and which consolidated all aspects of personnel management in its hands. The other was the change-over from voluntary enrolment of construction firms to their conscription into the OT. Both firms and their staffs became subject to this conscription and formed the nucleus of OT mobile units. OT's first operational test came in the 1940 campaign in the West. Its primary task then was to restore communications in the wake of the advancing German armies, assuring thereby the flow of supplies to the front lines. This type of operation was performed by mobile, specialised units consisting of OT firms and comprising their clerical and technical staffs, and the worker element assigned to the firms by OT. The unit carried two designations: one was that of OT Firmen-Einheit (OT Firm Unit) usually contracted to OT Einheit or simply Einheit. Thus the term Einheit in the OT has become synonymous with OT-Firmen, or concern, which is contracted to OT. The other designation for OT units was that of Bautrupps (Construction Detachments), a survival of the term given to the Army construction units before

Having served in the Luftstreitkrafte in the First World War, Fritz Todt was a keen aviator and is shown 'at the helm' travelling between construction site locations.

About to enter a Luftwaffe transport aircraft – it appears to be a Junkers Ju 86 – Dr Todt is greeted by Flugzeugführer Hotz. On 8 February 1942, Todt was killed when his aircraft crashed shortly after leaving the Wolfsschanze (Wolf's Lair) airfield near Rastenburg.

the OT came into existence. It indicates the fact that it was these troops that the new Organisation was expected to replace, especially in a more or less fluid military zone. The above kind of operation became one of the two basic types of OT's employments: mobiler Einsatz (Mobile Commitment or Operation), and the other type is the stationärer Einsatz (Static Commitment or Operation).

OT 1940–1941

As the military situation became stabilised in the West, evidence of a similar process of stabilisation became apparent in the OT. Most of the construction work in the West, from the end of the French Campaign to late in 1941, was on coastal installations along the Channel and the Atlantic, from Belgium to Brittany. The entire area was called Einsatzküste West (Coastal Operational Area West). The OT administrative HQ was at Lorient and controlled a number of construction sectors strung along the coast. Administrative control by the Lorient HQ was none too strong; administrative control from Berlin was still weaker. The OT Zentrale (Central OT HQ) at Berlin had not yet been established and the official name of the Organisation still was Inspektor-General des Strassenwesen, OT. Fritz Todt by 1941, however, had long outgrown the OT, and such administrative co-ordination as existed was provided by the autonomous corporate Wirtschaftsgruppe Bauindustrie (Economic Group: Construction Industry) which issued directions to OT firms. The result was that influential OT firms in the West coalesced and formed a firm hierarchy, making a bid for control of the Organisation. OT firms reaped a golden harvest during the period from autumn 1940 to early spring 1942. Long-term projects of dubious priority and doubtful value were begun and abandoned. Large numbers of fictitious personnel were carried on payrolls inasmuch as the Reich Government granted premiums to firms for each worker recruited by their efforts. Not only was centralised administration on the part of OT weak during that period, but OT's operational sphere was limited to Army projects. The Air Force and the Navy, while they took advantage of OT's proximity for operational liaison, made separate contracts with individual firms for the construction of their projects. Construction of such coastal installations as submarine bases and such installations as landing fields for the Air Force comprised a considerable part of the military construction programme in the West from 1940 to 1942. Consequently large firms like Strabag – contraction for Strassenbau Aktien Gesellschaft (or Road Construction Company) – either worked exclusively for the Air Force or the Navy, or they contracted only part of their personnel to the OT and kept the rest of their personnel outside of the OT in their capacity as private firms. The West (France, Belgium and Holland) is drawn upon as an example, but the above situation was also basically applicable to Norway and Denmark. On the other hand, the military situation in Russia during the first

Todt's funeral procession passes through Wilhelmstrasse, in Berlin, headed by this over-sized wreath from the Führer. He was buried in the Invalidenfriedhof (Invalid's Cemetery), the traditional resting place of the Prussian Army, which is located in the Scharnhorst Strasse.

year of the war in the East (1941) was too operational to allow any centralised administration there, let alone administration from Berlin.

Speer's Innovations

Fritz Todt died on 8 February 1942, in an aeroplane accident, survived by his wife, a son and a daughter. He was succeeded in all his functions by Prof. Albert Speer. Shortly afterwards, a new basic policy made itself felt. It consisted of a series of internal moves all tending toward co-ordination within, and centralisation of, the Organisation. The central HQ at Berlin, OT-Zentrale or OTZ, was established about that time, and its full official name became Generalinspektor für das Strassenwesen, OTZ. At the head of it was (and still is) Ministerialdirektor Dorsch. Another move was the establishment of a uniform basic pay tariff (to become effective 1 January 1943) for all OT worker personnel, equalling, except for those wages paid to forced labour, Wehrmacht basic pay. In addition a new and elaborate scale of bonuses, allowances, compensations and allotments was drawn up, and Dr Schmelter was appointed Sondertreuhänder der Arbeit für die OT (Special Labour Trustee for the OT). A third move was the gradual tightening of central control over OT firms, including issuance of a uniform type of contract between the OT and its firms.

A fourth move is discussed in some detail below. It was an attempt at greater organisational co-ordination within the various German-occupied territories in Europe, that is the West (France, Belgium, Holland), Norway and Denmark, Russia and Finland, the Balkans. (The OT did not become active in Italy on a large scale until the autumn of 1943. The first area of any size within Germany proper, the Ruhr area, was not established until about 1 May 1943.) This move, part of the general trend toward stabilisation, already begun late in 1941 in the West in the form of Einsatzgruppe West, was undertaken on a comprehensive scale by OTZ, but never became a reality in the occupied territories with any degree of uniformity. The organisational scheme was, with minor variations, to establish administrative levels in the following order:

OT Zentrale, Berlin (OTZ: Central OT HQ)

Einsatzgruppe (EG: Area Control Staff, Army Group level)

Einsatz (E: Area Control Staff, Army level)

Oberbauleitung (OBL: Basic OT Construction Sector and Admin. HQ)

Bauleitung (BL: Sub-Sector)

Abschnittsbauleitung (ABL: Local Supervisory Staff)

Baustelle (not abbreviated; Construction Site)

The scheme established a consistent chain of command in the organisation, but the inconsistent manner in which it was applied was so common in formerly occupied Europe that it became an utterly unreliable guide to the status of an OT operational area. Most of the confusion resulted from the fact that the term Einsatz had been indiscriminately used for sectors, irrespective of size, in which the OT had committed itself to operational activities. Many of these so-called Einsätze, some of them merely local construction sites, retained their original designation because of the impracticability of reorganisation within their area. Others persisted in clinging to their original designation even after a change of status had been ordered in their case by the OTZ. One fact did, however, emerge from this attempt at co-ordination: the Oberbauleitung (OBL) definitely became the basic operational sector of the OT.

The various moves toward administrative co-ordination and centralised control culminated in an edict issued by Hitler (through the Reich Chancery) on 2 September 1943, containing four clauses:

1. The Reichsminister für Bewaffnung und Munition Speer is head of the OT. He is under the Führer's direct orders and is responsible only to him. (The Ministry has since been changed in name to that of Reichsministerium für Rüstung und Kriegproduktion – Reich Ministry for Armament and War Production and now commonly referred to as the Speer Ministry).

2. The OT can be committed to work by order of its chief anywhere in Greater Germany and in annexed or occupied countries.

3. Clauses 1 and 2 also apply to all transport organisations assigned to the OT.

4. The head of the OT will issue directives for the internal organisation of the OT.

At the same time the OTZ was removed from under the Inspectorate General of German Roadways and became an office in its own right within Speer's Ministry.

Organisation Todt 1942–1943

Internal reorganisation was not the only change which the OT underwent during a period from May 1942 to late 1943. The status of the Organisation itself was revised so that it was included within the priority scheme of war production which by the winter of 1943/44 had encompassed the entire resources of the production machinery of Germany and occupied territory and to the highest degree that in Western Europe. During this period of stabilisation on the Western Front, the greater part of the OT lost its character as a paramilitary engineer corps and became, in essence, a defence industry, constructing not only military installations, but becoming more and more involved in the repair of air-raid damage to vital communications and essential war production plants, and in the construction of new and extensive underground depots, factories and other subterranean installations. It can therefore be pointed out that, from the economic standpoint, the OT became subject to the policies dictated by two public figures. One is the policy dictated by Albert Speer in regard to the comparative priority in supplies allotted to the various armament industries, including OT's great constructional tasks such as the Atlantic Wall begun in May 1942. The other is the policy dictated by SS-Obergruppenführer Fritz Sauckel, the Generalbevollmächtiger für den Arbeitseinsatz (Plenipotentiary-General for Manpower Allocation), in regard to comparative priority in manpower allotment. Speer and Sauckel are at present the two dominant personalities in German war economy.

Speer's Career

Professor Albert Speer's background and career, except for his lack of military experience, are reminiscent of that of Fritz Todt. Like Todt, Speer's early career was in the field of construction. But, whereas Todt's special interest lay in methods of engineering technique, Speer's early interest was in architectural planning and ornamentation. He was born 19 March 1905 in Mannheim, Baden, and attended the Technical Institutes at Karlsruhe, Munich, and Berlin.

Above: Hitler on the left facing both Albert Speer and Fritz Todt, on the right.

Speer had joined the Nazi party in 1931, and through his architectural skills he rose to prominence within the party. In 1934 he was appointed as the head of the Chief Office for Construction, and in 1937 Hitler made him the General Building Inspector for the Reich Capital. In both roles Speer produced a series of notable works including the Zeppelinfeld stadium, the 'cathedral of light' which hosted the Nuremburg rallies, as well as ambitious plans to rebuild Berlin. Following Todt's death he was appointed as the Minister of Armaments and Todt's successor in charge of the OT. *(CMcC)*

He obtained his engineering degree (Dipl. Ing.) from the latter, and stayed on for three years as a research student and faculty assistant. Speer joined the Nazi Party comparatively late, in 1932, and formed personal friendships with both Hitler and Göring. Hitler, as is well known, prides himself on his proficiency as an architect. In fact, he is known to have made suggestions for the plans of what is Speer's best-known work to the outside world – the reconstruction of the Reichskanzlei.

Two of Speer's early appointments in the Party are that of Leiter, Amt 'Schönheit der Arbeit' (Chief of the Bureau 'Beauty of Labour') of the 'Kraft durch Freude' (KdF) Strength Through Joy Movement (a branch of the German Labour Front) which involved the architectural ornamentation of public buildings and that of Unterabteilungsleiter der Reichspropagandaleitung technische und künstlerische Ausgestaltung von Grosskundgebungen (Chief of the Sub-section 'Technical and Artistic Arrangements for Public Mass Demonstrations and Official Meetings' of the Reich Propaganda Ministry). Another early appointment was to the newly created office of the General Bauinspekteur der Reichshauptstadt (Inspector General of Construction for the Reich Capital). Although this office was mainly concerned with the remodelling of Berlin from an aesthetic point of view, it represented an important increase in Speer's functions and powers. For one thing, it led to the creation of the Baustab Speer (Construction Staff Speer). For another, it put Speer in control of the Binnenflotte or Inland Waterways Fleet, which he promptly renamed Transport-Flotte Speer.

It was, however, not until the outbreak of war, and through his contact with Göring, that his stature as a functionary began to increase appreciably, and eventually placed him in a position to become Todt's successor, if not actually his rival, during the former's lifetime. The Baustab Speer was enlarged to form a construction organisation of somewhat over 100,000 men, specialising in construction of airports and airport installations within Germany. The number of NSKK (National Sozialistische Kraftfahr Korps or National Socialist Motor Corps) Units, or NSKK-Baustab Speer as they were called, which had always provided transportation for the organisation, were likewise increased and renamed the NSKK Motor Transport Standarte Speer (NSKK Motor Transport Regiment Speer). As already mentioned, upon Todt's death on 9 February 1942, Speer inherited not only the leadership of the OT but also all of the former's party and government offices and functions. The most important of these numerous government functions is naturally that of head of the 'Speer Ministry' or Ministry of Armament and War Production (which under Speer underwent a reorganisation during the summer and autumn of 1943, and another in the late summer of 1944). He is besides a member of the Zentrale Planung (Central Planning Board), the functions of which are comparable to that of a War Economy Cabinet responsible directly to Göring under the Four

Year Plan. His most important Party rank is that of Reichsleiter (Member of the Nazi Party Supreme Directorate). To return to the OT, Speer incorporated his Baustab into the Organisation when he took over its control. Most, if not all, of the original NSKK Motor Transport Standarte Speer was attached to the DAK (Deutsche Afrika Korps) and to the Army units in Russia. It is nevertheless from the transport aspect that Speer's name has become most prominently connected with OT: the various stages by means of which the Legion Speer (the present transportation unit of the OT) was created are described in the section on Services. The Transportflotte Speer was likewise attached to the OT and performs similar services in bringing up supplies by waterways to coastal and canal sectors of the Organisation.

Comparison of Todt with Speer
In a comparative estimate of the two men, Fritz Todt and Albert Speer, there is a decided temptation to describe the former in favourable terms at the expense of the latter. Todt, was from all accounts, a dynamic personality, impatient with administrative regulations. One might almost say that he executed a job by executing it. He had the true technician's ability of adapting the method of execution to the nature of the operation. Without detracting from Todt's abilities in this respect, Speer obviously is a skilled politician. His abilities as an organiser seem to be on the administrative, rather than on the operational, side. He is said to be a good judge of men as far as picking executive assistants is concerned. Whether any one man, however, even of Todt's stature, could have met Germany's critical problem of war production with anything like the efficiency with which at one time Todt built the Siegfried Line is quite problematical.

OT Construction Activities 1942–1943
As to the OT's activities from May 1942 to autumn 1943, broadly speaking, they were concerned with defensive construction, e.g. the Atlantic Wall in the West, the Ost-Wall in the East, coastal fortifications in Norway and Jutland, and with the beginning of underground installations in Germany proper. Diversion of OT personnel and equipment from the above activities to the repair of Allied air-raid damage in Western Europe including Germany proper (Einsatz Ruhrgebiet) began in the summer of 1943 and had reached the culminating point by the spring of 1944.

OT in the West Before D-Day
The intensity of Allied air raids in the winter and spring of 1943/44 caused a series of readjustments in OT activities in the West, particularly in NW France. Related in chronological order, these readjustments form a pattern of OT

operation under pressure. It not only provides a documented record of the OT's activities in anticipation of D-Day; at the same time it may be assumed to hold good, in general, in regard to its present operations in Germany.

First of all, as a reaction to increased Allied bombing, the Speer Stab für die Ruhr (Speer Special Staff for the Ruhr Area under Dipl. Ing. Sander with HQ at Essen) was established in July 1943 in order to co-ordinate the activities of the agencies engaged in rescue, salvage, repair and reconstruction work in the Ruhr and Rhine valleys. Besides the OT, the Wehrmacht, the DAF (German Labour Front) and Industry were represented on this staff. OT's task was 'to adjust to individual conditions'. As part of this 'adjustment, an OT Bergmann Kompanie (Miners' Company) was created and incorporated in the OT. Einsatz Ruhrgebiet (OT Einsatz Ruhr Area). Its function was to use the skill and experience of its personnel in rescuing people and salvaging property after air raids. Its members belonged to the OT, but their wages continued to be paid by the mine owners. They were housed in barracks and kept almost continuously on the alert. They came from all parts of Germany, mostly, however, from the Rhineland and Westphalia. In most mining districts, each mine had to release one man of its rescue service to work with the OT. Previously these men had been part of the Selbstschutz (Civilian Self-protection Organisation). A report, dated January 1944, mentioned the OT Bergungsregiment Speer (Rescue and Salvage Regiment Speer), which was formed late in 1943, and which worked first in the Ruhr District and subsequently in bomb-damaged locations throughout the Reich. Consisting almost exclusively of German personnel, it used equipment especially developed for reconstruction and salvage operations and was also equipped with steam-shovels, derricks, dredges, etc. At present, the OT in the Ruhr and Rhine valleys continues to carry out these tasks. Manpower for the OT in these bomb saturated areas of the Reich is obtained from prisoner of war personnel in Germany, especially Russian.

In work of a technical and strategic nature, such as repairs to communications systems in large cities, OT skilled personnel is under the over-all direction of the Technische Nothilfe, or TENO (Technical Emergency Corps). Members of TENO, while at work directing repairs for the resumption of normal activities, are at the same time on the alert for signs of sabotage and incipient uprisings.

In January 1944 an order prescribed that employees of OT firms be organised into training units for rifle and pistol practice. The units were termed Wehr- und Ausbildungsgemeinschaften (Defence and Training Units), and elaborate regulations concerning their training programme were laid down. The programme, however, fell through, mainly owing to lack of fit personnel.

Persistent bombings of France by the Allied Air Forces, especially of V-sites and lines of communications, created a restive atmosphere among OT personnel in the affected areas. The lowered morale facilitated desertions amid the confusion following bombing attacks, and reduced periods of productive work. The cumulative effect was to lower output to a critical point. Contributing to all this was the acute shortage of transportation fuel and the disruption caused in the general transport system, which affected OT movement of supplies and personnel.

Consequently, early in 1944, in danger areas, the OT authorities had already decided to continue construction work on only the most essential type of installations, such as, for example, V-sites, and to leave essential repair work, such as vital communication links to mobile Katastropheneinsätze (Major emergency crews). Damage to secondary communications had to be left unrepaired. In line with the above policy, therefore, as soon as work in bomb-target areas was considered completed, OT personnel was shifted to construction work on the Atlantic Wall where it could work under more favourable and stable conditions.

Preparations for Allied Landings

Mobile Emergency Bautrupps (Construction Crews), which were characteristic of the early days in France, when OT was restoring communications during the 1940 campaign in the West, were then reactivated to cope more effectively with air-raid damage. In May 1944, preparations in anticipation of Allied landings really got under way, as far as OT's tasks were concerned. Work on the Atlantic Wall was strictly limited to completing whatever local construction had already been in progress, especially to camouflaging and clearing of fields of fire. On 18 May orders were issued by the German Seventh Army changing the composition of the entire OT in its command area, to mobile units. These units were to serve a twofold purpose. One was to aid the army engineers both in the battle zone and rear areas; the other was to function as emergency air-raid salvage and repair crews. (As things turned out, after the invasion, all of OT's resources in NW France were employed exclusively on the second of these purposes, the repair of air-raid damage, as outlined in an order signed by von Rundstedt on 18 June 1944.) The administrative organisation of the Oberbauleitungen (OBL), however, remained the same, even after the invasion when their HQs were shifted. The firms, however, became the operational units in the field, each firm being responsible for feeding, billeting and paying its entire personnel including the non-German labour units.

Liaison between the Army and the OT was established through the Gebietsingenieur (Army District-Liaison-Engineer to an OBL). The OT units were at this time divided into five main categories:

Type 1

Festungbautrupps (Fortress Construction Detachments). This was the most advanced OT echelon inasmuch as it stayed with the army units defending the coastal fortresses such as St Malo, Brest, and St Nazaire. It consisted of three special types of components: Construction, Harbour and Power supply units. These sub-units were placed at the disposal of the Festungs Kommandeur (Fortress Commander).

Type 2
Bautrupps (Construction Detachments) in the battle zone and zone of communications. These were OT's forward echelon, mobile units which were to work under the direction of army engineers in case of Allied landings. In the meantime, according to an order of the Seventh Army Höhere Pionier Kommandeur (Chief Engineer), their tactical disposition was to be arranged by Festungs Pionier Kommandeur XIX (Fortress Construction Engineer Commander XIX) of that area. These construction units contained many types of special components such as bridge construction, highway construction, demolition, mine clearing, motor vehicle repair, munition handling, railway construction and general construction units. One railway construction unit in Brest was put directly under the Transportoffizier (Transport Officer).

Type 3
Bautrupps (Construction Detachments) in rear areas. These units were placed at the disposal of the General Ingenieur West (Chief Engineer of Army Group West). They contained the following special components: railway and general construction, power supply and guard units.

Type 4
Bautrupps (Construction troops) for German Air Force. They were placed at the disposal of the GAF, through liaison with the Chief Engineer of Army Group West. They consisted of the following components: motor repair, bridge construction, general construction units.

Type 5
Nachschubtrupps (Supply troops) in the battle zone. Remaining (exclusively German) personnel were formed into armed labour groups attached to Divisional and Seventh Army supply units.

Type 6
Arbeitstrupps (labour Detachments) in rear zone. Remaining 'reliable' non-German personnel were formed into un-armed labour detachments and under German guard evacuated to new zones. They were assigned work at supply installations (such as the construction of unloading ramps) in the rear areas, and were placed at the disposal of the Chief Supply Officer of the Seventh Army. Their German personnel were, if possible, to be supplied with small arms.

Type 7

NSKK Transport Units. These were attached partly to Army Supply, partly to OT. The twelve companies of the four battalions so formed, were to be supplied with one or two machine guns each.

On 18 June, as has already been mentioned, a general order was issued by von Rundstedt by which OT units were exclusively assigned to tasks of air-raid salvage and repair work. This order did not materially affect the mobile organisation of OT, as described above. Some changes in the chain of command did occur, however, owing to the fact that the area of activity was to be well in the interior. Only local French labour, not subject to evacuation, was to continue work on the Atlantic Wall. Repairs on highways, bridges were to be carried out under the direction of Army Fortress Engineers in liaison with the Feldkommandantur (Military Regional Command). For the repair of railway bridges, tracks and stations in areas subject to enemy infiltration, the Kommandeur Eisenbahnbaupioniere – West (Commander of the Railway Construction Engineers of Army Group West) was responsible. Repair work could be carried out either under the direction of Army Railway Engineers or of OT engineers.

For repair work on railway tracks and stations in the rear areas, such as the transportation zones Lille, Paris-Nord, Paris-West, Bordeaux and Lyons, the Chief Engineer of Army Group West was responsible. OT worked on these repairs in conjunction with the Chef des Hauptverkehrsdienst (Chief Traffic Officer) of the Wehrmacht in France who supplied the technical personnel, both German and French. The repair of aerodromes was also the responsibility of the Chief Engineer of Army Group West. On this work, OT worked in conjunction with the Luftwaffe Feldbauamt (GAF Field Construction Bureau).

Salvage work on the waterways, on the other hand, was undertaken by the French and Belgian Waterways Authorities under direction of the German Chief Traffic Officer. If repairs were necessary, they would be undertaken by the OT, at the request of the Chief Traffic Officer and by command of the Chief Engineer of Army Group West.

Military Regional Commanders were charged with:

1. Inspecting the scene of damage together with OT engineers and the appropriate Army Administrative Officer, such as the Traffic Officer in the case of railway damage

2. Sending reports on the damage and the requirements for repair measures to the Militär Befehlshaber Frankreich (Commanding General of France)

3. Providing the OT with manpower on a priority basis in the case of air-raid damage repair.

4. Conscripting the locally unemployed in France so as to co-ordinate the supply of manpower over the entire region.

Evacuation of the OT from France

Evacuation of OT foreign personnel to the rear areas in case of invasion was left to the individual field divisions stationed in the corresponding OT sectors. The order of priority was as follows:

1. German female personnel,
2. German male personnel,
3. Foreign volunteers,
4. Skilled foreign labour necessary to carry out building projects planned by the military authorities, and
5. Unskilled foreign labour, including French colonials in private industries and French inductees into the French compulsory labour groups.

Order of priority in regard to equipment was:

1. Dredges and steam-shovels.
2. Locomotives.
3. Rails.

Factors militating against complete evacuation of foreign OT personnel were:

1. Lack of transportation fuel.
2. Belated evacuation plans.
3. Ignorance of date of invasion.
4. Ignorance of Allied tactical plans.
5. Low priority rating of foreign personnel in the evacuation schedule.
6. Unwillingness of a majority of foreign personnel to be evacuated.
7. Difficulties arising from battle conditions.

One factor favouring complete evacuation:

1. The concentration of Allied landings at one point which gave OT personnel in other areas a chance to get away.

An American soldier poses beside an uncompleted bunker. The mesh of steel reinforcement rods is laid bare, and the timber shuttering forming the inner mould for the concrete is clearly visible. *(US Dept of the Army)*

Transportation was provided only for priority German personnel such as women, officials and employees in key positions. Otherwise German personnel able to walk was assigned to the supervision of marching columns. Material was transported by train. The evacuation plans were circulated on 18–20 May throughout coastal areas in France. Moreover the commanding generals of the individual sectors were empowered to order a partial evacuation if, in their judgment, Allied landings were a feint or a diversion.

The foreign personnel were the last to be evacuated. Portions of it were intercepted by the Allied advance across Brittany and in the Cherbourg peninsula. There were forced night marches. Most French personnel, comprising about 35% of all foreign workers in the West, deserted at the first opportunity. The total OT personnel in the West almost certainly numbered less than 300,000, of which about 85,000 were French. It is likely that the Germans managed to evacuate toward the Reich border between 100,000 and 150,000 non-German workers, especially as, excepting in Normandy, they encountered little Allied interference.

B. After D-Day

Manpower and Personnel in Autumn 1944

Speer, in a confidential declaration made on 9 November 1944, stated that the OT had 850,000 workers at its disposal inside Germany, and that this number was expected to be increased to approximately 1,000,000 men in the near future, with most of the increase to consist of Hungarian Jews. It was not expected that the 1,100,000 mark, necessary for carrying out the construction programme contemplated at the time would be reached. As can be gathered from these figures, the OT has been assigned an all-important role in German plans for continuation of total warfare.

Composition of OT personnel at the present time can be described in general terms only. It is estimated that of its approximately 300,000 foreign workers in Einsatzgruppe West (EGW), the Organisation managed to evacuate about one-third. Such personnel as was lost during the process, mostly French, Belgian, Dutch and Spanish, has been replaced by new forcible levies of Hungarians, Slovaks, Czechs, and Italians. It is furthermore estimated that the proportion of foreign personnel to Germans remains at least as high as 75%. As to the disposition of the mentioned manpower, little is known beyond the fact that it is apparently a basic OT policy to allocate foreign personnel as far away as possible from their homeland.

Effects of Allied Landing

The evacuation of EGW, until D-Day the biggest and most important of the OT Einsatzgruppen, together with the radical change in the military situation, threw the OT inside Germany in a temporary state of confusion. Not only was an estimated two-thirds of its foreign EGW personnel lost, but it afforded German personnel the opportunity for unsanctioned transfers to other employers within OT. Conversely, it gave certain OT-Firms an opportunity, once they were back in the Reich, to hold on to personnel which had been put in their charge for evacuation purposes only.

Such a state of disorganisation did not last long. By 15 July 1944, Germany had already been divided into eight Einsatzgruppen, twenty-two Einsätze, and an unknown number of Oberbauleitungen (estimated average is three to four OBLs to one Einsatz). Shortly afterwards a series of directives were issued by Speer, having the following results:

Einsatzgruppe 'Deutschland' I	East Prussia and Rear Area of Army Group North Russia.
Einsatzgruppe 'Deutschland' II	Pomerania, Brandenburg, West Prussia, Wartheland.
Einsatzgruppe 'Deutschland' III	Westphalia, Schleswig-Holstein.
Einsatzgruppe 'Deutschland' IV	Hessen, Thuringia, Saxony, Brunswick, Hanover.
Einsatzgruppe 'Deutschland' V	Württemberg, Oberrhein, Westmark-Mosselland, Rhein-Main (Hessen-Nassau).
Einsatzgruppe 'Deutschland' VI	Oberfranken, Upper Palatinate, Lower Bavaria, Swabia, Upper Bavaria, Upper and Lower Danube.
Einsatzgruppe 'Deutschland' VII	Bohemia and Moravia, Sudetenland, Lower and Upper Silesia.
Einstazgruppe 'Deutschland' VIII	Steiermark, Kärnten, Tyrol, Salzburg, Alpenvorland and Adriatic Coastal Regions.

1. Rationalisation, on a nationwide basis of OT-Firms, their technical staffs and worker personnel.

An allotment was made to each of the eight Einsatzgruppen on the basis of their individual assignments and tasks. The chiefs of the Einsatzgruppen in turn made manpower allotments to the OBLs within their respective areas (Einsätze, being in essence programne control staffs, were omitted as far as administrative channels were concerned).

2. Replenishment of trained German personnel.

Shortage of trained German personnel of foreman calibre and with qualities of leadership is now partially met by training of lower-grade German OT workers.

Courses being given after working hours. A specialist in economy engineering, sent by the autonomous economic group 'Construction Industry' to each OBL, acts as efficiency expert and consultant. An intensive canvass of suitable prospects for taking part in this training is being made, and even foreigners are admitted, provided they are officially classified as collaborationists. The shortage of foremen and NCOs was also partially offset by the acquisition of trained personnel from the Air Force and Navy construction agencies, when, in July 1944, the OT was permitted to use their administrative facilities for the purpose of programme co-ordination. A third source of supply came from among civil servants who came into the OT as a result of the comb-out connected with the administrative reorganisation of Amt Bau-OTZ. Finally a fourth source of supply, one of mainly supervisory and disciplinary rather than technical sub-leaders, came from the pool of partly incapacitated members of the armed forces who are regularly assigned in small groups to the OT, particularly to the Frontführungen (see above). Selected and qualified PoW labour, mostly Russian, are also detailed to construction sites which lag badly behind schedule.

3. Premiums for efficiency.
Efficient firms are awarded priority in equipment and spare parts. Competent foremen, especially in the case of foreigners and PoW labour, are awarded efficiency bonuses.

4. Drawing up of a basic, irreducible programme, called 'Mindestbauprogramm'.
This schedule is planned to draw on Germany's resources for construction to not more than 40%. Construction and repair of hydroelectrical installations have the highest priority, inasmuch as steam and electric power must be used to replace petrol to the greatest extent practicable.

5. Reinforcement of the emergency construction crews or units, acting as 'shock-troops'.
Each large OT-Firm, or combination of smaller firms working on the same construction site, was instructed to form Sondereinsätze (Emergency Units) from amongst their personnel, in order to deal with major breaks in communications, and damage to vital installations by Allied bombing, both in the zone of communications and in the interior. In connection with these duties, the units may be transported across the boundaries of Gauarbeitsämter (District Labour Control Bureaux). They consist of men picked for their skill and initiative, and their equipment is likewise complete, of the latest type and highly mobile. In the event of major air raids, a sufficient number of units consolidate in order to cope effectively with the resulting problems of repair. They are formed, however, only in case of emergency within their sector; between such emergencies, their

personnel revert to their normal daily assigments at their Baustellen (Construction Sites), in this case usually known as Stammbaustellen (Home Construction Sites). The entire arrangement is a development of similar measures taken in France, as described above.

'OT Special Brigades' – Reported in October 1944

The recent creation of Front-OT has led to some misconceptions. The Front-OT is an area comprising Germany's border region and German-occupied Europe – Norway, Denmark, N. Italy, etc. – within which OT personnel receives distinctive treatment in regard to pay, and so forth. The misinterpretation apparently was caused by an order of Hitler's, 13 October 1944, for the activation of a special OT force (Brigades) of 80,000 men to operate within the OT-Front area in Germany. This special force should consequently not be confused with the Front-OT itself. A secondary version of the order has been given in the paragraph below, however, inasmuch as the original captured document has been interpreted elsewhere and is not available.

The order signed by Hitler on 13 October defined the scope and purpose of the Front-OT. As the plans for it were developed, the Front-OT was to consist of 80,000 men, equally divided between Germany's East and West front zones. At least 25% of the personnel was to be German. Units were to be militarised, that is to say, formed into companies of 150 battalions of 600–750, regiments of 3,000, and brigades of 30,000. The tasks of the new formations were to be the reconstruction of damaged communications systems, and so forth (in other words they were to be identical to those of the emergency units previously discussed). To achieve its purpose the Front-OT was to be equipped especially with mobile compressors, cutting tools, motor rams and carpenters' tools. Basic units (probably companies) were to be sufficiently mobile and carry enough equipment to effectively control operation of a force three times its normal strength.

Evaluation of OT 'Special Brigades'

This project was apparently nothing but a further development of the so-called shock troops already mentioned, which in turn were merely a development of the emergency crews in France (see above). Weighing the pros and cons of the probabilities of the actual existence of such a formation of 80,000 men with sufficient equipment to expand at need to a force of a quarter million, it would surprise no one to find that Allied raids have been effective enough to cause its creation. That would mean a permanent nucleus of shock construction troops allotted in the form of two brigades comprising together about 20,000 men to each of the four Einsatzgruppen comprising Germany's eastern and western frontiers. This would in turn mean that such special personnel has been relieved altogether of its former routine duties between emergencies, and assigned permanently to mobile emergency work. There is, however, basis for belief that units of this type are still administered by the various OBLs in which they are stationed, just like ordinary OT personnel. In fact, their individual assignments to high priority tasks are allotted to them by subsection D of the Einsatzgruppe HQ, known as Fliegerschädensofortmassnahmen (Air Raid Damage Emergency Measures) of Referat Bau (Construction Section) in that HQ. Such allotment is effected through the appropriate OBL HQ which includes a similar subsection for Emergency Measures.

The project itself cannot be accepted at face value as a *fait accompli*. There are indications that it fell through, in the first place because equipment was found to be too valuable to allow its concentration in such mass, for the exclusive use of a comparatively minor branch of the Organisation; in the second place, because present conditions and the diversity of OT's tasks virtually preclude any rigid regimentation which, going beyond personnel administration, attempts to make itself felt in operational matters. Even if the project had been actually realised in its entirety, it still should not be assumed – as has been done – that the rest of the OT has been dissolved. Obviously, after having been put in charge of *all* civilian and military construction in Germany by highest authority, as discussed in the following paragraphs, the OT was not stripped of nine-tenths of its personnel on practically the same day.

Amt Bau-OTZ

While the Reich was being divided into Einsatzgruppen, etc., in preparation for the homecoming of the OT, higher policy in regard to its status as a governmental agency was likewise being revised, with the result that at present the OT is found to be in control of all construction inside Germany.

The first step was taken on 29 April 1944, when Amt Bau (Bureau of Construction) in the Speer Ministry was placed under the official who already was (and still is) head of OTZ, Ministerialdirektor Dorsch. Inasmuch as Amt Bau controlled the construction and building industries in Germany, the step effectively put OTZ on an equal footing with Amt Bau. The reason officially given was that it was Hitler's specific desire that it should be made possible for the OT to 'perform its tasks smoothly and unfettered, also in the Reich'. Its tasks prudently were defined as 'construction work for the war production industry'. The step was ratified by a decree of the Führer, dated 24 August 1944, placing Speer, in the capacity of Chief of the OT, in control of all official administrative construction agencies within Germany. In effect, the decree by implication placed the OT in control of Amt Bau's administrative organisation. Before the intermediate steps leading to this development are discussed, a brief outline of the history of Amt Bau is given below.

Amt Bau was created as part of the Speer Ministry, when the latter was reorganised in the autumn of 1943. The specific decree establishing the Bureau is dated 29 October 1943. The creation of the office put its chief, the Generalbevollmächtigter Bau (Plenipotentiary General for Construction) – at that time Stobbe-Dethleffsen – on an equal footing with the chiefs of the other Ämter (Bureaux) of the Speer Ministry. Stobbe-Dethleefsen, however, in addition to being head of Amt Bau, also represented Speer in the latter's capacity of Generalbevollmächtigter für die Regelung der Bauwirtschaft im Raume des Vierjahresplan (Plenipotentiary-General for the Regulation of the Construction Industry within the Four Year Plan). This dual function is reflected clearly, however, in the subordinate echelons.

Thus the Bau Bevollmächtigter im Bezirk der Rüstungsinspektion (Construction Plenipotentiary for the District of the Armaments Inspectorate) derived his authority from the Plenipotentiary General (Stobbe-Dethleffsen) and exercised full control over the priority programme for construction and allotment of building supplies. The Baubeauftragte im Gau (Construction Deputy in each Party Gau), on the other hand, derived his authority from the Chief of Amt Bau (also Stobbe-Dethleffsen). The Baubeauftragte, acted as liaison official between the Gauleiter in the latter's capacity of Reichsverteidigungskommissar (Reich Defence Commissioner) and the Construction Plenipotentiary of the Armament Inspectorate District in whose sphere the Party Gau was wholly or partly situated. As for the administration of construction within the Gau, such as e.g. the issuing of permits for construction of a non-military but high priority nature, or public and Party institutes, the Deputy was subordinate to both the Gauleiter and the Plenipotentiary, although primarily to the latter.

On 3 June 1944, Amt Bau and OTZ were consolidated. While the resultant agency, as to organisation, follows the lines of the Amt Bau rather than that of the OTZ, most if not all heads of its Amtsgruppen (Branches) are former OTZ departmental heads. It can be said, therefore, that the transformation is one in name rather than fact, and that all OTZ key personnel have continued in their functions. The next step, accomplished by 15 July 1944, was the formation of the eight Einsatzgruppen, etc. inside Germany and the establishment of the next chain of command. The most radical feature of the latter was the elimination of the Construction Plenipotentiaries and their staffs, and the creation of four Baubeauftragte (construction deputies) for each Gau, instead of one, on the staff of the Reich Defence Commissioner; one for civilian construction permits, one for inspection of civilian construction, one for air-raid shelters construction, and one to act as efficiency or economy engineer.

The reorganisation of the OT in Germany was thus practically completed about 15 July 1944, and Hitler's decree of 24 August of that year was therefore a ratification of an already existing arrangement. The change in the chain of command, eliminating the Construction Plenipotentiaries and replacing them by the Einsatzgruppenleiter as the highest regional executive authorities, subordinate only to Amt Bau-OTZ, was inevitable if duplication was to be avoided. On 16 October 1944, Speer, empowered by Hitler's decree, issued a series of directives defining the relative spheres of authority of the Chiefs of Einsatzgruppen, the Chiefs of Einsätze, and the Construction Deputies on the staffs of the Reich Defence Commissioners (Gauleiter). Both documents are rendered in translation at the end of this section. Construction agencies of the German Air Force and Navy were taken over by the OT in late summer 1944.

Significance of Front-OT

There are strong indications that the pooling of a million men in one industry, and their sudden redistribution on a rationalised basis, disrupted the economy of those construction firms which had not been conscripted into the OT. Such a reallotment caused resentment on the part of firms who lost employees attracted by the comparatively high wages paid by the OT. The movement of masses of OT personnel, over whom they had no control, across their administrative boundaries disturbed the Gau Labour Control officials, as well as the Gauleiter in their capacity of Defence Commissioners. A compromise was consequently effected. Zones were established, which, because of their susceptibility to enemy action, were designated front zones, and the collective area was designated Front-OT. Within this area of highest construction priority, the OT has the status of a military organisation, and its personnel, as 'Angehörige (member) of the Wehrmacht', commensurate basic pay plus the extra allowances, bonuses, compensations, etc., which – with certain exceptions – OT has been uniformly paying to their personnel working in exposed areas, since January 1943. Its German personnel are called Frontarbeiter, its foreign personnel, OT Legionäre. The Front-OT may also move its personnel across regional labour boundaries inside the Reich without interference from the Reichstreuhänder für die Arbeit (Reich Labour Trustees) who are Sauckel's regional representatives, or from the Reich Defence Commissioners (who are also the Gauleiter). This Front OT consists of (1) the operational zones fronting the Allies in the West, and the Russians in the East; (2) heavily bombed areas within the Reich; (3) Einsatzgruppe Italy; and (4) Einsatzgruppe Wiking (Norway and Denmark). The extent of the zone may be changed at the discretion of the Wehrmacht. That part of the Organisation which is not active in front zone is not designated Front-OT, and its skilled personnel receive only such specialist pay above their basic pay as is uniformly regulated by the Plenipotentiary General for Manpower Allocation (Sauckel) for all labour in Germany. And inasmuch as the OT has always distinguished between Fronteinsatz (Service performed in the operational area) and Heimatseinsatz (Service in the zone of the interior), there is consequently no basis for assuming that the OT has been reduced either in sphere of authority or in strength of personnel. Nor is there any basis for assuming that there has been a partial dissolution of the OT. All indications point to the contrary. It is well to remember, however, that even in the Zone of the Interior, the OT is, in respect to manpower priority, classified as a vital industry.

Hitler's Decree of 24 August 1944:

DECREE OF THE FÜHRER CONCERNING THE WAR COMMITMENT OF THE ADMINISTRATIVE AGENCIES FOR CONSTRUCTION,
24 August 1944

I. The Reich Minister for Armament and War Production and Chief of Organisation Todt henceforth heads the war activities of the Administrative Agencies for Construction. I empower him to issue directives for the above purpose to all administrative National Municipal construction agencies of Greater Germany and incorporated territories. He may dispose over the personnel and facilities of these agencies according to his Judgment.

The administrative organisation remains unchanged by thus being placed on a war footing.

II. The decisions under paragraph I apply also to state-controlled public corporations insofar as they have administrative agencies of their own.

III. The Reich Minister for Armament and War Production and Chief of the OT will issue, henceforth, the legal and administrative regulations necessary for carrying out and amplifying the above decree in agreement with the Plenipotentiary General for the Administration of the Reich (Himmler).

IV. This decree lapses at the end of the war.

Führer HQ. 24 August 1944,
The Führer. Adolf Hitler.
Reich Minister and Chief of the Reich Chancellery, Dr Lammers.

Speer's Decree of l6 October 1944:

FIRST EXECUTIVE ORDER FOLLOWING THE DECREE OF THE FÜHRER CONCERNING THE WAR COMMITMENT OF THE ADMINISTRATIVE AGENCIES. FOR CONSTRUCTION,
16 October 1944

With reference to paragraph III of the Führer's Decree Concerning the War Conmitment of the Administrative Agencies for Construction of 24 August 1944, I order, for the territory of Greater Germany and incorporated territories, in agreement with the Plenipotentiary General for Reich Administration (Himmler), the following:

I

1. The Chiefs of Einsatzgruppen of the Organisation Todt may henceforth commission administrative agencies of the Reich, the provinces, municipalities and communes, as well as those of state-controlled public corporations, to execute such scheduled and projected construction as they have consented to exempt from the Building Restrictions (para 7 of the 31st regulation concerning the Building Restriction of 8 August 1944 – Reichsanzeiger No. 206).

2. They may avail themselves of the building facilities of the Wehrmacht according to existing arrangements with the various departments of the armed forces.

II

1. The Construction Deputies to the Reich Defence Commissioner may group together construction agencies of the Reich, the provinces, and communes, as well as those of state-controlled public corporations, for the execution of construction assignments, according to the requirements of their commitments.

2. The Construction Deputies will be appointed by the Reich Minister for Armament and War Production and Chief of Organisation Todt, in agreement with the Reich Defence Commissioners. They are subordinated to the Reich Defence Commissioners and are assigned to the executive offices of the Reich Defence Commissioners.

3. The Reich Minister for Armament and War Production at the same time, in his capacity of Plenipotentiary General for the Regulation of the Construction Industry, has competence over the Reich Defence Commissioners (through the Construction Deputies) in the matter of directives.

III

1. The Reich Defence Commissioners will (through the Construction Deputies) examine the possibilities for combined management of current administrative business and the reshuffling of duties for the purpose of reducing personnel and administrative overhead, and for putting the facilities of the public agencies for construction to the most efficient use.

2. The Reich Defence Commissioner may (through the Construction Deputy)

regulate at his own discretion transfers from one agency to another of the management of current administrative business.

3. The Reich Minister for Armament and War Production and Chief of Organisation Todt, in concert with the Plenipotentiary General of Reich Administration (Himmler), decides in the matter of reshuffling of duties from the sphere of competence of one agency to that of another. Insofar as the possibility for the elimination of agencies is thereby created, the procedure will be regulated by the ranking official of the eliminated agency involved.

4. The Reich Defence Commissioner in whose Gau (Party District) the seat of the competent, regional office is situated has the final responsibility for measures taken in the case of state-controlled public corporations and administrative agencies whose spheres extend over several Reich Defence Districts.

IV.

1. The Reich Defence Commissioners (through the Construction Deputies) are obliged to put all available personnel and establishments (office buildings), equipment and diverse installations at the disposal of the Chiefs of the Einsatzgruppen of the Organisation Todt for use in construction as named in para. I.

2. The Chiefs of the Einsatzgruppen will specify their requirements for personnel and facilities to the Reich Defence Commissioners (through the Construction Deputies). Should the latter, on compelling grounds, believe themselves unable to comply with the requirements, they must, having so informed the Chief of Einsatzgruppe, obtain directly the decision of the Reich Minister for Armament and War Production, which will be rendered in concert with the Plenipotentiary General for Reich Administration (Himmler).

7. The above standing orders do not apply to administrative agencies for construction of the Reich State Railways and the Reich Postal Service.

VI.

The Chief of the Einsatzgruppe in the Protectorate of Bohemia and Moravia has no competence of direction and disposition over the autonomous (Protectorate) officials and agencies. Liaison will be established only through the German State Minister for Bohemia and Moravia.

Berlin, 16 October, 1944.
The Reich Minister for Armament and War Production and Chief of
Organisation Todt, Speer

PART II

An Artilleriebeobachter, artillery spotter, on the Westwall. This photograph was published in 1941 in *Unsere Wehrmacht*, a collection of colour images of various aspects of the German fighting machine. Hitler had planned the defensive line of forts and bunkers in 1936 and it was constructed between 1938 and 1940. Ironically the line was rendered obsolete by the Blitzkrieg tactics of the early stages of the war, but was reactivated in 1944 in the face of the anticipated Allied landings.

Organisation, Administration and Operation

A. Organisation

Introduction

The OT in the winter of 1944/45 is a radically different organisation from what it was in the spring of 1938, in regard to status and scope of function. Seven years ago it was a Wehrmacht auxiliary charged with military construction, ranging from the tactical to the strategic, in the various zones of operation. It has by now become the sole agency responsible for the entire war production programme in the Reich, insofar as it is, directly or indirectly, affected by Allied air raids, not to mention the part it plays in Nazi plans for a 'fanatic' defence. None of these functions, however, are representative of the role assigned to it in German plans for the reconstruction of a Nazi post-war Europe.

Whether the OT is to be assigned any role at all in Allied plans for the reconstruction of the Continent, or whether it will be demobilised, its internal organisation is of considerable importance. For this reason the OT structure and chain of command is being presented in two characteristic forms. One concerns itself with the stabilised, permanent organisation, as it operated in German-occupied Europe, and as exemplified by Einsatzgruppe West (EGW) (France and the Low Countries) in 1943, before the effects of Allied air raids had made themselves felt. The other concerns itself with as up-to-date a description of OT internal organisation, at the present time, inside the Reich, as can be given on the basis of available documentary material. For the sake of brevity the first will be henceforth referred to as the 'permanent organisation' and the second will be termed the 'current organisation'.

(a) 'Permanent Organisation'

'Permanent Organisation' – The OT High Command

Reich Minister for Armament and War Production, Albert Speer, succeeded Todt as Chief of the OT in February 1942; a decree by Hitler, signed on

2 September 1943, made Speer, in his capacity of Chief of the OT, responsible only to the Führer himself, without intervening channels. Speer's administrative director since 1942 has been Ministerialdirektor Dipl. Ing. Xaver Dorsch. Dorsch is responsible solely to Speer, and his HQ is the OT Zentrale (OTZ: OT Central HQ) last known to have been located in Berlin. He is at the same time chief of the Abteilung Wehrbauen und Ausland (Section for Military Construction and Foreign Countries) of the Inspectorate General of German Roadways.

The OTZ issues the fundamental directives for operational and administrative functioning, and the basic territorial distribution of manpower. Its most important task is in the field of economy engineering: the standardisation of material, building specifications and methods of construction. Apart from that, its functions are confined to the administration of the OT: it keeps the records, it checks incoming reports and accounts, it regulates the relationship between OT-Firms and the OT administration, as well as those between the firm and the workers, and finally it issues, through the Frontführungen, directives for the entire working and social routine of all OT personnel.

Matters of policy, as decided upon by the German Supreme Command of the Armed Forces, and insofar as they affect the OT, are put into execution by the chiefs of the Einsatzgruppen in conjunction with the commanding general of the corresponding military theatre or sector of operations. Construction plans affecting EGW, for example, were drawn up under direction of its Chief, Oberbaudirektor Weiss. (He is at the same time Rundstedt's chief engineer – General Ingenieur beim Oberbefehlshaber West.) To carry the example further, estimates of requirements for raw material, drawn up on the basis of a long-term construction programme (of at least six months' duration), were then submitted to the OTZ by EGW, along with the actual plans. Approval by the latter was a matter of routine, provided the plans submitted conformed in general to the strategic policy laid down by the Supreme Command for the theatre of operations occupied by EGW (France, Belgium, and the Netherlands). The material was then allotted to EGW through the OTZ by virtue of Speer's authority in the matter of priority allotment of essential war material. The actual shipments were made through Wehrmacht channels (Hauptverkehrsdienst or Central Traffic Service) and were labelled Wehrmachtgut (Armed Forces property). OTZ's sphere of authority in the matter of recruitment of manpower is discussed in Part IV on Manpower.

'Permanent Organisation' – Chain of Command

A decree, signed by Speer on 24 September 1943, ordered the normalisation of OT administrative levels in all theatres of operation along the following uniform chain of command.

1. Einsatzgruppe (EG: Area Control Staff: Army Group Level)
2. Einsatz (E: Area Control Staff; Army Level)
3. Oberbauleitung (OBL: Basic OT Construction Sector and Administrative HQ)
4. Bauleitung (BL: Sub-Sector)
5. Abschnittsbauleitung (ABL: Local Supervisory Staff)
6. Baustelle (Construction Site)

All of these terms, with the exception of that of Einsatzgruppe, had existed in the OT since its inception in 1938, but they had never been uniformly defined. This was particularly true of the designations, Einsatz and Abschnittsbauleitung. The uniformity in terminology which the decree attempted to establish in German-occupied territory was not realised in practice until the OT evacuated into Germany (see 'Current Organisation').

'Permanent Organisation' – The Einsatzgruppe. (EG: Area Control Staff, Army Group Level)

The term Einsatzgruppe was first identified in October 1941 in connection with the creation of Einsatzgruppe West (see Part V). *From Einsatzgruppe downwards, the OT should be visualised, not in the form of a hierarchy of units, but rather as a theatre of construction operations controlled by various levels of administrative staffs, of which the Einsatzgruppe (Area Control Staff on Army Group Level) is the highest.* The Einsatzgruppe West (EGW) comprising France, Belgium and the Netherlands is used throughout this book as a model, inasmuch as it represented the 'permanent' type of OT organisation to a greater extent than any other Einsatzgruppe. Other Einsatzgruppen are, however, discussed wherever they are believed to be of interest for purposes of comparison.

Although the OTZ issued the general regulations governing administrative and operational policy, the Einsatzgruppe is an executive and operational unit in its own domain. The administrative organisation of each Einsatzgruppe is basically alike; there are, however, regional differences in structure. These differences arose from the following three factors:

1. Political status of the occupied country or countries.
2. Nature of the terrain, strategic importance and natural resources of the occupied region.
3. State of military security in respect to partisan warfare and organised sabotage.

These factors resulted in variations of the regional OT organisations. Such variations manifest themselves in the following:

1. In the relationship between the regional OT and the Wehrmacht in the occupied country or countries.

2. In the relationship between the regional OT and German civil authorities, both in Germany and in the occupied country or countries.
3. In the internal administrative and structural organisation of the regional OT.
4. In the composition of work units.
5. In the proportion of technical and administrative personnel to manual labour and in the proportion and organisation of OT police personnel.
6. In the proportion of various nationalities, including Germans.
7. In the differences in type of tasks, the prevalence, for example, of road and bridge building in the North, in the East and in the Balkans, and the prevalence of fortification construction in the West.

Especially marked is the difference in organisation of the EGW and that of the EGs in the Eastern and the Balkan sectors. In Russia, for example, all essential systems and installations had to be built from the ground up: roads, bridges, communication cables, water supply lines, railways, administrative quarters, barracks and other living quarters for soldiers and workers, supply depots, warehouses, motor vehicle repair and maintenance shops, dams, factories and industrial plants, not to mention the building of all military fortifications and the exploitation of such resources as oil and coal. OT administrative personnel and Army administrative staffs were often quartered together for reasons of military security, climate, transport difficulties and especially because of the close interdependence which existed in the early days in Russia between the OT and the Wehrmacht. This situation put the OT's constructional capabilities to the test, earned it greater respect from the Army than in any other sector, and led to the most direct co-operation between the two. In addition, recruitment of labour, after a brief trial period of conscription through collaborationist agencies, soon reverted into German hands so that the manpower problem was much simplified on that front. The firms there, being German, were comparatively free from administrative supervision by EGs and still less from control by the OTZ. As the German Army advanced further into Russia, and the OT with it, the shortage of administrative personnel in rear areas was met by allowing the regional Reichskommissar to set up staffs to run the projects the EGs had brought into being.

The picture in the West as reflected by the EGW was different. Until the Allied air raids reached effective proportions, there was no state of emergency. Living comforts for rank-and-file personnel were immeasurably greater than in the East. Military security, until the time when Maquis activity broke out in France, was confined to the suppression of local sabotage. Excellent communications of all types between Germany and the West made administrative supervision from Berlin easier, but, at the same time, the administration itself was more complex. International law and official representation, such as it was, had to be observed – if only for the sake of formality – in the requisitioning of supplies, and in the recruitment and welfare of labourers. Relations with the Wehrmacht and with civil authorities were on a much more formal footing and were carried out through liaison and official channels. Political and social control of the OT by the Nazi Party organisations brought with it further administrative ramifications. The following captured German document from the West is submitted as an illustration of administrative frustration, owing mainly to shortage of manpower and deterioration of morale.

Organisation Todt   19 November 1943
Einsatzgruppe West
OBL-Cherbourg.

To the
Organisation Todt
Einsatzgruppe West

Reference: Inventory and issue of materials.

At the beginning of this year we attempted to take an inventory here although it was much too late. The first storekeeper was GREB. He did not take any inventory but sold all the goods and put the money into his own pocket. For this he was sentenced to imprisonment. His successor was Pöltl. He was an administrative employee who, although he did not actually sell anything, also did not attempt any inventory. The third storekeeper was Heckman. This man also failed to take any inventory but blackmailed everyone to whom he sold OT goods in exchange for tobacco and brandy. He too had to be replaced. His successor was Hipper. His only shortcoming was the fact that he could neither read nor write, and mixed up all the accounts. The fifth storekeeper within the ten months is Trumann, employed here since 20.9.43. This man was released by the Personnel Administration on 18.5.43 and was transferred to this branch. At that time I was grateful for personnel and took in anyone who seemed suitable. But as it happens, the reason for Trumann's reassignment to this post is his near-blindness, and consequently he cannot even attempt inventory because he positively cannot see a thing.

   Nevertheless, now, after nearly a year, the inventory must be undertaken. Stock must be taken of all Reich property. Among all men employed here, there is not one capable of performing this task. If all instructions issued by headquarters are to be carried out I must request the assignment to this branch of a suitable and capable man to replace Trumann.

To summarise, then, the OT is to be regarded as a generally flexible organisation, evolved to meet local conditions throughout Europe over a period of years.

The Organisation appeared to best advantage in the Einsatzgruppen situated in Russia; it began to give definite evidence of deterioration in the stabilised West.

'Permanent Organisation' – The Einsatz (E: Area Control Staff Army Level)

Einsatz as a subdivision of Einsatzgruppe is primarily a control staff concerned with co-ordinating the construction programme of the Oberbauleitungen (OBLs) under its control. Thus the largest administrative section in its headquarters is the Referat Bau (Subsection Construction). The above conception of Einsatz, however, represents a late stage of OT organisation, and there are frequent allusions to Einsatz in the OT which cannot be interpreted in this sense. The reason for this can be traced to the fact that the word Einsatz in the sense of 'commitment' is one of the most frequently and indiscriminately used terms in present-day German military language. Thus, in Russia, and to a lesser extent in the West, the term Einsatz was used to designate any area 'committed' to OT construction work, regardless of size, e.g. Einsatz OBL Terek (Caucasus) or Einsatz (Hakelberg) in Hafenbau (Harbour Construction) Einsatz Heidenreich. In the West, the Islands of Alderney, Guernsey and Jersey are to this day referred to as Insel (island) Einsätze, even though their administrative status is that of Bauleitungen. Similarly, the term Sondereinsatz (Special Commitment) will refer, at times, not to a subdivision of an Einsatzgruppe, but rather to a special type of construction commitment (e.g. Sondereinsatz Wolga, subordinate to the OTZ without intervening channels). On other ocassions Sondereinsatz will refer to an operational sector which was created too late to be fitted into the already existing schematic organisation of the larger sector in which it was situated. To give a further example, OT Einsatzdienststelle (OT Personnel Office of an operational sector, or sector committed to OT construction) does not necessarily refer to the personnel office of the HQ of a subdivision of an Einsatzgruppe but may refer to that of the HQ of a section of any size whatsoever.

The intention of the OT authorities was to normalise administratively all the irregular Einsätze, as soon as the military situation warranted stabilisation over large areas in conquered territory. The plan did not work any too well in Russia because the military situation over vast sectors of the East Front remained fluid and precluded a stabilised administration. It did not work too well in the West for exactly the opposite reason. The trend there toward stabilisation had begun as early as spring 1942, long before the publication of the decree of September 1943, ordering the term Einsatz to be uniformly employed as a designation of the administrative level below Einsatzgruppe. The result was that, with notable exceptions (Normandy and Cherbourg), the EGW omitted the Einsatz level, its next lower echelon in the chain of command being the Oberbauleitung (OBL). This shortened chain of command worked effectively enough in the West because of the comparatively small distances between the various OBLs and excellent means of communication between the latter and central control in Paris, where the EGW HQ was located. The mentioned exceptions, Normandy and Cherbourg, which had previously been OBLs, were raised to the level of an Einsatz in the autumn of 1942 and the spring of 1944 respectively. The construction programme in those sectors was heavy, of a highly technical nature, and of vital military importance. A larger technical control staff was consequently required than was normally provided by the TO/WE for an OBL. The necessary increase in staff was thereupon obtained by raising the Normandy and Cherbourg sectors from the level of an OBL to that of an Einsatz. Up to D-Day, however, the EGW HQ made no concerted attempt to obey Speer's decree of September 1943 for uniformity in designations of OT levels. In fact, even Normandy and Cherbourg were persistently alluded to, in official correspondence, as QBLs right up until July 1944.

'Permanent Organisation' – Oberbauleitung (OBL: Basic OT Construction Sector and Administrative HQ)

The Oberbauleitung (OBL) is the basic operational sector of any large OT region of activity, and its personnel consequently forms the OT's basic operational unit. The two levels above the OBL, that is to say, the Einsatzgruppe and the Einsatz, are operational staffs, controlling a number of OBLs. The levels below it (Bauleitung, Abschnittsbauleitung and Baustelle) are merely sub-sectors of the OBL, administered by the OBL HQ. In short, the OBL is the only OT sector, the HQ of which controls its own construction programme through direct contact with and supervision of, the OT-Firms which do the actual work. This is only the first of its two basic functions. The other is OT personnel administration in its broadest aspect, ranging from the exercise of disciplinary authority to the investigation of discrepancies in pay and including such duties as the messing, billeting and clothing of all OT personnel in its sector. The two main sections in an OBL HQ are consequently Referat Technik (Technical Subsection) and Referat Frontführung (Front Area Personnel Section). For the other sections and sub-sections of the OBL HQ, see below. For the performance of its functions, the OBL Frontführung controls all Lager (Camps and Warehouses) connected in any way with the administration of personnel within the OBL sector, such as barracks and food and clothing depots. The chief of an OBL has the rank of either Oberbauleiter (Lt.-Col.) or Hauptbauleiter (Col.).

The normal TO/WE for an OBL HQ is (including detached personnel in the field) approximately 3% of the manpower operating in its sector. This percentage figure does not include the clerical and field construction firms active in the OBL sector. In order to meet the problem of manpower shortage, the establishment of the OBL HQ has, since March 1944, been cut down to about one-half of this normal strength of 3%. The saving has been effected by making OT-Firms practically self-contained and self-operating units, responsible for feeding, clothing and caring for their men, but remaining accountable for their actions in these respects, to the OBL Frontführung.

Liaison between the OT and other Reich and Party agencies does not go below OBL level.

Reference has already been made to inconsistencies in the terms designating OT echelons. Thus a number of operational sectors in Russia were designated Einsätze even though they performed the basic functions of an OBL. Terms like Oberabschnitte (Main Sectors) were, although on a less frequent scale, similarly used on the eastern front. A third term, Linienschef (Line Chief), was also used there, to denote the HQ of a sector and its executive on an OBL or Einsatz level, when specialising in railway construction.

'Permanent Organisation' – Bauleitung (BL: Sub-sector of an OBL)

Although the term Bauleitung is used inconsistently in captured German documents, it was never as loosely employed as 'Einsatz'. Whereas 'Einsatz' at one time might have referred to an area of any size, from a local construction site consisting of only one OT-Firm, to a sector comprising half of Norway, 'Bauleitung' on the other hand always was and still is a subdivision of an OBL. It had also been used quite frequently to designate a subdivision of Abschnittsbauleitung (see below). The above mentioned decree for uniformity of September 1943 ordered, however, the term Bauleitung to be exclusively employed as a subdivision, directly under an OBL. As a matter of fact, the decree was not generally effective in remedying the situation in German-occupied territory. The BL at present, however, may be assumed to be a sub-sector, directly under an OBL and controlled by a staff, the strength of which depends on the size and importance of the BL. Basically that staff consists of an Abteilung Technik (Technical Section) and – if the BL is a large one – of a Frontführung (Front Area Personnel Section). The chief of the Technical Section is at the same time chief of the entire BL, usually with the rank of Bauleiter (Major). As a rule he is an OT firm executive appointed over all executives of other OT firms operating in the same BL. In this aspect he is also the ranking OT Officer (in a military sense) in his sub-sector. His main function consists of supervising the adherence, on the part of all local OT firms, to building specifications and to the time schedule as laid down by OBL HQ, and as called for in the contracts made between the OT and the individual construction firms. No payment may be made for construction in his sub-sector without his approval. All records, accounts, reports and so forth having to do with construction are also forwarded by the Abschnittsbauleitungen (Local Supervisory Staffs) subordinated to his BL, to his office, for checking and transmittal to the higher OBL HQ. The chief of a BL is directly responsible to the chief of his controlling OBL. The head of the BL

Front Area Personnel Section – provided there is one – is mainly concerned with personnel administration of the men in the sub-sector. For this purpose his office checks personnel records and reports sent in by the Abschnittsbauleitungen or, more often, directly by the local construction firms through their individual personnel offices.

A considerable part of the reports to BL Front Personnel Area Sections originate from the Lagerführer (Camp Supervisors) of the camp or camps situated in the BL. The head of the BL Frontführung then, reports directly to the corresponding section in the competent OBL.

'Permanent Organisation' – Abschnittsbauleitung (ABL: Local Supervisory Staff)
There is no specific ruling defining in what respects the ABL differs from the BL. Nor are all Bauleitungen necessarily subdivided into Abschittsbauleitungen. Usually when a BL, which previously had not been subdivided increases in importance and complexity to the extent that its staff can no longer effectively control it, it is subdivided into ABLs. If the BL sector continues to increase further in importance, it is then raised to the status of an OBL, and the ABLs within its area are raised to the status of BLs. The following will supplement what has already been mentioned about inconsistencies in the employment of the term Abschnittsbauleitung: in Russia special construction units, all on an ABL level, were designated as Wasserstrassenamt (Waterways Bureau), Hafenamt (Harbour Bureau) and Brückenbauleitung (Bridge Construction HQ). It should not be assumed however that the latter terms always denote a sector as small as an ABL. At times, it referred to a higher HQ.

The ABL is controlled by a staff under a Bauleiter (with a rank ranging from Bauführer, Second Lieutenant, to Bauleiter, Major, depending on the importance of his work) in much the same way as a BL is controlled by its staff. Generally, the staff of the ABL is similar though smaller than that of the BL, and its duties are usually confined to supervision of the local construction in hand. Individual ranks on the staff are of a correspondingly lower grade, personnel administration, as a function of the OT, (Front Area Personnel Section) as against that of the individual OT firms, does not, as a rule, go below BL level. Functions of the firms in this respect are outlined below. The chief of an ABL is ultimately responsible to the chief of the competent OBL and accountable to the chief of the competent BL.

'Permanent Organisation' – Baustelle (Construction Site)
The Baustelle (Construction Site) is the basic component of an OBL sector. The personnel of the OT-Firm (or firms) working on this construction site, comprise the basic operational unit and lowest entity in an OBL. There is no uniformity in the size of a construction site beyond the fact that when the site grows to such

proportions as to require a considerable staff for its control, it is raised to the status of an ABL, a BL, or even, in exceptional cases, to that of an OBL. Similarly two or more adjacent construction sites are grouped together and administered by an ABL or a BL. (See above.)

The executive of an OT construction firm is chief of the construction site on which his firm works. His authority, however, is limited in several ways. In his control of the construction at hand, he is limited by the terms of his contract with Organisation Todt. In his control of the manpower allotted to him by the OT, for the performance of the manual and mechanical labour at hand, he is limited by the basic regulations of the Organisation in regard to personnel administration, such as hours of work, rates of pay, bonuses and penalties, treatment of the various nationalities, and so forth. He has the right to invoke penalties for infractions of regulations without, however, having the authority to enforce punishment, which is left to the Frontführer (Front Area Personnel Director) of the BL or OBL. For the exercise of these functions, he is invested, as long as he is contracted or subcontracted to the OT, with the rank of an OT officer, normally that of Bauleiter (approximately equivalent to that of Major) but possibly one or two grades higher or lower, according to the importance of his firm and his own ability.

The OT firm executive must bring with him into his own OT staff of old employees, consisting essentially of technical and clerical personnel. He must do so because his staff, which is called Firmen Stammpersonal (Permanent Firm Staff), contains the German supervisory personnel without which the OT will not allot him any foreign labour. Inasmuch as foreign labour comprises about 80% of all OT personnel even at the present time, an OT-Firm is consequently helpless without a minimum of German supervisory personnel on its staff. If that staff drops below the irreducible minimum, there are three possible eventualities.

1. It is subject to dissolution as a firm, whereupon its manpower is withdrawn, the members and its equipment are temporarily requisitioned for use by other OT firms.
2. It may keep its entity in the OT, but not its status, by becoming a subcontractor to a more adequately staffed firm.
3. It may combine with several firms in a similar position to form an Arge (Arbeitsgemeinschaft or Working Combine) by pooling individual resources. It is only in exceptional cases that a firm withdraws completely from the OT. To do so would be an unwise step both economically and politically.

An important feature of the organisation of an OT firm is the increase in responsibility it has been given over all its personnel, including foreign workers. In fact, since March 1944, the OT firm has been charged with performing exactly the same functions in regard to its personnel as performed by an OBL

Frontführer toward the entire OBL Personnel. For this purpose each OT firm includes a Mannschaftsführer (Personnel Administrator) who is responsible to the firm executive, and accountable to the competent BL Frontführer, or lacking the latter directly to the competent OBL Frontführer.

Various phases of the OT-Firm as a basic unit will be discussed in more detail as follows: the economic and legal aspects in II D and the administrative and functional aspects in III B.

'Current Organisation'

'Current Organisation' – The OT High Command

Note: For the organisational structure of OT as it was intended to operate under normal and post-war conditions, see 'Permanent Organisation'.

Amt Bau and OTZ were merged under Generalbevollmächtiger Bau (Plenipotentiary General for Construction) Ministerialdirektor Dorsch, by an order of Speer issued 3 June 1944. The step can be regarded as unifying, under compulsion of circumstances, two governmental agencies which hitherto had performed similar functions; one (Amt Bau) inside the Reich, the other (OTZ) mainly in German occupied territory. Similarity in the functions of both agencies did not, however, entail similarity in organisational structure or methods of operation. The OT was essentially organised to co-operate with field and occupational armies, and its basic operational liaison was (and to some extent still is) with the former Festungspionier Stäbe (Fortress Construction Pioneer Staffs). Amt Bau, on the other hand, was organised to co-operate with civilian defence authorities and army officials concerned with vital war production. Its basic operational liaison was (and to some extent still is) with the Rüstungskommissionen (Armanent Commissions), and with the Reichsverteidigungsauschüsse (Reich Defence Committees). Now that extensive parts of the Reich are within the zones of operations, organisational characteristics of both OTZ and Amt Bau have been incorporated in Amt Bau-OTZ, as a result of the merger.

Complete information on the present structure of Amt Bau-OTZ is not available at present. A basic outline of Amt Bau, therefore, as it functioned prior to its merger with OTZ (3 June 1944) will, it is believed, be helpful in an evaluation of the merger. The Amt Bau was a Bureau of the Speer Ministry, and as such (as Bau-OTZ still does) represents a subdivision on the highest administrative level within that Ministry. Beside the organic Amtsgruppen (branches) which comprised Amt Bau, the latter relied (as Amt Bau/OTZ still does) on the collaboration of the following three special agencies attached to it.

The first of these is the Hauptausschuss Bau (Central Committee for Construction). This committee may be described as a HQ staff concerned with ways and means of procuring from outside agencies all finished products which are used in building and construction. Part of its mission consists of making recommendations for further simplification and standardisation of such products. The Central Committee controlled (as it still does within Amt Bau-OTZ) a number of Sonderausschüsse (Special Committees). In addition, a number of Zentralstellen (Central Offices) are reported to have been attached to Amt Bau. Their function is said to be co-ordination with agencies controlling the supply of building materials, as for example the Zentralstelle für Zement und Massivbarracken (Central Office for Cement and Permanent Hutments). It is not clear at present whether these Zentralstellen now under Amt Bau-OTZ act as liaison between the Rohstoffamt (Raw Materials Bureau) of the Speer Ministry and Amt Bau-OTZ, whether they act as liaison between, for example, all firms manufacturing cement, and Amt Bau-OTZ, or whether they act as liaison between the Hauptringe ('Main Rings), of the Speer Ministry, and Amt Bau-OTZ.

The second is the autonomous corporate Wirtschaftsgruppe Bauindustrie (Eoonomic Group: Construction Industry). This 'Group' is represented in Amt Bau-OTZ by a representative who is subject to directives from the latter. This liaison is the link at highest level, between Amt Bau-OTZ and the construction firms in Germany, which, without being OT-Firms, perform similar work. Inasmuch as the OT has the right to conscript firms in case of emergency, the entire question of 'OT-Firms' and the entire question of 'OT-Firms' in Germany, has by now become somewhat academic. Apparently a rather fine dividing line separates non-OT-Firms at present from those which contracted themselves to the OT for service abroad and – more recently – for service inside Germany. The former cannot be regarded as being at any time and in any respect independent of the OT, because the OT now controls all the administrative agencies from which these firms formerly had to accept directives as to priority construction, building permits and so forth. The OT, moreover, now has at its disposal all construction facilities of the armed forces and the SS, comprising their administrative agencies, establishments and equipment. On the other hand, these firms, for three main reasons, cannot be regarded as OT firms in the accepted sense of the word. One, their work is, relatively speaking, not of an emergency nature, and is performed under comparatively safe conditions, on sites probably not beyond the jurisdiction of their local labour control office, and certainly not beyond that of their Gauarbeitsamt (District Labour Control Bureau). Second, the firm personnel, foreign and German, is paid not according to the OT wage scales valid in the zones of operations (Front-OT), but according to the industrial wage scales as fixed for the entire Reich. Thirdly, non-OT firms enter into individual contracts with the parties directly involved, rather than sign uniform types of contracts with the OT. Finally, it must be added that it is probable that all personnel of these firms, except key personnel, can be called out for civilian defence work such as trench digging, by the Reichsverteidigungskommissar (Reich Defence Commissioner). OT firms proper are, on the other hand, active in the zones of operations or concentrated in rear areas which have suffered major air damage to vital installations, in short, are Front-OT. These firms and their personnel are considered military units not subject to control by civilian labour authorities, or by Party Gauleiter in their capacity of Reich Defence Commissioners (a government function).

The third special agency which was attached to Amt Bau and is still attached to Amt Bau-OTZ is that of the Reichsbeauftragter für den Holzbau (Reich Deputy for Timber Construction). This office was created because of the acute shortage of timber. Its mission is to assure the supply of timber for OT's high-priority programme.

The three above-mentioned attached agencies constitute the parts of Amt Bau, which at the present time continue their functions under Amt Bau-OTZ. Very little is known concerning the organic structure of the former Amt Bau itself, previous to its merger with OTZ beyond the fact that it contained an indeterminate number of Amtsgruppen (branches). At any rate, as a result of the merger some sections of the combined Amt Bau-OTZ have now been designated Amtsgruppen, of which two have been so far identified: Amtsgruppe Bauplanung und Baueinsatz (Construction Planning and Commitment Branch) and Amtsgruppe Verwaltung und Personal (Administration and Personnel Branch). Functionally, however, the entire structure of Amt Bau-OTZ has been organised along the lines of the former OTZ rather than along those of Amt Bau. Moreover, OT personnel has now replaced Amt Bau personnel in most, if not in all, key positions.

The scope of authority of Amt Bau-OTZ, is substantially the same as was that of OTZ, with some extension of authority in the matter of allotment of building supplies. The Construction and Planning Commitment Branch now not only apportions allotments to the various Einsatzgruppen, but also issues directives for their further apportionment within each Einsatzgruppe.

The following is a basic list of industries in order of priority, in respect of the procurement of supplies:

1. Armament finished products industry.
2. Armament component parts industry.
3. Chemical industry.
4. Mining industry.

5. Water and Power industry.

6. Transportation industry.

7. Armed Forces.

8. Housing and non Government projects.

9. Air defense.

'Current Organisation' – Chain of Command.

The decree signed by Speer on 24 September 1943, ordering the normalisation of OT administrative levels in all theatres of operations, was for the first time consistently adhered to, with the division of Germany into OT regions (eight Einsatzgruppen, twenty-two Einsätze, etc.) in July 1944.

'Current Organisation' – Einsatzgruppe (EG; Area Control Staff, Army Group Level).

There are eight Einsatzgruppen in Greater Germany. The Einsatzgruppe staff in Germany has in substance the same latitude in executive authority, as was previously enjoyed by Einsatzgruppe West (France and the Low Countries). Correspondingly, the sphere of authority and scope of function of a Chief of Einsatzgruppe within Germany, encompasses the following:

1. The drawing up and management of a building programme for the entire Einsatzgruppe under his control. This is done in conjunction with Amtsgruppe Bauplanung und Baueinsatz (Construction Planning and Commitment Branch) of Amt Bau-OTZ, and through liaison with OT's chief employers (the Army, the Air Force, the Navy, Reich Defence Commissioners, etc.)

2. The decision as to which construction agency's facilities are to be employed in tha execution of building tasks (i.e. those of OT or those of the Air Force, the Navy, the SS, the Reichsautobahnen (Reich Highway System) etc. In case of major assignments, the basic directives, as issued by Amt Bau-OTZ, are to be adhered to.

3. The right to enlist the help of the construction agencies of the above-mentioned organisations, for tasks in which OT agencies are already engaged. This right does not include the authority to change the internal structure of any of the above-mentioned construction agencies. Nor does it include the authority to deviate from the construction programme as laid down in this connection by Construction Planning and Commitment Branch. Consent in these two respects must be obtained from the ranking officials of the construction agencies involved.

4. The obligation to inform the appropriate Reichsverteidigungskommissar (Reich Defence Commissioner) within the Einsatzgruppe area of all important new projects, and to keep them advised as to the difficulties as they arise.

Since the creation of the Rüstungsunterkomissionen (Armament Sub-Commissions) (Speer's decree of 3 Aug 1944), OT representation on the Armament Commissions has been raised from Einsatz to Einsatzgruppe level. That is to say, the Chief of EG is now a member of the Armament Commission. Usually, however, he is represented by the subordinate Chiefs of the Einsätze situated within the respective areas of the Rüstungsinspektionen (Armament Inspectorates) corresponding to the particular Armament Commissions (see next para).

'Current Organisation' – Einsatz (E: Area Control Staff, Army Level).
There are twenty-two Einsätze in Greater Germany, roughly one to each Rüstungsinspektion (Armament Inspectorate). The Einsatz in Germany is mainly a liaison staff between its higher Einsatzgruppe Staff, on the one hand, and the Rüstungsunterkommission or Rustungskommission (Armament Sub-Commission or Armament Commission) and the Reichsverteidigungskommissar (Reich Defence Commissioner) on the other. The Armament Sub-Commission is situated in those Gaue in which there are no Armament Commissions. The Sub-Commissions were created by order of Speer, 3 August 1944, for the purpose of remedying this lack. (The Gauleiter in his function as chief of all types of civilian contribution to the war effort is also Reich Defence Commissioner.)

OT Einsatz liaison with the Armament Sub-Commissions is established through one of the four OT Construction Deputies assigned by the Einsatzleiter (Chief of Einsatz) to the Reich Defence Commissioner or Commissioners competent in the OT Einsatz area. The Construction Deputy as a member of the Armament Sub-Commission represents his Chief of Einsatz, and acts as expert consultant to the Chairman of the Armament Sub-Commission. The latter determines the priority programme of reconstruction and repair to be undertaken by the OT on, e.g., armament factories, in his district.

OT Einsatz liaison with the Reich Defence Commissioner or Commissioners competent in the area which the Einsatz covers is established through the above-mentioned Construction Deputies, of whom there are four if the entire Gau is situated in the Einsatz Area. It is the function of the Chief of Einsatz, through his four Deputies, to grant exemptions from the Building Restrictions Act, in order to allow the construction and repair of building and installations 'vital' to the civilian population and to the war effort in this respect. Included in this exemption is construction for the Deutsches Wohnungshilfswerk (German Housing Auxiliary Project), for the NSV (National Sozialistische Volkswohlfahrt or National Socialist People's Welfare), for construction of quarters for the Hitler Jugend (Hitler Youth Organisation) in connection with the children evacuation scheme, for the construction of farm buildings, and finally for civilian construction which can no longer be delayed. Such exemptions from the Building Restrictions Act as mentioned above, are granted by the Chief of Einsatz through one of his Construction Deputies, on the strength of directives issued to the latter by the Reich Defence Commissioner.

To summarise, the Einsatz Staff is essentially concerned with the technical aspects of control over the construction programmes as executed by the individual Oberbauleitungen operating in the Einsatz area. The Chief of Einsatz, besides being subordinate to his Chief of Einsatzgruppe, is, in respect to civilian defence, subject to directives (through the Construction Deputies) from the Reich Defence Commissioners whose Gaue are entirely or partly situated within his Einsatz. The Chief of Einsatzgruppe allots supplies and manpower to the various Einsätze under his control, more or less on the basis of requirements as submitted by the individual Chiefs of Einsatz. The latter base their requirements on the result of their conferences with the Chairman of the Armament Commissions or Sub-Commissions on the one hand, and on the directives as issued by the Reich Defence Commissioners on the other. If the Chief of Einsatzgruppe finds himself unable to comply fully with Einsatz requisitions, the matter goes through Amt Bau-OTZ to be taken up by Speer himself for final decision.

'Current Organisation' – Oberbauleitung OBL: Basic Construction Section with Administrative HQ

The present number of OBLs in Germany is not known. They are located mainly in industrial centres, subject to Allied air raids, in areas now being fortified, such as the Alpine regions and in the zones of communications.

The OBL is functionally in liaison with the competent Rüstungskommando (Armament Command) just as Einsatz is in liaison on a higher level with the competent Armament Commission or Sub-Commission.

c) Structure of QT HQs on various levels

Nomenclature of OT Units

The names given various OT construction units represent geographic terms, personal names, compass directions, numerals, administrative boundaries, or code designations. The following examples will illustrate this nomenclature:

Geographical Names:
    Einsatzgruppen: Deutschland I-VII, Einsatzgruppe Italien
    Einsätze: Apeninnen, Kertsch, Nordnorwegen and Polarbereich

Sondereinsatz: Wolga

OBLs: Wiesbaden, Garda, Holland, Isonzo, Normandie

BL: Caen

ABL: Granville

Personal Names:

Einsätze: Zinth and Wedekind

OBL: Gittinger

ABL: Kundt

Compass Directions:

Einsatzgruppe: West (covering France and the Low Countries)

Einsatze: Ost, West (in EG Italien)

OBLs: Nordwest and Mitte (in OBL Cherbourg)

Numerals:

Einsatzgruppen: Deutschland I–VIII

Einsätze: I, II etc. (in EG Russland-Süd)

Bauleitungen: 1, 2, etc. (in EG Russland-Nord)

ABLs: 1, 2, etc. (in OBL Bruges)

Einheiten: I, II etc. (in EG Russland-Nord)

Einheiten: 27, 33 etc. (in EG Russland-Nord)

Administrative Boundaries:

Einsatz im Bereich der Rüstungsinspektion XIIa

Code Designation:

OBLs: Alarich, Geisreich, Theoderich (in EG Italien)

Bauleitungen: Adolf, Gustav, Julius (Alderney, Guernsey and Jersey Isles)

ABLs: Linz etc. (in EG Russland-Nord)

Einheiten: Berlin, Essen etc. (in EG Russland-Mitte)

Miscellaneous:

Einsatzgruppe Wiking (covering Norway and Denmark)

Einsatze: Freie Fahrt NO (in EG Russland-Nord), Seefalke (in EG Italien and EG Russland-Süd)

OBL: W-2 or Soissons (in EG West)

Bauleitung für Energie (in EG Russland-Süd)

ABL: Weisser Sumpf (in Sondereinsatz Wolga)

Structure of OT Headquarters

The basic structure of the OT HQ is similar in all echelons. But it is only natural to find the organisation of the higher echelons more extensive and complicated than that of the lower echelons. Certainly a much larger organisation is needed to manage an Einsatzgruppe, for example, than a small Abschnittsbauleitung.

Under the direction of a chief of a sector (Einsatz and downward) we find usually four important sections:

1. Büro des Leiters or der Leitung (Chief's personal office staff)
2. Technik (Construction)
3. Nachschub (Supply)
4. Frontführung (Front Area Personnel Section)
5. Verwaltung (Administration)

Plus four less important sections:

6. Kraftfahrwesen (Motor Transport)
7. Nachrichtenwesen (Signal Communication)
8. Sanitätswesen (Medical Services)
9. SS Verbindungsführung (SS Liaison)

Only in higher echelons (EG and Amt Bau-OTZ) are the following sections in addition found:

10. Personalabteilung (Personnel Section)
11. Arbeitseinsatz und Sozialpolitik (Manpower allocation and Social Policy)
12. Kultur, Presse und Propaganda (Education, Press and Propaganda).

The sections in the highest echelons (OTZ and EGs) are usually called Hauptabteilungen and these in turn are subdivided into subsections called Abteilungen or Referate. The lower echelons are usually subdivided into Abteilungen and Referate. But many inconsistencies in terminology account for a considerable number of deviations from this pattern.

The above organisation is illustrative of HQ structure in all echelons at a time when the OT was mainly still operating outside the Reich. The structure of OT headquarters on the various levels, in the Reich at the present time, embodies no radical changes.

Former Hauptabteilungen in OTZ have become either Amtsgruppen or Abteilungen in Amt Bau-OTZ; Hauptabteilungen in EG HQ have become Abteilungen, subdivided into Hauptreferate and Referate; Abteilungen in Einsatz HQ and echelons below have become Referate. A more significant development is the present function of the Einsatz which, as a control staff over the construction programme within an area corresponding to that of a Rüstungsinspektion (Armament Inspectorate), has become a liaison staff between the OT on one hand, the Speer Ministry, Wehrmacht and civilian authorities on the other (Armament Inspectorates and Reich Defence Commissioners). This subject has been discussed in detail earlier. The absence of sections 10 and 11 (Manpower allocation and Social Policy and Culture, Press and Propaganda) on EG level in the Reich is a characteristic of OT administration inside Germany. EG Wiking (Norway and Denmark) and EG Italy have retained these two sections. Inside Germany the functions of these two sections are directed by Amt Bau-OTZ, in liaison with the DAF (Deutsche Arbeitsfront; German Labour Front).

Functions of OT Headquarters
The following is a brief description of the functions of the HQ subdivisions as enumerated above.

(1) Leitung (Executive Directorate)
At the head of each OT Unit is a so-called Leiter (Chief) as follows:

> Einsatzgruppenleiter at the head of an Einsatzgruppe
> Einsatzleiter at the head of an Einsatz
> Oberbauleit at the head of an Oberbauleitung
> Abschnittsbauleiter at the head of an Abschnittsbauleitung

These designations are functional and denote temporary duties and assignments and should not be confused with permanent OT ranks. Thus, for example, a man in charge of an Einsatz is called Einsatzleiter, but his OT rank may be either OT-Einsatzleiter or OT-Oberbauleiter or even lower.

There are great variations in the Chief's personal staff or staff organisation of the Leitung. Some illustrative examples follow: the Leitung of the EGW consisted of a Dienststellenleiter (Section Administrator), his Stellvertreter (deputy), a Sekretariat (Secretary's Office) composed of several planning engineers and a Vorzimmer (Reception Room) with clerical help. In the OBL St Malo there existed an Oberbauleiter (OBL Chief) and his Vertreter (Deputy), a Hilfsarbeiter (Assistant) of the Oberbauleiter and his Vertreter and a clerical staff. In the OBLs St Malo and Cherbourg such subdivisions as Vertragswesen (Contracts), Preisbildung (Price and Cost Control), Stollenbauangelegenheiten (Subterranean Tunneling), Baudispositionen (Assignments of Project locations), Firmeneinsatz (Assignments of firms to Construction Sites) which would normally be placed in either the section Verwaltung (Administration) or Technik (Construction) were included in the Leitung.

(2) Technik (Construction)

This section is variously known as Technik, Baubüro, Bau, Landbau, Technisches Büro or Technische Abteilung. in different OT units and takes care of all matters pertaining to construction. It contains subsections devoted to such specific matters as Vermessung (Surveying), Statistik (Statistics), Baustoffprüfung (Testing of Building Materials), Hochbau (Building above Ground), Elektrowirtschaft (Electrical Power Supply) and others.

(3) Nachschub (Supply)

All the matters dealing with the supply of materials, machines and implements needed in construction are centralised in the section Nachschub, which is also charged with the supervision of the extensive material depots.

(4) Frontführung (Front Area Personnel Section)

This section deals with the Frontarbeiter (Front Zone Worker) in all his activities on the 'front', which is to say in the front operational area as defined by OT. It takes care of the indoctrination of the Frontarbeiter in the spirit of the National Socialist ideology and of basic military training in defence against Allied attacks. The Frontführung gives counsel (but renders no decisions) in matters pertaining to wages, tariffs, furloughs, family problems, and also controls the Dienstbücher (Pay and Identity Books) and Erkennungsmarken (Identification Discs), distribution of Marketenderwaren (Canteen or PX goods), weapons, clothing and other equipment. It organises entertainment and is also in charge of libraries and e.g. the distribution of newspapers and magazines.

(5) Verwaltung (Administration)

This section deals with all matters pertaining to finances, bookkeeping and the internal administration of the OT units. Its subsections include Kasse (Treasury), Inventar (Inventory), Abrechnung (Auditing), Buchhaltung (Bookkeeping) and others.

(6) Kraftfahrwesen (Motor Transport)

This section takes care of motor transportation for men and materials, the actual task itself being performed by NSKK – Transportkorps Speer and Transportflotte Speer.

(7) Nachrichtenwesen (Signals Communication)

This is not always an independent section within the administration of a unit. Sometimes it forms a subsection within another main section. Thus, for example, Nachrichtenwesen formed a subsection within the section Verwaltung in OBL Cherbourg, within the section Technik in the OBL St Malo and within the section Nachschub in the Einsatz Seefalke (EG Italien).

(8) Sanitätswesen (Medical Services)

Medical conditions in a unit are taken care of by this section. It comprises medical personnel consisting of physicians, dentists, orderlies and nurses.

(9) SS-Verbindungsführung (SS Liaison)

Every OT unit from Amt Bau-OTZ down to an OBL has a representative of the SS to serve as security and political control officer. More specifically the tasks of an SS-Verbindungsführer (SS Liaison Officer) are the following: guarding against sabotage, political crimes and other transgressions, checking on German and foreign personnel; issuing of permits and passes of all types; keeping a card index of all OT personnel and of SS counter-intelligence operatives and tracking down fugitive workers, this last by means of the Schutzkommandos (SK: Security Guard Units).

(10 to 12) The Personalateilung (Personnel Section)

Arbeitseinsatz und Sozialpolitik (Manpower Allocation and Social Policy sections) and Kultur, Presse und Propaganda (Education, Press and Propaganda; are found only in the highest echelons, namely Amt Bau OTZ and in Einsatzgruppen. On lower levels such as Oberbauleitungen, the above matters are parceled out to subsections within the sections Frontführung Verwaltung.

   The lowest construction units, from a Bauleitung down, have a very restricted administrative organisation composed of a technical staff which takes care of construction and, if they are sufficiently important, a deputy Frontführer.

B. Chain of Command and HQ Sections

Einsatzgruppe West (EGW)

The procedure for the planning and construction of large projects of a military nature in the EGW up to June 1944 was as follows: After strategic policy had been decided upon by the German Supreme Command, the execution was entrusted to the Commander in Chief of Army Group West, who in turn called in the Chief of corresponding OT sector (Einsatzgruppe) as his executive engineer. Thus, in the case of the Atlantic Wall, General Field Marshal von Rundstedt was responsible for the project on the basis of plans as evolved by Oberbaudirektor Weiss, Chief of the Todt Organisation in the West and Chief Engineer on Rundstedt's military staff. In the planning of so large a project as the building of the Atlantic Wall, it can naturally be assumed that Hitler, Speer and other high functionaries showed varying degrees of professional interest, Speer and his staff, for example, concentrated on standardisation methods and construction specifications. The experience gained in the building of the West Wall was used in the selection and standardisation of the best type of fortifications for a particular terrain down to the smallest detail. This procedure simplified immensely both the planning and the estimating of material requirements. Moreover Weiss had at his disposal, beside his own staff, a special liaison staff of Army Fortress Engineers, and the Engineers from the staff of Army Group West. The blueprints were then sent to OTZ Berlin for approval, normally given as a routine procedure provided the plans did not depart radically from the original conception of the Supreme Command of the Armed Forces.

The Army exercised control through periodic inspections, first by Lt-General of Engineers Schmetzer, Inspector of Fortifications in the West, and then by General of Engineers, Alfred Jacob the Inspector General of Fortifications. Similar control for Naval and Air Force installations was exercised by the Navy and Air Force High Commands. Finally General Field Marshal Rommel inspected the entire Atlantic Wall in the capacity of Inspector General of Defence. In the exercise of this function, Rommel, like Speer was responsible only to Hitler.

After blueprints had been drafted and estimates of total requirements had been prepared in Paris, responsibility for the actual construction was divided amongst the various Oberbauleitungen. Each OBL was allotted the amount of material considered adequate for the construction of the fortifications in their sector. A certain latitude in the tactical arrangement of the defence installations was allowed, inasmuch as local engineers were better acquainted with local terrain. They were also expected, if necessary, to draft specific blueprints (Sonderzeichnungen) for special types of bunkers and similar projects, for which no provision had been made in the standardised plans. For this purpose, there were sittings of a Wehrmachtausschuss (Armed Forces Committee) composed of Army, Air Force, Naval Engineers of Corps level, and OBL technicians.

Once detailed blueprints were drafted and construction had begun, the Fortification Engineers were charged with supervising the satisfactory completion of that part of the fortifications which they eventually had to take over. For this purpose, each OBL established liaison with the Fortification Engineer staff stationed in their sector. Their authority was confined to supervision; modifications of the original specifications had to have the approval of Weiss. Abteilung (at present Referat) Technik (Technical Section) of each OBL administrative HQ managed the entire building programme for its own (OBL) sector. Referat Statistik (Statistics Section) planned the building schedule according to priority ratings and time limits. The schedules covered approximately a six-month period. Estimates of requirements of material, as well as machines and manpower (as represented by the firms), were figured on that time basis. It was the Statistics Section which kept the records on technical matters which firms were required to furnish in the form of periodic reports. The link in this respect between OBL and firm was the Betriebsführer (Executive Manager, very often identical with the owner) of the firm who co-ordinated the reports of the various construction supervisors employed by the firm on its building sites. He also sent in the reports of the firm's bookkeeper on all construction expenditure.

While the above outline gives the basic picture of the echelons involved in the planning and building of OT projects, it should be pointed out that the picture as presented is that of the EGW. Deviations, however, will be found even in the EGW. The German Air Force in France, at least, preferred (until July 1944) to control Air Force installations, which were being built by German firms through its own administrative bureau for Air Force construction – Luftwaffe Feldbauamt. Firms working directly for the Air Force were consequently not OT Firms. The German Navy (until July 1944) through its local administrative bureau, Marine-Bauamt, would furnish plans for such projects as for example emplacements for naval guns to the HQ of the Army Fortress Engineers (Pionier Festungs Baustab) which would take over the work, in conjunction with the OT. On small local jobs, the Army Engineers sometimes 'borrowed' OT supplies and manpower on an unofficial basis, and thus avoided 'red tape'. The Army, sometimes, and apparently for the same reasons, hired local labour directly, and had work performed without any control by the OT. This practice fell into gradual disuse in France partly because of objections made by the OT authorities, mostly, however, because the shortage of manpower in France finally became so acute that there was hardly any manpower available which had not already been allocated. The last evidence in the West of this practices, was in Zeeland (Netherlands) in April 1944, when the local population was conscripted directly by the Army for the construction of coastal fortifications under supervision of Army Engineers.

Russia

The situation in Russia was quite different. Not only did everything have to be built from the ground up, but there was also the constant need of protection from guerillas. Above all, the military situation was kept fluid, by the necessity of reckoning with the Russian counter-offensives. Relations between Wehrmacht and the OT were, therefore, much more direct than they were in the West. On the 23 July 1942, for example, the chief OT liaison officer to Army Group A ordered a preliminary survey detachment of the Brückenbauleitung Ertl (Bridge Construction Sector Ertl) to make a report on the construction site for a bridge which was to span the River Don at Rostov. The survey was started on the 25th, while the site was still within range of Russian artillery fire. On the 30th, presumably after the survey group had turned in their report, orders for the actual construction came through from the General of Engineers, Army Level. The construction itself was then left in the hands of the OT Bridge Construction Sector Ertl.

Balkans

Exploitation of the bismuth, manganese, antimony, molybdenum, chromium and bauxite mines in the Balkans was of great strategic importance to Germany. It was, therefore, the Generalbevollmächtigter für die Wirtschaft (Plenipotentiary General for Industry) in Belgrade who made the initial request for the construction of roads to facilitate exploitation on a large scale. The channels on this occasion were as follows. The Plenipotentiary for Industry in Belgrade made out his report to Berlin, whence it was forwarded through Army channels to the Commanding General, South East, who approved it and finally it was forwarded to OT in Belgrade.

Germany

The first evidence of organised OT activity on a considerable scale in Germany was the creation of Einsatz Ruhrgebiet in May 1943, later expanded to an Einsatzgruppe. The Ruhr Valley was declared an emergency area as a result of the Allied air raids which had destroyed among others the Mohne Dam. At that time the OT was only part of this reconstruction scheme, which was directed by Dipl. Ing. Sander in a dual capacity. His regular post was that of Baubevollmächtigter des Reichsministers Speer im Bezirk der Rüstungsinspektion VI. On 1 May 1943 he was given the additional task of repairing the damage caused in the Ruhr Valley, in connection with which he was appointed Baubeauftragter Ruhr des Generalbevollmächtigten Bau (Construction Deputy for the Ruhr of the Plenipotentiary General for Construction), that is to say, of Speer's representative, at that time Stobbe-Dethleffsen. In the latter capacity he was Chief of the special Speer staff for the Ruhr. The members of this staff were the OT Chief of Einsatz Ruhrgebiet, the chief of Armament Inspectorate VI and all Gauleiter whose Gaue totally or partially fell within the Ruhr Valley.

To list OT's activities in Germany at the present time would be equivalent to listing all repair and construction of any type whatsoever now being undertaken in the Reich. For the performance of its present tasks, the OT has absorbed all previously civil and official agencies in the Reich subordinated to Amt Bau with which construction Plenipotentiary Sander was connected.

C. Tasks and Methods of Operation

a) Activities of the OT

Activities of the OT in General

A list of OT building activities includes the following:

1. Roads.
2. Railway beds, ties and tracks.
3. Underground cables and pipes (communication and sewage).
4. V-sites.
5. Fortifications including bunkers, blockhouses, tank-traps, pillboxes, tunnels, roadblocks, laying of mines and gun emplacements.
6. Camouflaging.
7. Dredging and excavation.
8. Bridges.
9. Naval installations including harbours, piers, docks, coastal-gun emplacements.
10. Aircraft installations including aerodromes, hangars and runways.
11. Dams, dykes, draining and breakwater systems.
12. Mining industry including petroleum wells.
13. Exploitation of quarries, gravel and sand pits.
14. Electrical installations such as power houses, hydroelectric plants.
15. Factory buildings.
16. Water supply systems.
17. Barracks, camps, warehouses, hospitals, etc.
18. Snow removal (e.g. in Russia).
19. Air-raid damage repair.
20. Demolition work.
21. Underground supply and munition dumps.
22. Ventilation systems.
23. Water reservoir.
24. Surveying.
25. Painting and landscaping.

Activities of the OT According to Location

Broadly speaking, as has already been remarked, the emphasis, in the West, Norway and Italy, was on fortifications, and in the East and the Balkans on communication systems. In these latter countries besides, the emphasis was

One of three hundred-thousand: *A worker who has been employed for one and a half year on the West Wall. His wife and three children live in a village in central Germany. Every half year he comes home on leave like a soldier from the "front" ...*

The Men of the OT

Picture series
of the work done
by the Todt-Organisation
in the West Wall fighting zone

A steel helmet for every worker in the fighting zone
Enemy fire can be expected daily. The men then leave their posts and rush through shrapnel-proof trenches to the next dugout or bunkers in the rear

In the "labyrinth" of the fighting zone: the "pilot" takes the lead ...
Each group of workers is looked after by a soldier who knows the lay of the land and can safely lead the men to their posts through mine-fields and barbed wire entanglements. Additional bunkers and embrasures are being built here. The front workers, who are not soldiers, are instructed by the Todt-Organisation's trained leaders concerning the proper conduct in a fighting zone

A double-page spread from an English-language edition of *Signal*, the German propaganda picture magazine, featuring 'The Men of the OT' in the Westwall fighting zone.

Behind protecting trees
and screens . . .
*Invisible to the enemy the
West Wall workers carry on.
Between them and the front
line soldiers there is an active comradship. Machine-
guns protect them against
enemy shock-troops and re-
connoitering units. Everything looks quiet behind
the barbed wire, but . . .*

. . . Things hum in the
excavation
*The last planks are being
applied. Concrete mixers
are already on hand. Pro-
tected by a front line soldier
the German front line worker
works for — the front line
soldier*

Tunnels eat their way
through the hills . . .
*Connecting galleries lead
from one fortification to the
next. The compression ham-
mers are in the hands of
miners who have come to the
West Wall from all parts of
the Reich.*

'The last planks are being applied. Concrete mixers are already on hand. Protected by a front-line soldier the German front-line worker works for – the front-line soldier.'

A German infantry garrison entering a heavy fort through the heavily armoured and gas-proof door.

The German army has special soldiers to man the Line. The majority are young but veterans are interspersed.

Fully-equipped German machine-gun soldiers manning one of the concrete forts in the Siegfried Line.

Troops can be moved from place to place swiftly by this light railway installed deep within the Siegfried Line.

A typical tunnel in the Siegfried Line showing the rails for the light electrically driven railway that runs through it.

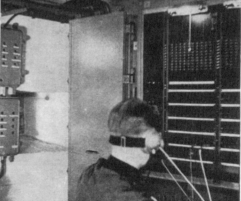

The German fortifications have a telephone system, the wires of which are buried deep underground like the exchanges.

A photo-feature on the Westwall, published in the UK during the war. *(CMcC)*

German infantry cleaning their rifles in an underground fort. These forts are plentifully stocked with food and ammunition.

In the observation room of a fighting unit. Information received here can be telephoned to all parts of the sector.

A mess-room in an anti-aircraft defence tower with its own water supply.

Siegfield Line soldiers receiving their orders from an officer.

Machine-gun outposts of the Line have deep entrances and underground alleys.

A concrete Siegfried Line observation post from which the orders for firing are given to the German gunners.

German soldiers leaving an underground fortification of the Siegfried Line.

These images reveal the elaborate facilities underground – see cutaway in colour section.

Opposite: Dragon's teeth anti-tank obstacles snaking through the landscape. Above: Two post-liberation photos showing Allied troops at the Westwall and passing through with apparent ease. In the lower image note that the girders fit into the toothed side-sections to block the road. Manyof the Allied soldiers went to great pains to pose for photographs hanging out their washing on the 'Siegfried Line', bringing to life the words of the popular song. *(NARA)*

also on the rebuilding of power plants and factories and on the exploitation of natural resources. Some of the important construction work in both West and East carried out/ by the OT are listed below.

i) The 'Westwall' (Siegfried Line)

Hitler gave the order to start fortifications in the West in May 1938. As can be learned from German sources, as early as 1936, there were about 100 fortresses at tactically important locations along the Rhine. These were augmented at the rate of 500 a year till Hitler harnessed all available means for the construction of the Westwall, which extends from Wesel (near the Dutch border) to the Swiss frontier in the South. Emphasis was put on the fact that the Westwall was to be built in depth. More than 22,000 fortresses stretch over its entire length, including dugouts, anti-tank positions, anti-aircraft strong points, and so forth. The manpower employed consisted roughly of:

Festungspioniere (Fortress Engineers)	90,000 men
OT	350,000 men
Reichsarbeitsdienst (German Labour Service)	100,000 men

To these 540,000 must be added additional help from the Army, which brought units for training purposes to the Wall to establish obstacles, blocks, and lay communication cables. About 6,000,000 tons of cement were used. The daily supply of stones came to 140,000 tons, and 695,000 cubic metres of wood were employed.

A cast 'Panzerturm' turret and exposed steelwork during construction of the Westwall.

Firms which worked on the Westwall were chosen from the neighbouring towns (Aachen, Saarbrücken, Köln, and others) and were later moved to the Atlantikwall, or Atlantic Wall.

The following, taken from *Infantry Journal* in 1943, gives some idea of the magnitude of this project:

> From his headquarters in Wiesbaden, Fritz Todt organised the work as a gigantic problem in excavating, steel and cement procurement, concrete mixing and transporting, concrete pouring, labour, transporting and housing problem, all put on a twenty-four hour basis. As the Nazi and German military press depicted this enterprise, a variety of organisations and enterprises were called upon to contribute – the German cement industry threw in one-third of its total production; private construction firms furnished the largest excavators available and fully a third of all concrete mixers in the Reich as well as pneumatic drills, tractors and 15,000 trucks, or over one-third of the whole German truck fleet. The Reich railways put at Todt's disposal 6,000 freight cars per diem, later raised to 8,000, and the Reich Postal service, which runs the larger part of the German rural bus lines, 68% of its total fleet. The National Socialist Motor Transport Corps (NSKK) furnished numerous truck drivers, dispatch riders and traffic control officers.
>
> The OT began its work with 35,000 men of its own on 20 July 1938, practically all building workers; this number rose to 45,000 a week later and thereafter in the following acceleration: 77,000 on 3 August; 191,000 on 7 September; 213,000 on 14 September; 241,000 on 21 September; 278,000 on 28 September; and to its maximum of 342,000 on 6 October. While these numbers rose and the work got actually under way, Hitler, speaking at the Annual Party Day rally on 12 September, called it 'The most gigantic fortification work of all ages'. To the labouring contingents were added 90,000 workers employed by the Staff of Fortification Engineers (Festungspionierstab), who did the surveying, cable-laying, camouflaging, etc. and 100,000 men of the Reich Labour Service (RAD), on whom Todt increasingly drew as a labour force.

ii) The Atlantikwall

Work on the 'Atlantic Wall' proper, excluding the Channel defences, was begun in the spring of 1942. The Wall extends from the Bay of Biscay in the south to the North Cape, Norway, in the north and covers about 1,700 miles. A conservative estimate of the number of men employed is 300,000. German propaganda figures put the number at about a half-million, and it is possible that this number, given for a peak period (autumn of 1942), was not unreasonable. The same sources claim that 20,000,000 cubic metres of earth were excavated and moved in the period from May 1942 to May 1943. It was also officially stated that it took

Above: The Batterie Todt, one of the major fortresses on the Atlantikwall, is located near Cape Gris on the Pas de Calais. Operational from February 1942, it consisted of four casements, or blockhouses, armed with Krupp 380 mm calibre guns with a range of 55.7 km. Turm 1, the main casement, now houses the Musee du Mur d'Atlantique – see colour section

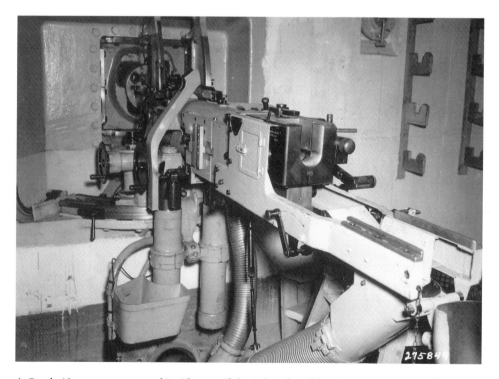

A Czech 40 mm gun mounted inside one of the Atlantikwall bunkers, photographed by Allied troops in 1944. *(NARA)*

Two post-D-Day images of Atlantikwall casements. The upper example shows some remnants of the camouflage netting. The construction is crude with the shuttering markings clearly visible and what appears to be groves made in the drying concrete. In the lower photo, the almost routine ritual of hanging out the washing. The original caption reads, 'Allied soldiers do laundry in captured German pillbox'. *(NARA)*

Interior of a Schiffsbunker, one of the large structures intended to protect ships.

17,000 cubic metres of cement per single gun of a super-heavy coastal battery. (There were at least two main types of such batteries: Battery Todt and Battery Lindemann, named after the well-known artillery general.) Four batteries of the Todt type, complete with living quarters for the personnel, were said to have been installed within ten weeks, the work of 15,000 men with 400 trucks.

iii) Channel Defences

The Channel Defences were started soon after the 1940 campaign in the West, one noteworthy feature at the present time being the fortification of Alderney. The code name for the island is 'Adolf'. Work of a military nature had been carried out ever since the seizure of the island by the Germans. Much of this work is concentrated on the construction of tunnels and heavy coastal gun emplacements. Beside native conscripted labour, Russians, Jews and African Negroes have been employed there by the thousands, and to some extent Frenchmen and Spaniards in lesser numbers. The Island also contains a penal colony to which recalcitrant and habitually delinquent workers are consigned. These, along with the Russians, Jews, and Negroes, are generally assigned the onerous tasks, while Frenchmen and Spaniards are given the task of supervising. An interesting sidelight is the disclosure that about a half-dozen German overseers were sentenced to various penalties by court-martial in March 1944 (Commanding General of 319 Inf. Div. presiding). The courtmartial was held as a result of a written report that 600 Russians had died on the island within the space of nine months. Besides work on Alderney, submarine bunkers, or 'pens', were constructed at St Lazaire, Lorient, Brest and Marseilles.

iv) Norway and Denmark

The OT undertook the construction of the Reichsstrasse (National Trunk Road) connecting the southern part with the northern part of Norway from Nordland through Karasjok and on to the Finnish border at Rovaniemi. Apart from German propaganda statements, it is not certain in what state of completion this project is at the present time. Construction of coastal fortifications has been going on for approximately two years. Fortifications have been erected on Jutland.

v) Finland

Exploitation of nickel mines was undertaken by the OT in the Petsamo area.

vi) Russia

Aside from road and bridge building and reconstruction of industry in cities like Stalino, OT activity in Russia was extended over such a vast area that there does not appear to be any outstanding single piece of construction. Most of the

Above: A replacement Kriegsbrücken, literally a 'war-bridge', constructed by the OT on the Eastern Front, using timber which is immensely strong and was far more readily available than steel. Below: This new steel-framed, free-standing bridge crosses a frozen river. The harshness of the conditions in the east made the construction work difficult. The OT also had responsibilites for clearing the roads after heavy falls of snow.

reconstruction work carried on by the OT, aside from installations essential to military operations, was in the southern part, starting at Kiev and extending through the Crimea and Kerch. Reconstruction of industry was centered in the Donets Basin. Kerch, Nikopol and Kherson were the centres of bridge building activities. In Nikolaev the Crimea and Kherson, the harbours were reconstructed. As to roads and fortifications, the claim was made that 700 miles of roads were improved and kept under repair during the period from July to December 1943. According to German documents, 400,000 men were engaged in the building of the so-called 'Ostwall' (Eastern Wall) in April 1943. At one time OT was investigating the possibility of trunk highways to Berlin from Riga and from Lemberg (Lvov).

vii) Slovakia

A building programme was inaugurated in Slovakia in 1939 by Fritz Todt whereby OT began a network of roads, the completion of which was left to Slovakia. OT completed its share, but the present state of the project is unknown.

viii) Balkans

A Balkan trunk highway (Balkan Durchgangstrasse) was planned in the summer of 1941. It was to extend from Belgrade to Salonika via Kragujevac, Nish, Skoplje, Veles, with a side road from Nish to Sofia. Its total length was to be about 400 miles and 7,000 to 10,000 men, mostly Serbs and Greeks, were employed on it.

Another type of OT construction typical in the Balkan Area was that of funicular railways.

ix) Rumania

The Derubau (Deutsch-Rumänische Bau Gesellschaft), the German-Rumanian Building Corporation, was established in 1940 and entrusted with the development of roads and the laying of oil pipelines. The arrangement was that the OT should initiate the programme. It was then to continue under Rumanian technical supervision. Improvement and expansion of the strategically important network of roads in the Moldavia region and in Bessarabia and beyond the Dniester were part of the scheme.

x) Bulgaria

In June 1942 the Bulgarian Minister for Labour concluded an agreement with the OT whereby, under a Five-Year Plan, the OT would complete 900 miles of asphalt roads during the period from 1942 to 1946. Each year some 200 miles of roads were to be built. OT also improved Bulgaria's Danube Port of Rushchuk.

xi) Albania

Two important roads were built in Albania by the OT, one linking Serbia near Prizren with Northern Albania; the other from Elbasan, connecting with the Bulgarian road network near Bistoly in the south, was improved with the help of Italian Army engineers.

xii) Germany

Except for Einsatzgruppe Ruhrgebiet (established May 1943), the OT did not become a factor in construction within the Reich until the summer of 1944. At the present time Germany is divided into eight Einsatzgruppen, twenty-two Einsätze and an unknown number of Oberbauleitungen (see Part V). The OTZ has been merged with Amt-Bau to form Amt Bau-OTZ which, as a paramilitary agency, now has comprehensive control over all aspects of construction within Germany.

The present tasks of the OT can be divided into four main types:

1. Mindestbauprogramm which may be translated as an irreducible minimum of most urgently needed repairs construction, formulated in the form of relatively short-term programmes (three to six months).

2. Repairs to communications, in support of the German armies on the western and eastern fronts. This zone, comparing roughly with the zone of communications and rear areas of the zone of operations, is the essential part of 'Front-OT'.

3. Strategic fortifications, underground construction of factories, supply depots and reduit installations. Not enough is known at present about this type of construction for anything but speculative discussion. It is, however, a virtual certainty that locations indicating OT and SS co-operation are locations of activities of type 3.

4. Civilian construction. This work overlaps, to some extent, with type 1.

b) Methods of Operation

'Stationäreinsatz' or Static Method of Operation

The OT employed two methods of operation, the mobile, as exemplified in Russia where it worked closely in the wake of the advancing German Army, and the static method as exemplified in the West. The Germans named these two methods Mobileinsatz and Stationäreinsatz. There is a certain temptation to associate the first method with Fritz Todt and the second with Speer. Todt was essentially a technician who thought in terms of large operations and who possessed the great ability of adopting methods of execution to the nature of the operation. Speer, on the other hand, was forced by the economic situation of Germany to concentrate on mass production and standardised operative procedure. It would, therefore, be inaccurate to imply that the OT developed organisationally according to one man's volition. Rather, it developed as dictated by the pressure of war strategy, as expressed in economic and political terms.

There are indications that the static or 'semi-permanent' type of operation was to have been continued and further developed after the war in the event of a German victory. The OT was organized not only administratively but also operationally on the lines of a military organisation. Before the German collapse in France, the OT in Germany could be somewhat compared with the German Ersatzheer (Replacement Army). OTZ could be compared with the administrative offices in Berlin of the OKW (German Supreme Command), Oberbauleitungen, with the divisions of an army of occupation and EGW with the HQ in Paris. In the West, the Oberbauleitung was, with some isolated exceptions, the smallest operational sector possessing a full administrative HQ, just as division is the smallest army unit with a General Staff HQ. The OBL consequently represented the 'basic unit' as conceived in terms of the German 'Einheitsprinzip' or standardisation of 'basic units', leaving, however, the composition of higher units on a flexible basis, by grouping 'basic units' together, according to the requirements of the task to be performed.

Most of the OBLs in the West had a strength of from 10,000 to 15,000 men, with indications that the OT/WE strength called for about 16,000 men or that of a division. Apparently a self-contained building organisation of the above size was considered to be the smallest unit able to cope with the construction of large scale installations, without at the same time, being unwieldy. In short, it was considered to be the most efficient unit. Specifications of raw material and of building parts had already been standardised, so had the costs of material and labour. If each OBL had approximately the same manpower strength, therefore, it obviously would also have the same productive capacity. If building activity should increase appreciably in the sector of a particular OBL, its sector of operation was to have been decreased proportionately. Conversely, if building activity were to decrease appreciably in a particular OBL, its operational sector was to have been increased proportionately. Inasmuch as building programmes were planned to extend over six month periods, such realignments would not have occurred too frequently. Readjustments of OBL sectors for this reason did occur several times in NW France.

Standardisation of specifications simplified the manufacture of parts and their assembly, as well as the drafting of plans and preparation of estimates of material requirements. Standardisation of costs, beginning with the raw material and ending with the finished parts used in construction or installation, simplified the budgetary and financial administration. Standardisation of the productive capacity of the OBLs would thus have immensely simplified estimates of time requirements over the entire Western sector, as well as simplified the allotment of material and the problems of personnel administration.

Actually, things did not turn out as anticipated. OT's operational efficiency deteriorated progressively in the West as the chances for a German victory began to dwindle. Specifically, the reasons were; OT demands for manpower and material grew apace with Germany's territorial conquest, which, as the military situation became more unfavourable, necessitated the construction of comprehensive defence systems. For a while OT had to compete with German essential industries for material and manpower. Then, as Germany began to strain to keep up with Allied production, OT had to accept an economic policy which gave armament production a priority in respect to manpower, essential machinery and parts, and especially transportation fuel. Later this priority enjoyed by the competitors of the OT came to include a variety of accessory materials. This, in turn, meant not only greater control of the OT by various Reich agencies, but showed up in such small, yet effective, means of work stoppage as delay in the shipping of new machine parts intended to replace worn out parts, lack of material and lack of transportation owing to lack of fuel. As for manpower, it was largely because of the refusal of the non-German workers to leave their native country for war jobs in Germany that OT, at least in the West, managed to control the amount of manpower at its disposal. Allied air raids in the winter of 1943 and spring of 1944 were such a demoralising factor that OT authorities had to arrange for mass transfers of personnel from Allied target areas, such as V-sites, to the comparative safety of the Atlantic Wall. These factors, combined with desertions and slow-downs began to affect output materially. The situation had become so desperate in fact that not only could the Germans not afford to discipline working personnel as long as they could get any work out of them at all, but they even made arrangements with the French authorities to employ French convicts who enjoyed the dubious distinction of not even having served their full term.

'Mobileinsatz' or Mobile Method of Operation

Mobileinsatz, as it operated in Russia worked as follows. Highly mobile and self-contained engineering units (bridging, harbour construction units, and others) followed closely in the rear of the German advancing armies, and, if the project was a large one, were given their assignments as a result of OT liaison with the CG of Army or Army Group engineer units, and if the project was a small one as a result of indirect co-operation with the Railway and Fortress Construction Engineer staffs. The chiefs of these OT mobile units had complete responsibility for the execution of their mission. In this connection, it should be pointed out that there were practically no OBLs in Russia and consequently no stabilised administrative HQ. Captured Russian officers with engineering experience provided they were ideologically tractable, were retained for their technical knowledge, their knowledge of Russian and their ability to handle Russian workers. Manpower was obtained simply by stopping convoys of Russian prisoners of war on their way to rear and by putting them to work until relieved by the next convoy of prisoners. (This practice of impressing manpower was used not only by the OT but also by the Army engineers).

Simplification and standardisation of building materials and of methods of construction have been intensified to a still higher degree inside Germany at the present time. Any attempt at uniformity in the productive capacity of 'basic' operational sectors, such as the OBL, has, however, been definitely abandoned in the face of OT's present tasks, 70% of which are estimated to be of an emergency nature.

For specific aspects of OT methods of operation, see the section and subsections on Supplies, Transport, Construction Personnel, Chain of Command, Specifications, Liaison, Firms and Contracts.

c) Construction Specifications

Standardisation of Assembly Parts

Standardisation – always dear to the Germans and carried almost to the level of a religion by the Nazis – is the keynote of all OT construction work. The OTZ worked out certain definite specifications for each assembly unit of a large construction project (pillboxes, shelters, gun emplacements, and so forth) and then allowed the individual Einsatzgruppen extreme latitude as to how many of these standardised and partly pre-fabricated construction parts were to be used and exactly where. This fact accounts for the uniformity in types of construction in, though not necessarily in the disposition of, the defences on the Westwall, the Atlantic Wall, the Gothic Line and those of the east. As terrain, however, played such a large part in the German defensive programme, the OTZ (now Amt Bau-OTZ) wisely allowed the individual Einsatzgruppen to execute independently special plans, 'Sonderzeichungen' which were submitted to the OTZ only for ratification. Thus, for instance, one particular type of emplacement which was especially designed to meet the defensive problems imposed by the African terrain became known as a 'Tobrukstand'. However, once the Tobrukstand had been found practical, it was standardised and used again and again in sandy terrain. Similarly, when France fell and a great many tanks with damaged bogie wheels and treads were captured, it occurred to the engineers working on plans for the Atlantic Wall to simply imbed these tanks in concrete, leaving only the turret above the ground, thus providing a practical and economical emplacement with tank turret. This original form of pillbox was subsequently incorporated into the standardised list of emplacements.

This standardisation was, of course, 'practical insofar as it allowed the OTZ to make a pretty accurate estimate of how much building material should be allotted to each project. For example: 1 Type A emplacement needs so and so much Type B concrete (mixture also prescribed: 400 kilos or eight sacks per cubic metre, added to 70% sand, 30% gravel, admixture 15% water).

Consequently ten Type A emplacements would need ten times the amount. In the event that unforeseen factors, such as swampy terrain, resulted in the need for more material than was originally allotted to the particular project, the competent OBL put in a requisition to the EG, or, in the case of strategic material, to OTZ (now Amt Bau-OTZ) for additional supplies.

Technical Data

Technical data on construction specifications are somewhat beyond the scope of this basic handbook. The examples given below, will serve as illustration:

Ref. No.	German Designation	Translation	Cubic Metres of Concrete Used	Dimensions etc
105	Beobachtungsstand	OP	325	12 m x 4–5 m. Reinforcement 8 mm iron rods
121	Verteidigungsstand mit Panzer Kuppel	Strong point for 7 officers and 32 EM/OR	350	Reinforcement 12 mm iron rods

Later on, when a periodic progress sheet was drawn up, always in connection with a map, it looked somewhat like the following:

Map Ref.	Stützpunkt (Strongpt.)	Programme from/to	Completed	Under construction	Not yet started
Sheet 39	Waldam (often only designated By number)	2 Beobachtungs-stände 105	1 x 105	-	1 x 105
		3 Verteidigungs-stände 121	1 x 121	2 x 121	

Information for these progress sheets was gathered at periodic intervals from the ABLs at each OBL and sent through channels to the Einsatz. Thence it was forwarded to Einsatzgruppe and finally to the OTZ (now Amt Bau-OTZ) where a constant check was maintained on all OT work.

Present State of Research

Research in respect to simplification and standardisation of component machine parts was intensified still further during 1944 and into 1945. At the present time, such research is directed through Amtsgruppe Entwicklung of the Technisches Amt (Development Branch of the Technical Bureau) of the Speer Ministry. It is in one of the latter's agencies that plans for reduced consumption of strategic material and labour, as used by the OT, are worked out on the basis of specific recommendations made by Hauptauschuss Bau (Central Committee for Construction) of Amt Bau-OTZ.

D. Firms and Contracts

a) Firms
Definition, Origin and Development of OT-Firms

The status of a firm in the OT is fundamentally similar to that of a unit or individual in the armed forces of the Reich. Whether such a firm applied of its own accord for enrollment as an OT-Firm or whether it was 'abgestellt für OT' (conscripted for the OT), it contracted itself to carry out construction under OT administration, just as a soldier, by taking the oath, contracts himself to Army Service. Once enrolled, the firm is designated 'OT Einheit' (OT Unit), and the term 'Einheit' became, as far as OT is concerned, synonymous with a building or construction firm contracted to it.

The Einheit is expected to operate as a self-contained unit, composed of a clerical and technical staff, possessing the skill and equipment necessary to direct and execute the construction tasks assigned to it. It is also expected, if the situation demands, to convert itself from a static unit working on a comparatively long term building programme of fortifications, depots and so forth, to a mobile unit combining the functions of army signals and engineer units which restore rear communications. As a unit, it is furthermore expected to abide by, and to confirm with the regulations of the OT Central HQ in Berlin concerning the daily routine of its own personnel and their relationship to the rest of the OT personnel. The supervision of these firms is the function of Oberbauleitungen which are the administrative headquarters in the basic construction sectors. It must be stressed at this point that the Oberbauleitung is the only direct link between a firm and the OT administration. Any request by a firm requiring action by a higher OT echelon has to go through the Oberbauleitung controlling the particular sector in which the firm operates.

Regulation of the status of OT-Firms was not only a gradual process, but also differed considerably in different localities, for example, the methods employed in France varied from those practised in Russia. At first, when the OT was organised by Fritz Todt in the spring of 1938, it was created for the one and specific purpose of completing the Siegfried Line or West Wall, In spite of the vast proportions of this project, there was considerable uniformity in the type of work that had to be performed which facilitated regulation by the OT. Bonuses for speedy and efficient work were offered by the government, and the patriotic aspect was duly stressed by the Nazi press. Consequently, enough large building firms offered their services so as to put the entire construction on a voluntary basis. (The individual firms even drew lots for the location of their particular building sector.) Nor is there any basis later for assuming that firms in any large numbers became so reluctant to work for the OT as to make mass conscription of such concerns necessary. This willingness is due to the attractive profits obtainable from OT contracts. The only possible instance of such reluctance occurred in late 1943 when a large number of firms had to be mobilised for the Russian winter Campaign.

From mid-year 1938 until about May 1942, OT firms, backed by the Reich construction industry, practically ran the OT, and it is only the unfavourable development of the military situation which strengthened the grip of centralized governmental administration at the expense of the private commercial building interests. Around May 1942, the OTZ, having taken over control of the OT from the General Inspektor für das deutsche Strassenwesen (autumn of 1941), began to issue uniform regulations in respect to OT firms. As it is, the Wirtschaftsgruppe Bauindustrie (Economic Group: Construction Industry) and the Reichsinnungsverband des Bauhandwerks (National Guild of Building Craftsmen) probably still have enough influence in the OTZ (now Amt Bau-OTZ) to restrain the government from making life unduly unpleasant for their member firms in the OT.

Although the main problem of the OT-Firm was that of manpower, it also faced a shortage of transportation fuel, lack of sufficient and serviceable equipment and spare parts and, more recently, lack of material due to damage to the communication system by Allied air raids. Those difficulties resulted in competition amongst the firms for manpower, transportation, equipment and material. Nor was all such competition or even an appreciable part of it open and above-board. In France for example, German and French officials were bribed to procure manpower and the workers themselves were bribed to change employment. French subcontractors who employed French workers were offered premiums. Building assignments of favoured firms were given an unwarranted priority rating by the local OT officials. Conversely, material, manpower, equipment and transportation were withheld or withdrawn on some pretext from firms with less fortunate connections. The OT firm is expected to keep at all times a minimum of German supervisory personnel and serviceable equipment. Should either drop below the minimum, the firm may find itself in the position of not being able to obtain foreign manpower from its competent OBL. In this struggle for manpower and supplies, it is the small firms which go under first. Unable to meet OT's minimum TO/WE requirements in respect to German

Fritz Todt addressing the crowd at the opening ceremony for the U-boat pens, or bunkers, at La Rochelle or possibly St Nazaire judging by the vertical, straight-sided portals. Note the flag-bearer displaying the cogged-wheel symbol of the Deutsche Arbeitsfront (DAF), the German Labour Front. St Nazaire is one of five large fortified U-boat bases built in occupied France. The others are at Brest, Lorient, Bordeaux and La Rochelle. U-boat bunkers were also constructed in Germany and Norway.

technical assistants on their staff, and the TE/WEs in respect to equipment, they are compelled – provided they remained in the OT – to choose one of two courses. One is to consolidate with other firms and form an Arbeitsgemeinschaft (Working Combine) commonly abbreviated 'Arge'; the other to descend to the status of sub-contractor to a larger firm, thus avoiding final responsibility, but on the other hand missing the larger profits of the main contractor (4% as against 6%). As subcontractors, OT-Firms can at the same time form part of an Arge, in which event a single main contractor may control a combine of subcontractor.

The evacuation of the OT from EGW and other parts of Europe into Germany (summer and autumn of 1944) has resulted in the tightening of central control in regard to the allotment of manpower to the individual OT firms. A German construction firm at the present time in the Reich is more than ever regarded as a unit of a regimented organisation: if, because of lack of competent staff personnel, it lags behind schedule in the performance of its mission, reinforcements for its supervisory staff are assigned to it by the OT authorities. Equipment is now similarly pooled. On the other hand the individual OT firm, at present operating within the Reich, has no authority to recruit its own manpower.

Organisation of OT-Firms

Within the framework of the OT, the internal administration of the individual OT firms is made uniform and standardised by means of preliminary instructions issued by Wirtschaftsgruppe Bauindustrie to firms entering the OT. As far as the personnel of an OT firm is concerned, a distinction is made between Stammarbeiter (German employees who already were with the firm before it entered OT) and all others.

Three distinct parts comprise the organisation of an OT-Firm:

1. The chief executive who may be the owner of the firm or a firm representative acting as executive manager. A firm may, moreover, have branches in the OT in two or more widely separated localities in occupied Europe (e.g. Norway and Italy). If the firm is assigned to that part of the OT operating within Germany, its entire personnel and equipment are likely to have been enrolled for OT work. If, on the other hand, the firm is assigned to what is left of German occupied Europe, only part of its personnel and equipment may be so enrolled, as an OT branch of the firm, the rest remaining behind with the main branch in Germany.

2. The clerical department whose general duties are the keeping of administrative, personnel, business and financial records and the making out of reports to the OBL according to OT regulations.

3. The technical department which contains statistical personnel and field

personnel. The statistical personnel is concerned with the building schedule including such matters as material and equipment. In connection with these duties, it keeps in close touch with the corresponding subsection Statistik in the OBL. The field personnel comprises the firm technical staff, supervising the various single pieces of construction on which the firm is working, as well as the manpower employed on them. The technical staff has a dual assignment and a correspondingly dual responsibility and status. In the exercise of the first it works in the interest of its employer, the firm, and is responsible for the efficient and speedy construction of the job which it supervised. Finishing a job before schedule means extra profit to the firm, aside from the advantages accruing from the good will of the chief of the OBL. In the exercise of the second, it works in the interests of the OT, and is responsible for seeing that specifications are strictly adhered to and properly carried out. In the latter function the construction supervisors are invested normally with the OT rank of Bauführer, corresponding to that of a second lieutenant in the army. Under the Bauführer who supervises a single building job or several adjacent ones, are the Poliere and Schachtmeister (Section Foreman) who supervise the labour gangs and have NCO ranks. The firm executive manager has similar functions and powers over the entire construction site in which the firm is active. His OT rank is frequently that of Oberbauführer, corresponding to that of a first lieutenant, but it can vary as it depends on the skill of the supervisor and the importance of the particular construction job.

About February 1944, owing to the shortage of German supervisory personnel and the desire of the OT to restore features of mobility to firm units which had become static, the firm and the body of foreign workers in its employ became a more self-contained unit than it had ever been before. In effect, the administration of the firm took on the features of a lower echelon of an OBL HQ. A new post was created as part of the firm re-organisation, namely that of the Mannschaftsführer (Personnel Administrator), who, as a deputy of the OBL Frontführer, took over the administrative duties over all personnel employed by the firm and carried the rank of Betriebsobmann in the DAF. His status can be either that of OT organic personnel, assigned to the firm, or he can be selected by the firm from among its own personnel provided the choice is acceptable to OBL HQ. In either event, his Wehrsold (Army Pay) is paid by the firm. His functions, beside those of feeding and billeting the personnel in his charge, encompass the supervision of their physical and mental welfare. The Betriebsführer (Executive Manager) is also responsible to OBL HQ for the actions of his Mannschaftsführer.

Under the new arrangement the Poliere and Schachtmeister took over the duties of OT's organic NCOs (Baustellen Truppführer). From then on, they were to supervise the German personnel in their charge not only at work but also in camp, where, as Company Sergeants, they are now to assist the Camp supervisors. They also are to keep an eye on their men in respect to morale and report to the Mannschaftsführer on the personal affairs of workmen requiring official attention. All the above personnel are Stammarbeiter. The Hilfspolier (Assistant Polier), who are assigned to the firm by the OBL, perform the same services on the construction site and in camp for foreign workers. (For more detailed description.of the working arrangement between the OT-Firm and the manpower allotted to it, see Part III.)

Firm Reports and Records

The firm has its advance and rear echelons in its administration. The construction supervisors possibly with the help of a clerk, keep records on the construction site, attendance, hours worked, supplies used, work completed, and so forth. Permanent records and periodic reports to OBL, however, made in the office of the firm usually located in the town nearest to the site of construction, which turns out, as often as not, to be near the OBL HQ. In some cases the permanent office records are sent to the firm's legal seat and main office.

The number of main firms controlled by OBL Cherbourg, a construction sector of average activity and strength, in January 1944, was thirty-four. Its TO/WE, which was almost filled, called for a strength of about 15,000 workers. That would put the average manpower controlled by one main firm at about 400. The margin of variation was, however, quite large. The number of subcontractors including French was seventy-nine.

The following is a list of basic records and reports made out by the clerical staff of the Firm.

1. **Schachtmeisterlohnliste** (Pay lists made up on the basis of a record of workers present, hours worked, etc, kept by the Schachtnieister (Section Foreman).
   These lists are made daily, and the total computed in a weekly list. There are special pay-lists for special types of work, such as work additional to that specified in the original contract.

2. **Bautagebuch (Daily Work Journal)** (Daily Work Journal)
   Report on number of work shifts, weather, progress of work since beginning date, occurrences affecting work and pay, equipment check including condition of service, visits of senior officials, changes in price lists, serious difficulties such as unavailable plans and blueprints, and so forth. To be handed in weekly.

3. **Baustellenbewertung** (Monthly Construction Report)
   A monthly report carrying over from the previous months statistical data which was not available for the previous month's report.

4. **Leistungszusammenstellung** (Monthly Work Progress Report)
   Report on work finished during the month giving contract and construction job numbers.

5. **Erfassang der Bestände** (Unused Material Report)
   Made out at completion of job. New material bought back by OT at 100% cost price; material in good state of preservation 60% cost price; still serviceable material, at 30% cost price.

6. **Abschlagsrechnung** (Fortnightly Quittance Accounts)
   Must be numbered consecutively.

7. **Schlussrechnungen** (Final Accounts)

8. **Personal Kartei** (Personnel Files)

9. **Geräte Kartei** (Equipment File)

10. **Geräte Meldung** (Semi-monthly report on unserviceable equipment)

11. **Geräte Inventar** (Monthly inventory of equipment)

12. **U Meldungen** (Daily absence without leave reports)

13. **Arbeitseinsatzstatistik** (Semi-monthly personnel strength reports)

14. **Starkemeldung der Belegschaft an die Deutsche Krankenkasse OT West.**
    Strength Report of Personnel to the German Health Insurance Agency of the OT West.

Construction Programme, Material and Equipment

Building schedules are tentatively made up on an approximately six months' basis. The schedule is drawn up by the statistical section of the Technical Section of the OBL on the basis of assignments apportioned to the OBL by the EG. Firms are accordingly apportioned their assignment by the OBL on the above basis. They are usually assigned jobs corresponding to their specialities such as bridge-building, excavating, and so forth. Prices, from the cost of raw material to the cost of the completed finished installation, including every intermediate operation, are fixed either by the Reichskommissar für Preisbildung or standardised by the OT. Material is sold to the firm by the OBL, unused portions of which are bought back at prices depending on the condition of the leftovers.

Arrangements are also made by the OBL if necessary, for the hiring of equipment by the firm from local contractors or dealers unable or unwilling to join the OT or thrown out of the OT. Equipment can, on occasion, be obtained from the Army Fortress Engineers. Otherwise the firm is expected to have its own equipment and to maintain and repair it. The OT reimburses the firm for the use of equipment and its normal wear and tear on the basis of standard price tables (Geräteabrechnung). The firm puts in a request for additional manpower, if such is called for by an increased assignment, with the QBL. In practice, however, many firms dependent on extraneous arrangements for extra manpower, most of which are contrary to labour regulations as established by the German labour authorities and controlled in occupied parts of Europe by the military authorities (e.g. Stülpnagel in France).

Control over military construction by firms is exercised through periodic inspection (Baukontrolle) of Army engineers in conjunction with OT engineers. Occasionally firms are penalised financially if there is too great a time lag between the scheduled and the actual date of completion. On the other hand completion of a job ahead of schedule is rewarded by a cash bonus. Time lost on a Job is debited to the firm or to the OT depending on the circumstances. (Pay, Allotments, and so forth are discussed in detail in Part III.) Following is a partial list of German terms commonly used in regard to the building programme:

1. Durcharbeit	24 hours uninterrupted work.
2. Sofortprogramm	Highest priority rating, emergency construction.
3. Grossprogramm	Large project construction, such as fortifications, underground tunnels, etc.
4. Schartenbau	Construction of hedgehog positions, strongpoints, emplacements, shelters.
5. Bauwerk	A specific piece of construction on a Baustelle.
6. Baueinsatz	(i) The collective building sites under the control of one firm or Arce in an OBL. (ii) A general term meaning commitment or allocation of construction.
7. Bauvorhaben	Construction projected.
8. Sonderbauten	Special Construction (V-sites, etc.)

Regelbauten – Standardised Construction

Transport is supplied to the firms by NSKK – OT units which pool their own vehicles and trucks with those of the OT firms and locally requisitioned vehicles. Transport is requisitioned from the NSKK by the firms. Owing to the shortage of fuel and the resultant competition for transportation, new regulations were issued in Feb 1944, whereby vehicles belonging to firms were returned to them and permission for hiring additional vehicles from local sources was granted.

Foreign Firms in Occupied Europe, Summer 1944

(i) France

Until February 1944 French firms could not sign a contract directly with the OT but were compelled to sub-contract themselves to a German OT Firm. Such contracts were to be approved by the Vertragsabteilung (Contracts Sub-Section) in the EGW. In February 1944, however, the French building industry established direct liaison in the EGW in order to represent the interests of French firms working for the OT. The office was called Service de Liaison et de Défense des Entrepreneurs Francais auprès de l'OT. In April 1944 the Comité d'Organisation du Bâtiment et Travaux Publics (COBTP) was established. Its function was to recruit reliable French firms for the OT and

Another Kriegsbrückenbau built by the OT, this time in Belgium. The ruins of the old bridge can be seen to the left. As the war progressed, the repair or replacement of bomb-damaged structures became an increasingly important part of the OT's role.

establish standard price quotations in connection with OT contracts. Members of the latter could sign contracts directly with the OT through the offices of the Service de Liaison which attempted to co-ordinate the resources of the French with those of the German construction industry, as well as to arbitrate differences between French and German firms. It proceeded through the intermediary of the German Wirtschaftsgruppe Bauindustrie (Economic Group: Construction Industry) which maintained liaison in the EGW (see below). French firms were financed, if necessary, by the German firm, especially if they brought large gangs of workers, adequate staffs of technicians and serviceable equipment.

(ii) Belgium and Holland
Aside from possible construction of V-sites, there was relatively little activity in Belgium and Holland after the Channel Coast defences had been completed and labour transferred to the Atlantic Wall in France. Consequently most of the Belgian and Dutch OT firms were active in France.

(iii) Norway and Denmark
Conditions as outlined in the case of France hold substantially true for EG Wiking (Norway and Denmark). A small number of German OT firms, however, dominate the field in this sector.

(iv) Italy
The number of Italian OT-Firms in 1943–44 was extremely small, possibly less than two dozen. An Italian firm always could sign a contract with the OT without the necessity of subcontracting itself to a German OT-Firm. There were even fewer German OT-Firms in Italy than Italian. Firms obtain their manpower mainly through the Azione Graziani Labour Agency. Relationship between German and Italian firms and the workers is comparatively free from outside administrative interference.

German Building Associations and Corporations
Wirtschaftsgruppe Bauindustrie (Abbrev. WGB) is the German Building Industry in the self-governing estate of Industry and Trade. It forms part of main group IV, the other groups being the allied industries, Stone and Earthwork, Woodworking, Glass, Ceramic and Sawmills. These, with the Building Industry, form part of Reichsgruppe I Industrie (Group I, Reich Industry). The entire set-up is under the control of Speer in his capacity as Chief of War Production, even though it is in the Ministry of Economics of which Funk is the head. The WGB established liaison at the EGW and the OBLs in the West.

Reichsinnungsverband des Bauhandwerks (Abbrev. RB) is the National Guild of Building Craftsmen. It forms part of the fifty-two Guilds of craftsmen which comprise the Reich Craftsmen Association. The RB, like WGB maintains liaison at the OTZ and also, like WGB maintained liaison at EGW and the OBLs in the West.

Strabag, Strassenbau Aktiengesellschaft (Road Construction Corporation) is a large corporation said to have Göring's financial backing. The GAF dealt with it directly in the construction of aerodromes and runways. In this connection it was active along the Channel Coast (Baugruppe St Malo) and in Italy where it seems to have been the OT's predecessor. In France, it was partly absorbed into the OT in 1942 and in Italy replaced by the OT in 1943. The GAF in France seems to have continued dealing with a branch of Strabag until sometime in June/July 1944 when the OT took over the construction agencies and facilities of the Luftwaffe.

b) Contracts

General Contract Regulations

The relationship between the OT and German, as well as foreign, firms of the Building Industry is regulated through a variety of contracts. In the early days of the OT, these contracts were drawn up with a fair amount of latitude taking into account the productive and capital capacity of the different firms. In early 1942 the Referat Verträge, in Abteilung V4, Hauptabteilung Verwaltung, OT Zentrale (Contracts subsection in section V4, Bureau of Administration, OT Zentrale) was established under Vertragsreferent Regierungsrat Walter Daub. Under this subsection, all contracts were standardised, thus placing all firms on the same level in their legal ties with the OT. The main object in designing the new standardised contract was to ensure the total commitment of the contracted firm in providing a staff of skilled personnel as well as the tools for the efficient performance of the assigned task, while the OT assumed the responsibility of getting the construction materials, machines and labour to the right spot at the right time. Since the bulk of all labour was apportioned by the OT to the firms, labour policies and social welfare also had to be regulated. A series of regulations issued during the latter half of 1942, tending to establish uniformity in pay scales, benefits and allowances, put these matters on a sounder basis than had been previously the case.

Out of this attempt to achieve standardisation, a set number of contracts have emerged of which the most important are discussed in this section.

An OT contract consists of two parts:

(i) The Job Specifications (Auftragsbedingungen)
(ii) The Legal Agreement (Vertragsurkunde)

The Job Specifications contain the conditions and legal relationship laid down by the OT regarding the assignment of all projects. The Legal Agreement contains additional agreements not covered by the Job Specifications, making special allowance for the peculiarities of a particular single construction project. In single incidences special annexes may be attached to the Job Specifications, such as lists of construction materials and equipment to be used or provided. The contents of the original Legal Agreement always takes precedence over other attached contract parts which are valid as long as they do not contain anything which conflicts with the original Legal Agreement.

Relation between the OT and Contracted Parties in Legal Matters
The following terms are used in connection with OT contracts:

Bauherr	(Construction Landlord) The German Reich, represented by OT.
Arbeitsgemeinschaft (Arge)	(Working Combine) A consolidation of firms
Hauptunternehmer	(Contracting Party) May be an Arbeitsgemeinschaft of single large firm.
Nachunternehmer	(Sub-contracted Party) To a larger firm or Arbeitsgemeinschaft.
Unternehmer	(Firm) Under OT contract or subcontract.

While the system of assigning contracts to single firms worked out quite well at first, it soon became obvious, with the increasing scope of tasks entrusted to the OT, that the individual firms performed given assignments on different efficiency levels. Small firms especially did not measure up to standards, while the larger concerns often employed different methods of administration and labour policies. As a result OT administration became confronted with problems growing more complex and creating an abundance of unnecessary detailed work which would make it necessary to maintain a large staff of administrative personnel.

For this reason, the OT conducted a vigorous drive whereby small firms were encouraged to consolidate into 'Arbeitsgemeinschaften' (work combines), often abbreviated into Arge. Under the Arge, one firm, usually the largest, would be elected as 'Federführendes Unternehmen' (deputised firm), to represent the Arge in all dealings with the OT. An OT document explains this system as follows:

> The large-scale construction work undertaken and the necessity of making use of all available resources in personnel and manpower demand the creation of a simplified administrative apparatus, and at the same time the accomplishment of great results. For this reason in single construction sub-sector (Bauabschnitt) a consolidation of firms (German and foreign) must be effected under the leadership of one single firm

hereby referred to as the 'Contracting Party' (Hauptunternehmer). The OT will deal directly with the Contracting Party with regard to all questions which are of the same nature for all 'subcontracted Parties' (Nachunternehmer) concerned.

The drive against small and inefficient firms was conducted with increasing effort, and it was quite a common practice to either force a small firm into an Arbeitsgemeinschaft or to make it a subcontractor (Nachunternehmer) to a larger firm. An inefficient firm could also be dissolved and its tools and machinery 'rented' by the OT, under the 'Gerätemietvertrag' (Contract for the lease of tools and machinery). (See para below.)

Legal relations between the OT and contracted firms (German and foreign) are now maintained, therefore, through standardised contracts. The first part of a contract, the Job Specifications (Auftragsbedingungen der OT), lay down the conditions under which all tasks on construction projects of the OT must be executed. The second part of the contract, the Legal Agreement (Vertragsurkunde), gives specifications of additional agreements to suit a particular project.

A contract may be assigned to a single firm (German or foreign) or a combine of firms (Arbeitsgemeinschaft). The single firm or Arbeitsgemeinschaft may subcontract smaller firms under the conditions laid down in the Job Specifications whereby the Arbeitsgemeinschaft or single firm acts as Contracting Party (Hauptunternehmer), and the (smaller) firms become the Contracted Party (Nachunternehmer). The Amt Bau-OTZ, Einsatzgruppe, Einsatz, OBL, representing the German Reich, is designated as the Bauherr (Construction Landlord).

Two examples of actual contracts, between Bauherr and a Foreign Unternehmer, and between Hauptunternehmer and Nachunternehmer, are reproduced in below.

Types of Contracts

(i) OT – Selbstkostenerstattungsvertrag (Cost Reimbursement Contract)
This contract provides for the reimbursement of overall costs of the contracted firm by the OT plus a commission, normally 4½% – the firm's Profit – upon the successful completion of the assigned task.

(ii) OT – Leistungsvertrag (Efficiency Output Contract)
On the basis of this contract, the OT provides all labour and building construction materials (except tools and machines which are rented from the Contracted Firm). All labour is paid by the OT according to standardised tariffs, and the profits of the firm are computed on the basis of the wages paid.

(iii) OT – Stundenlohnvertrag (OT Hour Wages Contract)

This contract is based on the number of working hours used to complete an assigned project. It is used chiefly in trades which are allied to the Building and Construction Industries (Baunebengewerbe) but not the main industry itself.

(iv) Deutsch – Französischer OT – Leistungsvertrag(German – French Efficiency Output Contract)

This contract is based on the 'Leistungsvertrag' (ii above) but was chiefly designed for French contractors.

(v) Richtlinien für die Bemessung der Gerätevorhaltung (Gerätemieten)(Contracts for renting tools and machinery)

Also referred to as Gerätemietvertrag (Contract for the lease of tools and machinery).

(vi) OT-Ostbauvertrag (OT Contract 'East')

Based on the Selbstkostenerstattungsvertrag and chiefly designed for Eastern Contractors. Ostbauverträge fall into several types, of which the two most important ones are:

(a) Rahmenbauvertrag Ost. The 'Rahmenbau' is a standardised method of building fortifications and strong points according to set specifications. Rahmenbau contracts, therefore, are used for a variety of construction projects, the costs of which, owing to the standardisation of separate parts, can be determined in advance. The largest Rahmenbau project in the EGW was named 'Bunkerbau West' (Bunkerbau = Construction of pillboxes).

(b) OT-Ostmontagevertrag. Same type of contract as 'Stundenlohnvertrag' (iii above), specially designed for Eastern contractors and only used in trades allied to the Construction and Building Industries.

Main Types of Contracts

The type of contract most frequently used today is the Leistungsvertrag. The reason for the popularity of this contract is that it is based on the favourite OT principle of efficiency output. The Selbstkostenerstattungsvertrag, being based on the practice of reimbursing the costs of the contractor, was practically abolished in late 1942, when the new labour policies and standardised tariffs were introduced by Dr Schmelter, and it is today mostly confined to the construction of barracks and camps. The Leistungsvertrag, therefore, is the common type of contract in use today. The Leistungsvertrag was also designed to call for the utmost achievement on the part of the contractor, because it is based on an incentive system of work. If a contractor succeeded in executing an assigned project in less time than the total number of hours specified in the contract, he was nevertheless paid on the basis of the contract hours and not the hours actually spent on the task, an inducement for both contractor and worker. All other types of contracts named above, are based on the principle of the Leistungsvertrag and only contracts with firms of industries allied to the Construction and Building Industries (Baunebengewerbe) are based on the Selbstkostenerstattungsvertrag.

Samples of Leistungsvertrag (Efficiency Output Contracts)

1. Contract Between the Greater German Reich Represented Through Organisation Todt.

Einsatzgruppe Italy, Einsatz Seefalke, Rome in the following paragraphs referred to as the Bauherr (First Party). Bauherr = Legal term to designate the Contracting Party which in this case is the Greater German Reich as represented by OT, Einsatz Seefalke in Rome: for purposes of this interpretation the Bauherr will be translated as the First Party.

Diplom-Ingenieur (Technical title – Dr of Engineering, Paul Andory, Rome, Via Philibetho 161 in the following paragraphs referred to as the Untemehmer (Legal term to designate the Firm as 'Undertaking or Contracted Party'; henceforth translated as the Second Party).

Building contract concluded between the First Party and the Second Party. The Second Party will first be granted costs in accordance with para 8; then as soon as it is possible, the parties will fix the amount of payment in accordance with Para. 8.

Para. 1 – The Undertaking

The parties will agree as to the amount of the payment, and lay it down in a specification giving details and plans for the undertaking. The latter must be approved by OT, Einsatzgruppe Italian. For all subcontracting, the permission of the local authority of the OT must be obtained. The Second Party commits itself and its subordinates to efficient and economical execution of the undertaking within the time set. The contract document consists of:

(a) The original contract.
(b) The specification.
(c) The diagrams.
(d) The technical regulations on building construction, VOB part C.
(e) The general contract regulations for building construction (DIN 1926–1985).
(f) The general contract regulations for building construction, VOB part B (DIN 1961).

Para. 2 – Scope of the Undertaking

The scope of the undertaking is laid down in the specifications and plans. The Second Party is normally responsible for all work necessary for the fulfillment of the undertaking. If it cannot provide all the material himself, the First Party will direct it to a source of supply. The details of the undertaking are to be decided by the First Party.

The price of the contract is given in the specification. The advance payment made to the Second Party will be reckoned on the basis of 30,000 lire for each workman employed.

The First Party is entitled to alter the details of the task at any time. If the Second Party loses by this, he will receive as compensation 6% of the value of that part of the task which will not now be carried out. No compensation may be paid if the task is to be carried out for the same payment but in another part of Italy.

Para. 3 – Special Duties of the Second Party

The Second Party is responsible for providing the necessary personnel. It must provide pay etc. for any extra personnel supplied by the First Party on the same scale as for its own employees.

Materials supplied by the Second Party which are declared unsuitable by the First Party immediately on delivery will be withdrawn.

Materials provided by the First Party remain its property; but when the Second Party has tested and approved them it has the same responsibility for them as for its own materials.

If required to, the Second Party will assume partial responsibility for the transport of materials, in lorries provided by the First Party.

The Second Party must submit to the local OT authority, in writing, any objections it has to the First Party's constructional plan. Work on the feature concerned will normally be suspended until a decision is given. Even if the First Party provides a guard, the Second Party is still responsible for the protection of the undertaking against damage and theft.

Para. 4 – Special Duties of the First Party

The First Party is responsible for collaboration with all German and Italian authorities involved.

If the Second Party cannot provide all necessary materials, equipment, labour, etc., the First Party will, as far as possible, assist it.

The First Party will ensure that OT personnel on the undertaking are boarded and lodged without cost to the Second Party, and provide transport for them.

It will provide land, premises, etc. for the work rent free, or give appropriate compensation.

Para. 5 – The Local Building Authority
The local building authority will take upon itself the rights and duties of the First Party as set out above.

The Second Party will also set up a local building authority to administer its side of the work, and to represent it in its relations with the First Party. The Second party may refer any differences of opinion to the First Party's superior authority.

Para. 6 – Rules for Contractual Obligations
Statements of accounts must be acknowledged correct by both parties. Personnel and apparatus for estimates will be supplied by the Second Party. Compensation for wages paid will only be granted at the standard rate.

A list of equipment required for the work will be submitted to the First Party.

If the price is fixed, time rates may only be paid by written order of the First Party. When work is done for the cost price, a daily report of hours worked will be submitted to the local building authority for signature. The First Party may demand reports on progress at all times.

Para. 7 – Compensation
Compensation will normally be paid according to fixed rates laid down in the specification. If the price of labour increases, the Second Party may request a revision of the rates.

Compensation according to costs will only be paid if exceptional circumstances require it.

Para. 8 – The Estimation of Compensation
I – Fixed Prices
Wages are fixed according to the standard rate, without reference to compulsory deductions.

The price of material is calculated from the lists appended to the contract. Supplementary payments will be made to cover increased prices, transport costs, and unavoidable waste; if prices fall, excess compensation granted must be repaid to the First Party.

Compensation for equipment maintenance is 115% of the rate laid down in the 'Wibauliste' (Economic Group: Construction Industry List).

A supplementary payment for running expenses will be made at the rate of 12% of the total cost of wages, material, and equipment maintenance.

On the basis of the total sum thus obtained, a further 8% is allowed to cover profit and risks incurred.

Workmen's insurance etc. will be paid by the First Party.

Special agreements will be made concerning use of the Second Party's own vehicles, extra maintenance costs, time rates, etc. Extra work will only be paid for if the First Party has agreed to it.

Payment of Expenses:
Compensation will be paid for the following expenses:

Wages, plus 40%

Workmen's insurance etc.

Equipment expenses, according to Wibauliste, plus 10%

Transport costs.

Revenue payments.

Special agreements will be made concerning the use of the Second Party's own vehicles, and material provided by it.

Para. 9 – Accounting and Payments
The Second Party will receive initially an advance of 3,000 lire for each workman employed. The First Party may demand a security for this advance.

The Second Party must keep accounts of all work carried out and all expenses, and submit a monthly statement based on these. The First Party will pay compensation within fourteen days. Minor queries as to the accuracy of items should not be allowed to hold this up.

The payment will be made, in lire, into an account with an Italian bank as designated by the Second Party.

A final settlement will be made at the conclusion of the work. No subsequent claims by the Second Party will be admitted.

Para. 10 – Period Laid Down for the Completion of the Work
The period will be agreed upon when making the plan of work, and the Second Party will undertake to observe it to the best of his ability. The period is automatically extended by any delays occasioned by the First Party. If, by increased expenditure, the work can be expedited such expenses will be made good. The First Party will institute bonuses to encourage faster work. If the Second Party fears it cannot finish within the period set, it must report this to the First Party.

Para. 11 – Acceptance and Guarantees
The construction will be accepted as soon as it is ready. The Second Party will guarantee it to be satisfactory for one year after the date of acceptance, and any defect arising during this time will be repaired by him or at his expense. If the First Party finds the work to be inferior, he may reduce the payment accordingly.

If the damage results from enemy action, or force majeure, no guarantee is required. For the duration of the guarantee, the Second Party will give 3% of the total cost of the construction as security.

Para. 12 – Insurance
The Second Party is responsible for adequate insurance of the project, out of its own funds.

Para. 13 – War Damage
In the case of war damage, the Second Party is entitled to payment for the work so far carried out, plus expenses for repairing the damage. Compensation will be paid for any damage to the Second Party's property.

Para. 14 – Security
The task, and all documents relating to it, will be treated as secret by the Second Party. He will observe all the security regulations, and not permit his employees to know more than is essential for the performance of their duties.

   The Second Party will make individual reports on all supervisory technical, or commercial personnel employed on the undertaking, and report immediately any changes.

Para. 15 – Termination of the Contract
The First Party may terminate the contract, or part of the contract, at any time, if circumstances require it (with compensation as in para. 2); or if the work is not being satisfactorily performed, or if its completion is too long delayed (with compensation for actual expenses only).

Para. 16 – Text of the Contract
The contract will be in German and Italian. In case of doubt the German version is binding.

Para. 17 – Commencement of the Contract
This contract comes into force on ....

Para. 18 – Amendments to the Contract
Require the written authorisation of both parties.

Para. 19 – Value of the Contract

Para. 20 – Extension of the Contract
The First Party is empowered to stipulate further tasks.

Para. 21 – Legal Disputes
Legal disputes will be settled out of court by an arbitration board, as laid down in an agreement appended to the contract.

2. Contract for German and Foreign Nachunternehmer (Subcontractors or Contracted Parties) between Messrs Deutsche Bau-Aktiengesellschaft, Berlin, W.50, Einsatz Normandy, represented by Director von Pein, Engineer and Leader Reichel, Merchant (hereinafter called the 'Hauptunternehmer') (First Party) and Messrs Thuillter, Public Works Contractors, 20, rue Esther Cordier, Chatillon (Seine), represented by Marcel Dhaille, Commercial Manager (hereinafter called the 'Nachunternehmer') (Second Party).

It is agreed as follows:

Preamble
The great extent of the building works to be carried out, and the need for making full use of all the forces available for the purpose, make it necessary to install an administrative organisation which will be as simple as possible, but, nevertheless a large output must be obtained. For this reason a group of Nachunternehmer (Firms) (German and foreign) will be put together in each building sector, which will be placed under the control of a single firm. The Todt Organisation will therefore in all cases deal only with the Hauptunternehner appointed as the manager on all those questions which are the same for all firms concerned.

The German State represented by:
The Organisation Todt, Einsatzgruppe West, OBL Cherbourg, commissions the First Party, hereinafter called HU, with construction tasks and works as set out in the annexe which the HU transfers to the Second Party, hereinafter called NU, on the instructions of and for the OT.

Para. 1 – General
1. The following apply as integral parts of the contract:

    (a) Auftragsbedingungen der OT für die Ausführung von Bauleistungen zu Leistungspreisen. (OT-Leistungsvertrag). (Job specifications of the Todt Organisation for the Execution of Building Works at Unit prices – Efficiency Output Contract) issue of May 1943.
    (b) Leistungsverzeichnis zum Rahmenbauvertrag Bunkerbau. (The Works Schedule to the Frame-building Contract, Pillboxes) West, of the Todt Organisation, issue of May 1943.
    (c) Die Verordnung über die Baupreisbildung (BPVO)
    (The Order on Calculating Building Prices).

2. Alteration of the details of this contract does not affect the contract provided they do not constitute a complete change in the order.

3. The NU must not further subcontract the carrying out of the work accepted, either in whole or in part.

4. This contract between HU and NU, including all extra work, requires the approval of the OT in order to be valid.

Para. 2 – Pricing and Accounting for the Work Done
1. The building work done will be charged for on the basis of the prices of the Leistungsverzeichnis (Works Schedule).

2. The prices which apply are those of the 'Leistungsverzeichnis zum Rahmenbauvertrag Bunkerbau West' (Works Schedule to the Frame-Building Contract, Pillboxes, West), issue of June 1943.

3. Modifications of the section PI of the contract prices are governed by Section 1B of the preamble to the Leistungsverzeichnis (Works Schedule). Sections Ps of the prices to be changed are to form the basis, without alteration, of the charge in accordance with Job Specifications Para. 14, section 9, in conjunction with Job Specifications Para.

4. For modifications of the sections PI of the contract prices, the modification factors (see preamble to the Works Schedule, Section IB) are fixed at:
   $F1 = 0.60$ and $F2 = 1.60$.

5. For ascertaining the supplementary prices, the same regulations with the supplements for overtime and general expenses, as in ascertaining prices for the contract, are to be employed.

6. If works become necessary which are not provided for in the Works Schedule, the prices for these extra-contractual works must be agreed upon between the HU and the NU before the work is started. Such agreements require the approval of the OBL.

Para. 3 – Pegging Out and Measuring
1. The fixing of all pegging, measuring and height figures on the ground which are necessary for the calculations, must be undertaken by the NU, with the collaboration of the HU, with full responsibility for their correctness. The NU must see to it that the checking of the pegging and of the work done can be easily carried out by the building control.

2. When measurements which are to serve as basis for charges are made, a representative of OBL must always be present.

3. For all measurements, etc., the necessary labour, measuring instruments, levels, etc. must be provided by the NU at its own cost, and if possible from its own stocks.

4. In the event of infringement of the foregoing orders, the measurements and the decisions of the OBL will prevail.

Para. 4 – Tariff Conditions

1. Whenever possible the NU must carry out its work to the greatest extent according to the Output Pay Principle (Reichstarif-Ordnung über den Leistungslohn im Baugewerbe, 2 June 1942, and Anordnung des Beauftragten des Sondertreuhänders bei EGW, 20 April 1943).

Para. 5 - Relation of the NU to the OT

1. In relations with the OT, the HU is the sole contracting party.

2. The HU is entitled, in connection with the completion and continuation of the building work, to issue instructions with which the NU must comply. If the NU considers that the instructions of the HU are unsuitable, it may appeal through the OBL to the OT, whose decision is final.

3. The NU is in all respects entirely responsible in its sector and within the scope of its order for the carrying out and completion of the building work. For the carrying out of the building work it will remain in constant touch with the HU. The latter will, as a general rule, only have to intervene if the steps taken by the NU appear to the HU to be inappropriate and inadequate.

4. The OT has the right to entrust third parties with the execution of the rights arising under this contract, or to authorise Government Departments to take its place in this contract.

Para. 6 – Services and Remuneration of the HU

1. The HU undertakes to render the following services to the NU:

> (a) It organises, and arranges for, the supply of all building material, building fuel and auxiliary building material, and arranges, as may be necessary, for the provision of railway wagons at the appropriate places.
> (b) It arranges for the provision of foreign labour.

(c) It installs the NU on the work in conjunction with the local building controller of the OBL.

(d) It arranges for the daily supply of the necessary lorries, omnibuses and other means of transport, and arranges for the necessary way-bills for the dispatch of the NU's plant.

(e) It calculates and negotiates additional price agreements, even when the work of the NU is concerned.

(f) It carries on all negotiations regarding the execution and completion of the building work and the necessary building measures with the OBL.

(g) It arranges for the necessary wages and makes them available to the NU at the proper time.

(h) It undertakes to provide all the intelligence reports and forwards the proofs of the prescribed guard measures. The NU, however, must provide it with the necessary proofs for this purpose at the proper time.

(i) The HU provides the necessary data for the preparation and putting through of the accounts, the HU checks the accounts of the NU and then passes them on to the OBL.

2. The HU on principle applies the same conditions and prices to the NU which it has itself received as a result of special arrangements with the OT, for the building work to be carried out by it. This also applies to any 'Erschwerniszulage' (Pay addition for dangerous work performed) which may be arranged with the OT, the amount of which is governed by the position of the locality and the degree of difficulty, and for which the same regulations are to be valid for the NU as are valid for the HU.

3. The HU receives for the services rendered under 1 (a) to (i) which he deducts from the approved accounts of the NU.

(a) For the works according to the Works Schedule.
(b) For specially agreed works, an allowance of 3%, which is charged to the NU, and which the HU can collect by means of a direct deduction from the accounts of the NU.

4. The HU is not entitled to make any deduction from the hourly wage basis, from the accounts for wages for building in spare time, from compensation for loss of wages and the like when authenticating accounts approved for payment.

Para. 7 – Services of the NU
1. The duties of the NU comprise the maintenance of a building office staffed with sufficient, experienced, capable technical and commercial staff, to see to the management and execution of the work.

2. The NU must see to it that, for the area of its construction there is regular co-operation between all offices or departments which are concerned with the carrying out of the works.

Para. 8 – Delivery of Building Material
The following duties are incumbent upon the NU in connection with the building material put at its disposal:

(a) To take delivery of the building material at the place of receipt and to be responsible for the same.
(b) To watch over the correctness of the deliveries as to quantity and quality, and institute any necessary inquiries and claims by the OT, through the agency of the HU.
(c) To keep the necessary books, stocklists and controls for the purpose.
(d) To provide for the storage and working up of the materials in accordance with the usual rules of good building practice.

Para. 9 – Change of Contract
1. If, during the course of the building, there should be an appreciable alteration in the conditions on which the prices were fixed, then either the OT, or the NU through the HU, may apply for a change in the prices. In such event the alterations in the conditions on which the prices were fixed must, from time to time, be reported in writing, as soon as the effect of the same becomes manifest. Any such alteration in prices, however, should if possible, not take place during the continuation of the construction. With the object of simplifying the accounting, any alterations in price which become necessary should only be agreed on in a lump sum on the completion of the building.

2. The NU can be released from the contractual relationship under the same conditions, and with the same effect, as the HU itself.

3. Alterations in this contract require mutual agreement and written confirmation, as well as the approval of the OT.

Para. 10 – Conditions of Secrecy
The NU must comply with all orders of the OT or other competent organisations acting for the same, regarding the maintenance of secrecy and regarding the reliability of the labour engaged.

Para. 11 – Regulations for Accounting and Payment
1. The advance required on each payday for wages, including social charges and tariff additions, will be made available to the NU, at the request of the

HU, in the same amount as the latter receives from the OBL, for payment to the workers and/or for payment to the social insurance undertaking. For this purpose the NU must apply in due time to the HU for the advance required. In so doing it must comply with the regulations concerning foreign currency and with the regulations of the OT regarding payments at the front to the Gefolgschaftsmitglieder (auxiliaries).

2. The HU is entitled, in order to protect the interests of the OT, to refuse to pay accounts which can be objected to and to return them for rectification.

3. In the preparation of accounts the headings demanded by the OBL must be adhered to.

4. Every account must be checked by accountant of the NU who is responsible for the accounts, and must be signed with his full name and provided with a note that it is correct.

5. All payments of the OT and of the HU are made without prejudice to the correctness of the accounts drawn up.

6. If subsequent examination of the accounts, after the final payments have been made, shows that rectifications are necessary, the NU must immediately refund to the HU any sum received in excess, upon application to the latter by the OT. It agrees that such liabilities to repay to the State may be set off direct against claims due to him in connection with other Government work.

7. The HU has the right, in the event of reasonable doubt, to make retentions from current payments of such amounts as to preclude over payments. The HU has the right to withhold payments on account which are due, if the NU fails to comply with his contractual obligations or with justifiable instructions from the HU or from the OT.

Para. 12 – Notice of Termination and Withdrawal of Order
1. The HU or the OT may at any time serve notice of termination of the contract in accordance with para. 33, Section 1, of the Job Specifications of the OT Leistungsvertrag (Output Efficiency Contract) issue of May 1943.

2. The HU may withdraw the work from the NU if it is not prosecuted with the necessary energy and competence, or if the NU falls into arrears in the time limits of the contract, or allows periods of grace allotted to it to make up the arrears to elapse without result.

In the event of the Order being withdrawn, settlement must be made with the NU in accordance with the contract for work done up to the date of the withdrawal of the order. The question of to what extent additional credits shall be allowed to the NU is left to the decision of the OT.

Para. 13 – Assumption and Warranting
1. The assumption of the construction work is to be applied for by the NU through the HU.

2. Should any claim be made against the HU in respect to the commitments of the NU, the HU is responsible.

Para. 14 – Guarantee
1. The HU is entitled to require from the NU a security of 5% of the total accounts of the NU – but not more than RM 150,000 – for the carrying out of the contractual obligations.

2. By agreement with the HU, the NU may either place this amount in an account, which must be blocked for at least two years for claims against the HU arising out of this contract, or it can be provided in the form of a bond or any other suitable manner.

3. The guarantee must at the same time constitute a guarantee for the OT.

Para. 15 – Assignment of Claims
Claims under this building contract may only be assigned with the prior consent of the HU. Any assignment without this consent is legally void under para. 399 of the Civil Code.

Para. 16 – Legal Disputes
1. AH disputes arising out of the execution of this contract will be settled by the ordinary courts of law. The competent jurisdiction will be determined by the HU.

2. See Arbitration Agreement.
Disputes between the HU and the foreign NU will be settled by the OT (EGW). If no final decision can be reached in this manner, the dispute will be submitted to the military commander in France in accordance with the Arbitration Agreement. In the carrying out of the proceedings, the chief contractor will be represented by the OT.

Para. 17 – Coming to Effect of the Contract
This contract takes effect as a continuation of the existing contract of 1 March 1943, being retroactive to .... o'clock on 1 August 1943.

E. Personnel Administration Policy

Multiple Factors Involved in OT Personnel Administration
The following is an outline of OT's policy in regard to personnel administration. This policy is peculiarly interesting because of the vast number of foreign workers in the OT. A reasoned attempt has been made to reconstruct official policy on the basis of available documents. How this policy operated in practice is discussed in Part III (Frontführung).

Personnel management was the basic administrative problem of the OT in the West. The variety and extent of construction work on which it was engaged at one time (May 1942 to May 1944) made demands upon the technical training, mechanical experience, occupational skill and administrative and professional knowledge of some 600 different professions, trades and occupations and upon the muscular effort of over one million unskilled and semi-skilled labourers of about forty different nationalities. For instance, the problem of pay scales alone must have turned the hair of conscientious officials a premature grey. Only a small proportion of OT personnel, not exceeding 5%, was paid simply according to rank. The other 9% were paid, first according to some fourteen different classifications of service status, from German Government Delegate to that of Forced Labour; secondly according to some forty tabulated levels of training, experience, skill and professional, and Trade Guild standing; thirdly according to age, location, family situation and marital status; fourthly according to individual dependability and work out-put; fifthly, according to categories of labour such as heavy, extra heavy and dangerous labour; sixthly according to temporary situations such as unavoidable delays and unforeseen difficulties owing to natural factors and delay and difficulties owing to enemy action.

The basic pay tariffs were made uniform on 2 February 1943 for all nationalities including German (German personnel was placed in responsible supervisory positions at every opportunity), but with the exception of Russians, Poles, Czechs and Jews. Discrimination based on race and nationality in matters of social insurance benefits, extra allowance and deductions for food, billets, clothing and personal items, however, prevented the factor of OT pay from becoming unduly simplified.

Nor was pay by any means the only factor susceptible to administrative complications. Rations, billets, issue of clothing and purchase of canteen articles, entertainment, furloughs, restrictions, security, discipline, sanitation and above all morale were, thanks to the political discrimination practised, some of the other factors involved.

Adaptations of Policy to Local and Immediate Situations.
It is conceded that in this respect the OT had a comparatively easy time of it in Russia and in the Balkans, where manpower was obtained by impressment without further formality, and fed and billeted after a fashion without many questions being asked. It is also conceded that the fortunes of war dictated a general policy of political conciliation in the West by the German Government, and a more specific policy of conciliation in regard to foreign workers in the West by the OT. It is furthermore conceded that the ever-growing shortage of manpower reduced the German supervisory personnel in OT to an irreducible minimum and consequently made a conciliatory policy all the more imperative, even while such a policy became in a large measure ineffective because of Allied propaganda and the growing self-assurance of native elements, hitherto only apathetic or at best lukewarm to the Allied cause. However, the severe policies from a chronological and a geographical standpoint which the OT adopted in regard to political discrimination, were, like the various types of operational organisation, dictated by military necessity and adapted to the immediate situation. To a victorious Germany, a post-war OT would have been as important as it was essential during the war. The OT had been counted on to kill two birds with one stone: to reconstruct Europe according to Nazi strategic schemes of economic exploitation, and to unite politically, the working masses of Europe by channelling their activities along Nazi lines of labour organisations. From a long-range point of view, therefore, neither the enforced labour system without perceptible regard for humane treatment, as it was practised generally in the East and in the Balkans, nor the other extreme of a conciliatory policy born out of necessity, as it was practised in France, can be taken as exemplifying OT administrative policy in regard to foreign workers. It was not until the end of 1943 and the beginning of 1944 that OT began to issue regulations with any indication that they were part of a definite political policy in regard to a 'United Europe'. These regulations may be constructed as in the following paragraph.

OT Personnel Administration Defined in Terms of Long-Range Policy
Under stable conditions there was no need envisaged for self-contained mobile operational units. The OT-Firms would consequently be relieved of the personnel administration which they had assumed over their employees and would be concerned once more solely with the building programme. Administration of food, billets and welfare would once more be taken over by OBL Frontführung, Foreign workers would continue to be administered according to Himmler's regulations governing racial and national discrimination. (Administered in the

OT by Sozialpolitik und Arbeitseinsatz Abteilung: Social Police and Manpower Allocation Section). Consequently no foreigners would be in a position to issue an order to a German. Supervision over foreign workers, however, would continue to be delegated to collaborationists in increasing number as they proved their trustworthiness, always under final German control. German Lagerführer (Camp supervisors) of foreign workers' camps might be replaced by collaborationists although this step would be obstructed in some sectors by local Frontführer. Supervise the treatment of the various nationalities of foreign workers would continue to be assigned to welfare workers of corresponding nationality, who would have no more than advisory authority in respect to unsatisfactory conditions or individual cases of ill-treatment.

It is quite conceivable that the German Government had intentions to continue some such arrangement in relation to execution of its post-war reconstruction dreams. Latitude allowed to foreign governments would of course, vary, possibly from an arrangement whereby the foreign government might run its own OT according to a construction programme controlled by German staff, down to an arrangement not far removed from the closer control described above.

F. Service Branches of the OT

a) Supply

Services of Supply
All matters affecting supply in the OT are taken care of by the Abteilung Nachschub which forms one of the four chief sections in the administrative structure of all OT construction units. The Abteilung Nachschub provided administratively for the procurement of all the essential materials needed by the OT in its construction projects, such as stone, rock, metals, sand, cement, lumber, dies, explosives and camouflaging materials. It also furnished the necessary water-power, electricity and fuel (gas, oil, wood, charcoal, coal and carbide) and provided for heat and ventilation.

The vast amount of materials needed in the various construction projects of the OT were stored in Nachschublager (General Supply Depots) under the control of the Einsatzgruppen. From these general depots, the materials were then distributed to smaller depots of the various operational units normally an OBL. Nachschublager are sometimes classified as to the type of material they contain, as for instance Eisenlager (Iron Depot), Gerätelager (Tool Depot), Verpflegungslager (Ration Depot, Ausrüstungs lager (Equipments Depot) and Ersatzteillager (Spare Parts Depot) and so forth.

Inasmuch as the cost of constructions performed by the OT for the three component parts of the Wehrmacht (Army, Navy and Air Force) was covered by the Wehrmachtshaushaltabteilung (Armed Forces Budgeting Department) it is therefore safe to assume that building materials not locally obtained must consequently come from Wehrmacht storehouses. For example, building materials coming from Germany for use by the OT in Norway, are labelled Wehrmachtsgut (Property of the Wehrmacht).

It is known also that the Wehrmacht supplied the arms and ammunition required by the OT, and. this fact is borne out by an order from OKH (High Command of the Army) dated 13 Feb 1942 which states:

> Weapons, equipment and ammunition for units of the OT employed by the Wehrmacht and working at the expense of the Wehrmacht shaushalt (Armed Forces Budget) and therefore called Fronteinsatz (Front Area Consignment) will be delivered without cost. The delivered material will still belong to the Wehrmacht.

Although building materials were furnished to the firms by the OT through the various OBLs, certain Bauhilfstoffe (secondary building materials) such as timber, nails, wire and so forth were supplied by the firms themselves. Usually the machinery and tools were also provided by them. The cost for the use of these materials, for the rental, repair and replacement of the machinery and tools, was included in the contract which the firm made with OT.

If a firm did not possess adequate machinery for a certain job it could rent machinery from a firm in the Reich or in occupied territories. Thus, for instance, according to one document date 18 July 1943 the firm Hermann Hibert of Nürnberg billed Arge Schiffer for a total of RM 4,060.74 for the rental of two dredging machines over a period of three months at RM 1,353.58 per month. Owing to the general shortage of equipment, the costs for renting machines were exceptionally high.

Some idea of the complexity of the supply situation in the OT can be derived from the following instructions on the acquisition of construction engines issued by the OTZ in October 1942. Following an order of the Bevollmächtigter für die Machinenproduktion (Plenipotentiary for the Production of Machinery) dated 17 July, 1942, all replacement parts of machine weighing individually less than 100 kilograms and in total less than 1,000 kilograms could be obtained from a firm in Germany without a special permit. In ordering parts weighing 100–300 kilograms a special permit had to be obtained from the Wirtschaftsgruppe Bauindustrie (Economic Group: Building Industry). In case this organisation was not willing to issue the necessary permit the OTZ was to be contacted by way of the appropriate OBL and Einsatzgruppe. No special permits were needed for replacements for locomotives. Replacements for motor-vehicles were to be obtained through the NSKK-Staffelführer. No permits were to be issued to buy

Above: Cutaway of a fort on the Westwall, revealing the various layers with the gun turret at the top, operations rooms, living quarters and, on the bottom level, generators and an electric train. Below: Soldiers closing a barrier on the Westwall. Openings were needed for the passage of traffic, but could be closed very quickly when required.

A romanticised image of the Reichsautobahn in this poster by Robert Zinner. *(Wolfsonian-Florida International University)* In truth it is not that far removed from the reality, and the bridges and roads were considered to be part of the beauty of Germany. This 1942 photograph, top right, shows the viaduct at Drackensteiner Hang in the Schwabian Alps, on Reichsautobahn 26, Munich–Stuttgart. Below: Published in 1941, a rare colour photograph of an OT work party during the construction of the Westwall. Narrow gauge rails were often laid for moving materials and building waste on large sites.

Dr Fritz Todt, founder of the construction organisation that later bore his name.

Remnants of the Atlantikwall: The 152-mm guns are still in situ at the Longues-sur-Mer battery in Normandy. Started in September 1943, this battery consisted of four gun emplacements and a two-storey observation post which was uncompleted by the time of the Allied landings. Below: Close-up detail of the main casement at the Batterie Todt in the Pas de Calais. Note the shell damage.

Todt Battery has lost its 380-mm Krupp guns, although their size is indicated by the scale model, top right. Turm 1 now houses the Musée du Mur de l'Atlantique Batterie Todt, above and right. The Battery at Azeville in the Basse-Normandie region, below, is set back slightly and with no direct view of the sea the gunners relied on spotters or signals from Crisbecq. (DSMD)

Channel Island Bunkers
Occupied by the Germans from 30 June 1940 up until the end of the war, the Channel Islands, because of their strategic position, became an integral part of the Atlantikwall defences, and the OT constructed many fortifications and bunkers. Overlooking the sea, this observation tower, above, is at Battery Moltke, Jersey, and, below, a bunker on Guernsey. *(Man vyi)*

Above: Looking down upon the Battery Lothringen at Noirmont Point, Jersey, plus old and new fortifications combined at Fort Hommet on Guernsey. *(Man vyi)*

Right: A close-up of the observation tower at Battery Lothringen. Note the impression left by the rough wooden shuttering on the concrete. The simplicity of the bold geometric shapes of these fortifications, sliced by multiple slots, is beguiling in its resemblance to Brutalist architecture, but to the inhabitants of the islands these are monuments to the tyranny of occupation and the brutal treatment of the foreign slave workers who constructed them. *(Pawl 'pbm' Szubert)*

Colour illustration of an unidentified U-boat base under construction in western France. It was published in *Bauen und Kämpfen* – 'building and fighting' – a collection of poetry and art in praise of the work of the OT.

The OT built U-boat pens at five main locations in France: Bordeaux, shown below, Brest, La Rochelle, Lorient and Saint Nazaire. *(Tony Hisgett)*

Interior of the U-boat bunker Valentin on the Weser River near Bremen, north-western Germany. Built between 1943 and 1945, although still unfinished by the end of the war, it was a manufacturing facility rather than an operational submarine base. The largest U-boat facility in Germany, it was second only in scale to the pens built at Brest in France. *(C. Mezzo)*

Another colour illustration of U-boat base construction. Compare this with the photo on page 101.

Above: The blockhaus at Watten with evidence of Tallboy damage visible on the roofline. The octagonal structure was an entrance to the lower levels, but as the photo on the right shows, these are now filled with water. Below: One of the tunnels through which V-2 rockets could be moved at the Cupola d'Helfaut-Wizernes. Constructed within a chalk quarry, this huge facility was designed to store and launch V-2 rockets on an industrial scale. As part of Operation Crossbow, in 1944 the site was subjected to a string of bombings, including with RAF Tallboy bombs, and it never became operational.

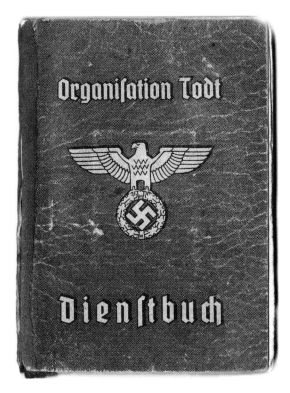 

Above: OT Dienstbuch, the personal workbook of an engineer serving in Southern Russia. Sample pages are shown below. Above right: Arbeitsbuch für Auslander, workbook for foreigners, issued to a Polish forced labourer in 1942. The 'P' patch was worn to distinguish them from the Germans. *(Sjam2004)*

1 Oberbauleitung	2 Name und Sitz des Betriebes (Unternehmers) — (Firmenstempel) oder der Dienststelle	3 a) Tag des Beginns der Beschäftigung b) Art d. Dienstverhältnisses*	4 a) Art der Beschäftigung (möglichst genau angeben) b) Stundenlohn bzw. Monatsgehalt	5 a) Tag der Beendigung der Beschäftigung b) entlohnt bis einschl.	6 Grund für die Beendigung der Beschäftigung	7 Unterschrift des Unternehmers
1	Der Generalinspektor für das deutsche Straßenwesen Organisation Todt — Zentrale —	a 10.8.41 b	a Dau-Ingenieur b Mon.-Geh.	16.8.41		
2	O.T. Linienchef der Dg Abschnittsbauleitung 6 — Dnjepropetrowsk —	a 16.8.1941 b	a Abschnittsbauleiter b Gehaltsempf.	5.8.1943 31.8.1943		
3 O.B.L. Kuban	Oberbauleitung Kuban Abschnittsbauleitung Starotiterowskaja/Kuban	a 6.8.1943 b	a O.T. bauleiter b Gehaltsempf.	17.3.44		
4	OT-Oberbauleitung Noris — Blto.2	a 18.3.44 b abg.	a Bauleiter b Mon.-Geh.	15.10.44		
5	O.T.Reg. Batl. 412	a 16.10.44 b abg.	a Oberbauleitung b Mon.-Geh.	9.5.45	Kriegsende	

*) Zu h: Angabe ob dienstverpflichtet, abgeordnet, freigestellt, Stammarbeiter, Stammpersonal.

TAG DER BRIEFMARKE 1942

ORGANISATION TODT

EINHEITSORGANISATION DER DEUTSCHEN SAMMLER

Abgabepreis 25 Rpf einschließlich Zuschlag für den Kulturfonds

3 3
DEUTSCHES REICH

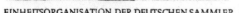

Above: 'Einheitsorganisation der Deutschen Sammler' – a propaganda postcard featuring the Organisation Todt. This was one of a series of similar cards depicting a range of occupations and organisations, promoting the role of the workforce.

Right: A similar pose showing an OT worker carrying his pickaxe over his shoulder like a soldier with his weapon. This illustration was originally published in the booklet *Bauen und Kämpfen*.

Brassards worn on left upper arm above Swastika Brassard

EM/OR and NCOs

Officers (Führer)

Officers (Stabsführer)

Officers   (Hohere Führer, left) (Chief of OTZ, right)

Classification insignia, worn on left upper arm below Swastika brassard.

OT – Organic Personnel

OT – Organic Personnel

Colour denotes construction branch: Yellow = Communications; Red = Construction (above);
Green = Administration; Black = Band; Brown = Propaganda; White = Frontführung; Blue = Medical.

Above: Bronze sculpture of Fritz Todt at the Batterie Todt museum. Above right: Albert Speer, with back to camera, in a colour photograph from the June 1944 cover of *Die Wehrmacht*. Below left: In November 1943 Hitler sent Erwin Rommel to Normandy with responsibility for defending the French coast against an Allied landing. Dismayed by the uncompleted state of the Atlantikwall, he instigated the building of new tank traps and obstacles, and is credited with restoring morale among the defenders. Implicated in the plot to kill Hitler, Rommel was compelled to commit suicide in October 1944. *(CMcC)* Below right: Fritz Sauckel was responsible for the use of forced and slave labour and, together with Speer, was tried for War Crimes and Crimes Against Humanity at Nuremburg – see page 247.

new construction equipment. Old equipment was to be bought or leased in Germany. In cases of emergency the OTZ was to be contacted to discover means of procuring new equipment.

In cases where more than one firm was employed on a construction site, the various firms identified their own equipment by the use of different coloured markings. The listing and controlling of these markings was done by the subsection 'Kennziffern' in the section Nachschub at the various OBLs.

b) Transport

NSSK – Transport Brigade Todt and Early Speer Transport Organisations

From the inception of the OT until the beginning of 1944, all motor transport for the OT was carried out by various organisations under the control of the NSKK – Nationalsozialistisches Kraftfahrkorps (National Socialist Motor Corps). Unlike the Wehrmacht, the OT seems to have found little use for horse-drawn vehicles. Certainly in the West no other form but motor-transport is known. It is reasonable to assume, however, that horses or mules may have been employed by the OT in Russia or in some of the Balkan countries where motor cars were scarce and the roads not well suited for motor transport.

Just as the OT in its final form, is the result of the conglomeration of several building organisations created by Todt and Speer, so the final OT organisational structure of the NSKK-OT transport services resulted from the unification of various transport organisations created by these two engineers in support of their building activities. There is no space here to give a complete history of these organisations but it may not be amiss to note some facts of general historical interest.

In 1938, when Todt took over construction of the West Wall on the western boundaries of Germany, the existing NSKK units, organised into LKW-Staffeln (Lorry Battalions), were commissioned to take care of the transport of the building materials and of the workers to and from the fortifications under construction. The immense task of transporting materials in 15,000 lorries for the 22,000 fortified construction sites in the West Wall and of moving 200,000 workers daily in 5,000 buses, required a well-knit and efficient organisation. The task was accomplished by an organisation called Kraftwagenleitung West, commonly abbreviated into Kra-West. By the time OT had been transferred to the construction of the Atlantic Wall, the transport units which had worked for the OT were organised into the NSKK-Transportstandarte Todt, soon to grow into an even larger unit, the NSKK-Transportbrigade Todt.

The units of this Transport brigade following NSKK procedure were called Kolonne (equivalent to platoon), Hauptkolonne (company) Staffel (Battalion) Standarte (Regiment), Brigade (Brigade) and Gruppe (Division).

The members of the NSKK-Transportbrigade Todt wore an olive-green field blouse, black breeches and (in winter) an olive-green overcoat.

At the time when Todt was busy on the West Wall, his younger rival Speer had already created and was using an organisation called Baustab Speer in projects involving the remodelling of Berlin and the building of aerodromes in the Reich. The NSKK units employed in these projects were organised into the NSKK-Baustab Speer which, at the beginning of the Second World War, had been amplified and renamed NSKK-Motortransportstandarte Speer and then further augmented into NSKK-Motortransportbrigade Speer. In contrast to the elastic organisation of the NSKK-Transportbrigade Todt, the NSKK-Transportbrigade Speer was set up along rigid military lines. The units employed were those of the Wehrmacht, i.e. Regimenter, Abteilungen, Kompanien and Züge. NSKK-Transportbrigade Speer served chiefly the German Air Force and to a lesser degree the German Army. It was subsequently widely employed by the OT in Russia, the Balkans, in Italy and Norway, but unfortunately it is not known exactly how the individual transport units were assigned to the various OBLs. The ranks in this particular branch of the NSKK are not known for certain, but it is suggested by certain evidence that they are identical with those of the NSKK-Transportbrigade Todt. The uniform was usually the grey-blue of the German Air Force; sometimes, however, the brown uniform of the NSKK-Baustab Speer was also worn.

Legion Speer

As the NSKK organisation is a 'Gliederung' (formation) of the Nazi Party, it could only employ personnel of German nationality. To satisfy the growing requirements for transportation personnel within the OT, Speer, when he became Reichminister in Todt's place, entrusted Gruppenführer Nagel with the formation of the Legion Speer. This organisation originally consisted of Russian emigrants but was soon greatly expanded by the inclusion of some 250,000 Russian prisoners of war. In Sept. 1942, the leadership of the Legion Speer was placed in the hands of NSKK-Gruppenführer Jost who then obtained the rank of Generalkapitan and the title of Kommandeur der Legion Speer. In its early inception the Legion Speer was called the transport and construction formation of the Generalbauinspektor für die Reichshauptstadt who was, in fact, Reichsminister Speer.

The original plan of including Russian prisoners of war evidently never took any real form. Instead, the Legion Speer was organised along voluntary lines and was open to all persons of any nationality as well as those who did not possess any nationality at all (Staatenlose). Only the leadership of the Legion Speer remained in German hands.

The oath taken by the legionaries was a personal oath of allegiance to Hitler:

I swear by God the Almighty, this holy oath that I will exercise unconditional obedience to the Führer of the German Reich, Adolf Hitler, and that I am ready at any time to sacrifice my life to honour this oath.

The uniform originally prescribed for all non-German personnel of the Legion Speer was of black material. Later (in April 1943), when it was found out that the durability of the material was impaired by the black dyes, the olive-green uniform was introduced for the legionaries, the result creating such a confusion of uniforms that in 1944 the members of the Legion Speer were found attired in black, olive-green and even brown uniforms, presumably taken over from the NSKK-Baustab Speer.

The directives concerning the employment of foreigners prescribed the following areas for different nationalities: in the West, Russians, Ukrainians, Latvians, Estonians and Lithuanians; in the North, Norwegians, Swedes, Danes, Dutch Flemings; in the South-West, (Balkans), French and Walloons; in Germany, Dutch and Flemings; in the Eastern Military Zone, Bulgars, Serbs, French, Walloons, Norwegians, Swedes, Denes, Slovaks, Croats and Czechs. The above programme, however, served only as a general directive. Modifications were permissible with one exception, Russians could only be employed in the West.

The training of personnel was performed in the several Ersatzabteilungen (Replacement Battalions) set up at Berlin-Nikolassee, Paris, Oslo, Belgrade and in the 'Ersatzregiment' at Kiev.

Organisation of the Legion Speer was military.

The Einstellungsverfügung or contract of a member of the Legion Speer is translated as follows (it was issued in both German and French, the legionary having been in this case a Frenchman):

NSKK – Gruppe Todt (Comprising Legion Speer after October 1942)
Abschnittsführung West   OU ....
Contract

1. Mr .... *(Surname)* .... *(Christian name)*
.... *(date and place of birth)* has as of .... *(date)*
enlisted as a legionary in the Abschnittsführung West.

2. a) During training the legionary will be paid at the rate of 4 RM per week.
    b) At the conclusion of training he will be posted for duty. From then on drivers, trained fitters and repair men will be paid 45 RM per week.
    c) All other legionaries will be paid at the rate of 40 RM per week.
    d) Pay issued, plus allowances, covers all overtime and work done on Sundays, etc.

3. Every legionary will receive in addition, rations, accommodation and uniform, service pay (Wehrsold) of 12 RM per ten-day pay period (plus any additional pay issuable by virtue of service in particular countries), and free medical attention.

4. Drivers of gas-generator-propelled vehicles will receive additional pay at the rate of 1 RM per day, during such time as they are actually employed on the vehicles.

5. After a minimum period of six months' service, the legionary will receive fourteen days' leave with full pay, including free travel to his home. He cannot claim any further period of leave during the service year.

6. Legionaries will be employed in the occupied Western territories. They may also volunteer for employment elsewhere.

7. The legionary will live in the quarters to which he is allotted and wear the prescribed uniform.

8. The legionary will at all times obey the orders of his superiors. He is bound to maintain secrecy as to his duties and remains bound to this after leaving the service.

9. The legionary is subject to German civil and military law. He may not leave his unit without the permission of his superior officer, not even for a short time. Such conduct will be punished as absence without leave, or even as desertion.

10. This contract is valid for one year. After this period it will be automatically renewed unless the legionary requests his discharge a week before expiry.

Read and approved .... *(Signature)*

Transportgruppe Todt

After Todt's death in February 1942, Speer became the Reichsminister for Armaments and War Production and at the same time the Chief of the OT and of all the transport formations in the service of the OT. The amalgamation of the building organisations created by these two men was now to be followed by the reorganisation of the entire transport system. A new organisation was set up in October 1942, called NSKK-Transportgruppe Todt or simply NSKK-Gruppe Todt and placed under the command OT of NSKK-Gruppenführer Willi Nagel. It Included the NSKK-Transportbrigade TODT, the NSKK-Transportbrigade Speer and the Legion Speer. The inclusion of the Legion Speer in the NSKK-Transportgruppe Todt did not mean that Legion Speer was to be considered part of the general NSKK organisation. At the time of the reorganisation, it is emphatically stated that its inclusion was done solely for administrative reasons. In 1944 the term NSKK-Transportgruppe Todt was often replaced by NSKK-Gruppe Speer, a term introduced in honour of the Reichsminister. The term Transportkorps Speer, was first found in several documents about the middle of 1944. It has since then officially replaced the old designation NSKK-Transportgruppe Todt. It is believed that the preponderance of foreigners in the transport units working for the OT as well as the desire to have all the transport units solely under the direct control of Speer were the two chief factors leading towards a gradual breaking away from NSKK ties. The Legion Speer may be the only transport unit left to the OT at the present time, there being some evidence that the other elements have been withdrawn from the organisation. The last known address of Transportkorps Speer is Berlin-Charlottenburg 9, A Meesedam (Westkreuz). Its staff was organised along the same lines as the General Staff of a German unit such as a division as follows:

Abt. Ia	Einsatz (Employment)
Abt. Ib	Quartiermeister (Quartermaster)
Abt. Ic	Nachrichtenwesen (Signals Intelligencc)
Abt. IIa	Personalverwaltung (Personnel Administration)
Abt. IIb	Entlöhnung (Wages)
Abt. IIc	Ausbildungswesen (Training)
Abt. III	Disziplinarwesen (Discipline)
Abt. III	Unterkunft u. Verpflegung (Billets and Mess)
Abt. IVa	Verwaltung u. Wirtschaft (Administration)
Abt. IVb	Sanitätsabteilung (Medical Service)

(A few further sections have been omitted because exact information is not available on them).

NSKK-Gruppe Todt assigned units of different strengths to each Einsatzgruppe. The sector of an Einsatzgruppe in which NSKK was employed was called an Abschnitt and its staff Abschnittsführung. The transport organisations working for the OT received their own HQ directives concerning general matters of transport, but in all matters of operational activities they were under the direct control of the OT units, especially the OBLs, to which they were assigned. There follows here a complete list of Abschnittsftthrungen as they existed in 1943:

1. Abschnittsführung West (France, Belgium, Holland)

2. Abschnittsführung Wiking (Norway, Denmark)

3. Abschnittsführung Russland-Nord

4. Abschnittsführung Russland-Mitte

5. Abschnittsführung Südost (Balkans)

6. Abschnittsführung Italien

7. Abschnittsführung Reich

The Abschnittsführung West, with HQ at Paris, was attached to Einsatzguppe West and controlled transportation for the OT units in France, Belgium and Holland. The staff was organized along military lines and the numbering system of individual sections corresponds almost exactly with that of the Berlin staff of the HQ of NSKK-Gruppe Todt (or Transportkorps Speer). The sections are, in part, as follows:

Abt. Ia	Einsatz (Movement of vehicles from one unit to another)
Abt. Ib	-
Abt. II	Personal (Personnel)
Abt. Ill	Gericht (Court and Discipline)
Abt. IVa	Truppenverwaltung (Administration)
Abt. IVb	Arzt (Medical Service)
Abt. Vk	Technik (Technique)

Abschnittsffthrung West distributed units called Kraftwagenstaffel or simply Staffel (Battalion strength) to various OBLs according to need. Usually one Staffel was assigned to one OBL, but sometimes one Staffel took care of the transport needs of more than one OBL. Units called Hauptkolonnen, Kraftwagenhauptkolonnen or Transporthauptkolonnen and smaller units called Kolonnen or Transportkolonnen served various construction undertakings within an OBL. With the introduction of Legion Speer, formations called Abteilungen, Kompanien and Züge were assigned to various OT units on a level with Staffeln, Hauptkolonnen and Kolonnen. The direct contact between the OT and NSKK was established through NSKK-Verbindungsführer (NSKK Liaison officers) who were attached to the various OBLs.

The size of the various transport units varied greatly according to need. The number of Staffeln and Abteilungen in an Abschnitt depended naturally on the number and strength of OBLs in an Einsatzgruppe. A Staffel attached to the OBL Cherbourg and OBL Normandie was subdivided into eighteen Hauptkolonnen which altogether contained 549 transport lorries, eighty-seven buses and thirteen motorcycles. Some Hauptkolonnen took exclusive care of the transport of material, while others specialised in personnel. Staffeln in other OBLs were considerably smaller, as they normally consisted of about six Hauptkolonnen. A Hauptkolonne was usually subdivided into three Kolonnen, each controlling about ten to forty-five lorries.

A schematic picture of the transport formations working for the OT in France and the Low Countries presents great difficulties because of the frequent changes which took place from time to time in the organisation of the units.

Even from later periods up to about March 1943, very little known about the organisation of the transport units. Such Staffeln as are known to have been employed in the OBLs in the West are as follows:

NSKK and Legion Speer Units in the West

OBL	St. - Staffel L.S. - Legion SPEER		
	Up to Feb. 1943	*Feb. 1943*	*became in Jan. 44*
Holland	?	St. 1	St. 60?
Belgium	?	St. 2	St. 61
Audinghem & Nordwest	?	St. 3	St. 62
Rouen	St.34	St. 4	St. 63
St Malo & Cherbourg	?	St. 5	St.64
Brest	?	St. 6	St. 65
Lorient	St. 22	St. 7	St. 66
St Nazaire	?	Abt. 1 (LS)	St. 67
La Rochelle	St. 36	St. 8	St. 68?
Bordeaux (Bayonne?)	?	Abt. 2 (LS)	St. 69
Marseille	?	St. 9	St. 70
Paris	?	St. 10	St. 71
Ardennes	?	?	St. 72
Cannes?	?	?	St. 73

[Question marks are as they appear in the 1945 Handbook.]

The first complete picture of the transport organisation in the whole West can only be given for the period from February 1943 onwards as the list above shows, ten Staffeln of the NSKK-Brigade Todt and two Abteilungen of the Legion Speer served the OT in France, Holland and Belgium.

Major reforms took place at the end of 1943. In this year so many foreigners had entered into the service of the Legion Speer that a dangerous situation was threatening the existence of NSKK units. The heads of the transport in the service of the OT were faced initially with two possibilities. They could open the doors of the NSKK to all foreigners or disband the NSKK formations because of the shortage of German personnel. The solution was found in a compromise. The members of the Legion Speer, which formerly had been organised in

Abteilungen, were directly incorporated into the Staffeln of the NSKK-Gruppe Todt. The picture as of from January 1944 onwards shows that fourteen Staffeln were employed in the West (Nos 60–73) and no Abteilungen. These Staffeln were composed predominately of foreign legionaries with only the leading executive and administrative positions reserved for persons of German origin. The example from OBL Süd (St Nazaire) will illustrate well the proportion of German to foreign personnel. There, the NSKK-Kraftwagenstaffel 67 employed 118 Germans, 380 Frenchmen and 265 Russians. The present situation is such that it is most unusual to find a German driver working outside of the boundaries of the Reich.

The foreigners in the employment of the NSKK-Gruppe Todt are composed at the present time of two classes of personnel:

1. The legionaries, that is, members of the Legion Speer
2. The so-called NSKK-Freiwillige, that is, short-term employees, such as non uniformed drivers, technicians, and menial help.

Other Transport Organisations

Besides the three main transport organisations discussed above, sometimes other transport units served the OT. In Norway, for instance, we have the NSKK-Transportbrigade Luft (or NSKK-Motorgruppe Luftwaffe) carrying supplies for the airfields, and NSKK-Transportbrigade Heer, working for the German Army. Both of these organisations were also placed at the service of the OT. The sea transport for the OT was provided by the Transportflotte Speer with HQ at Groningen, under Einsatzleiter Grosskapitän Seyd, employing in March 1944, about 10,000 men. This transport unit is also known to have worked in Russia, Italy and Norway. Transportflotte Speer was originally called Binnenflotte (Inland Waterway Fleet) and was charged with Berlin with coal along the river and canals leading to the capital. Transportflotte Speer combed all Norway for seamen and trained them in the Speerschule for Seamen at Sandefjord.

Requisitionings of Private Vehicles

When NSKK moved into occupied territories in the service of the OT, it brought along German-made vehicles. In course of time however, with the growth of the OT undertakings, the number of existing vehicles proved to be entirely inadequate for the new tasks. To satisfy the increased needs of transport, the NSKK was allowed to buy or hire vehicles in the occupied territories. From the NSKK, the transport was assigned to various building enterprises according to need. The centralised handling of motor vehicles did not, however, produce satisfactory results. In February 1944, it was decided to put the OBLs in charge of transport under the terms of a special Transportvertrag (Transportation

Contract). All the private vehicles which had been taken over by the NSKK were to be returned to the OBLs. In order to augment their motor park, the contractors were empowered to buy or to hire local lorries. The lorries owned by the OT could also be hired through the NSKK at a set hourly rental. The new arrangement enabled the OBLs to exercise direct control over their own vehicles and to hire vehicles without bothering about having to wait for permits or assignments from the NSKK. The latter continued to run its own vehicles chiefly for the general use of the various construction units. Its chief function, however, was that of an organisation in control of all drivers in the service of the OT.

Some cases are known in which the OT hired vehicles from the local military authorities. Thus in January 1944, QBL Cherbourg asked for the loan of 100 lorries from Militärbefehlshaber Frankreich Gruppe Verkehr.

Types of Motor Vehicles

In France 95% of the lorries and buses were French (Renault, Hotchkiss and Citroën) the rest were German, (Opel and Mercedes), American (Ford and Chevrolet), and Italian (Fiat). Only about 20% of the vehicles were Holzgas (Producer Gas) driven in early 1944, but this number must have increased later owing to the shortage of petrol.

As early as the beginning of 1943 the quality of the motor vehicles used by NSKK left much to be desired. Thus, out of 549 transport lorries used in OBL Cherbourg in May 1943, only 318 were in relatively good shape, 217 were in repair shops for replacement of spare parts and five were in the process of being transformed into wood-burning vehicles. The state of vehicles in OBL Rouen was supposed to be even worse than in OBL Cherbourg. There is no doubt that in the course of time the conditions must have worsened considerably. An order of 24 March 1944, provided that vehicles used for transport of men should, in case of invasion, be placed at the disposal of the Army.

c) Signals Communications

Signal Communications Services

All wire and wireless communication within the OT units was from an OBL level upwards, in the hands of the section Nachrichtenwesen, known also variously under the names 'Nachrichtendienst' and 'Nachrichtenführung. The executive staff in the communications section was under the leadership of a Nachrichtenführer or Nachrichtenleiter. The clerical staff in the section Nachrichtenwesen was composed primarily of 'Nachrichtenmädel' who were under the supervision of a Nachrichtenführerin. (An order from OTZ forbade the employment of Nachrichtenmädel below twenty-one years of age in the occupied territories or 'Fronteinsatz').

At the present time OT signal communications in Germany are directed from Einsatzgruppe HQ level, where Nachrichtenwesen is a Referat (subsection) of Abteilung Bau (Construction Section).

All official mail addressed to an OT unit such as an OBL was first turned over to the Geschäftszimmer where it was opened and registered in a 'Briefeingangsbuch'. Then it was placed on the desk of the Oberbauleiter from where it was distributed to the chiefs of the various sections. The reserve procedure took place in the case of letters sent out by the OBL.

All sections had to keep an orderly file following a scheme (Aktenplan or Geschäftsplan) approved by the Oberbauleiter. The right of signature was given only to the Oberbauleiter, his assistant, the chiefs of sections and to the Abschnittsbauleiter. All letters had to end with the greeting 'Heil Hitler'. Otherwise the name of Hitler was not allowed to be mentioned. Whenever necessary he was to be referred to as 'der Führer', or, more formally, as 'Der Führer des Grossdeutschen Reiches'. (In direct speech the Germans had to use 'Mein Führer' and foreigners 'Führer'.)

In countries where mail service was not well organised, as in Russia, the inter-OT correspondence was taken care of by means of special couriers. Even in France couriers were used on special duty runs. Letters very rarely quote the geographic addresses of the OT units. They are forwarded through the Army Postal Service and consequently bear Feldpost (APO) numbers. Letters of the alphabet were attached to the FPN (German abbreviation, equivalent to the American term APO number) to denote subdivisions of a given unit. Thus, for example, FPN 05925 represents OBL Cherbourg and FPN 05925 E or 05925 EO respectively represent the firms Eisenrieth and Ensle Ostertag both employed by the OBL Cherbourg.

d) Health and Medical Services

Medical Services

The OT provides medical services for all its members whether they are OT-Eigenes Personal (OT organic personnel) or Firmenangehörige (Firm personnel). This service is controlled by the section Sanitätswesen composed of German and foreign personnel. Originally all the doctors were German, but, in the course of time, the shortage of qualified German medical men became so acute that foreign doctors were freely accepted into the OT Medical Service. The picture as of 1944 shows foreign doctors surpassing in number those of German origin. The rank given foreign doctors, however, was very low, none being able to attain a grade higher than that of a Haupttruppführer (equivalent to that of a Master Sergeant in the American Army).

The organisation of the medical service in the various OT units can be best described by quoting some examples. OBL Cherbourg, which comprised about 15,000 men, employed one chief doctor, two assistant doctors, seven foreign doctors, one dentist, ten medical aid men and four nurses. Einsatz Seefalke in Rome was composed of four doctors, ten medical aid men, six Sankra (Ambulances) with drivers, four assistant drivers, one administrative officer, fifteen Italian doctors and fifty Italian nurses. In the organisational scheme for Russia, a Sanitätseinheit (Medical Unit) was composed of one doctor and ten medical aid men; one Sankra (Ambulance) and one lorry were attached to each unit of the size of an OBL. Every third or fourth Sanitätseinheit had as its chief a dentist instead of a doctor.

Every OT man is covered by medical insurance which varies for the different classes of personnel working for OT. The insurance is collected by the Deutsche Krankenkassen OT (OT Health Insurance Companies), one to each Einsatzgruppe and all part of the Krankenkassenverband OT (OT Health insurance Association) in Berlin.

OT has its own hospitals (Lazarette) and dispensaries (Reviere and Grossreviere) staffed chiefly with foreign personnel. Characteristic of the attitude of the OT to foreigners is the fact that the hospitals have separate wards for German nationals and for foreigners. Sometimes existing hospitals in the occupied territories were placed directly at the service of the OT. OT personnel, being part of the Wehrmacht, can also be treated in the Army, Navy and Air Force hospitals, but their bills have to be covered by the OT: moreover the foreign manpower in the OT is, as a rule, not granted Wehrmacht facilities in this respect.

There are also mobile units for First Aid Treatment as well as travelling dental clinics to take care of men who, presumably because of the urgency of work, cannot leave the construction sites.

Several convalescent homes (Erholungsheime and Kurhotele) beautifully situated in the mountains are at the disposal of OT personnel (e.g. Schloss St Märgen in Längsee, for NSKK-OT personnel; Island of Mainauon Lake Constance).

Sanitary Conditions

Although the Germans are rather proud of their achievements in improving the sanitary conditions of the camps, the reports at our disposal show that the picture is not so rosy as painted by German propaganda. While the Germans have cleaner barracks and generally live under all round better sanitary conditions than the foreigners, the conditions in some of the camps for the latter were appalling. The delousing process was one of the perpetual tasks of the personnel organised in the so-called 'Entwesungstruppe', mobile units which moved from place to place. No man could obtain furlough papers without first obtaining a stamped statement from the local OT doctor that he was free of vermin and from contagious diseases. (Frei von Ungeziefer und Ansteckenden Krankheiten). To quote an instance, out of 1,000 Russian prisoners who were deloused immediately upon their arrival in Cherbourg (May 1944), 750 had to be deloused again within a few days.

Inoculation, especially against typhus and cholera, is supposed to be given to all OT personnel. The date and dosage are also supposed to be entered into a man's Dienstbuch (Pay and Identity book). After examining several hundred such records, however, it is found that either the injections were overlooked entirely, or else, if given, no record of it kept. It is known that typhus, almost non-existent in civilised countries in recent years, was rampant in the West where sanitary conditions certainly must have been more favourable than in the East or Southeast. In the Balkans, the OT had also to contend with wide-spreading malaria. Since quinine was not available, malaria had to be treated with anti-pyrine.

e) Security Administration and Units

Rechts-und Diziplinarstelle (Legal and Disciplinary Subsection)
The services of security were well organised in the OT and were handled by units either forming an organic part of the OT or loosely attached to or co-operating with it. Each of these units is discussed separately below. The first is the Rechts-und Diziplinarstelle (Legal and Disciplinary Subsection). This is a subsection in the Section Frontführung in the administrative organisation of all OT units up to and including the Oberbauleitung. As the name implies, this sub-section takes care of legal and disciplinary matters. It has, however, only jurisdiction in relatively small matters and can commit offenders to a penal camp for a period only up to four months. All the more serious transgressions and crimes are dealt with by the military courtsmartial.

Schutzkommando
The second is the Schutzkommando (Security guard). The task of enforcing law and order in the OT Camps and building sites lies chiefly in the hands of the Schutzkommando, also known by the older name of Schutzkorps (both abbreviated as SK). The staff of the Schutzkommando, called Schutzkommandoführung, is headed by a Schutzkommandoführer, and is attached to the section Frontführung, as the Legal and Disciplinary Subsection discussed above.

The individual SK units are administered at OBL level; their duties comprise the guarding of construction sites, warehouses, machines, explosives, fuel dumps, motor vehicle parks, material equipment and food depots, and personnel camps within their respective OBL sectors. They are also employed in convoying prisoners, personnel and material. In convoys one SK man is theoretically assigned to guard twenty workers; in the case of 'untrustworthy' personnel, such as returned fugitives, the T O/WE calls for one SK man to ten 'guarded' personnel. Due to the shortage of SK men, the actual proportion is about one third of TO/WE requirements. In the Balkans, Poland and Russia, the SK units had to be perpetually on the alert against partisan raids and were often fortified into Stützpunkte (Strong Points).

In 1943 a critical shortage of SK men was caused by the Wehrmacht's drive to find suitable personnel for its armed forces. This weeding-out process left in SK only those Germans who were physically unfit for active military service. (One SK Identity Book discloses under the heading 'identifying scars or wounds', 'right arm amputated'). The resulting shortage of personnel forced the SK organisation to look for replacements among the foreign groups. In the EGW, for instance, most of the foreign personnel was recruited from among the French, Dutch and Flemish nationals, and came from the ranks of the collaborationists. Men accepted for the SK were trained for a period of six weeks or (in a short three-week course) in special SK camps such as the ones at Eichkamp near Berlin, at the OT Reichslehrlager (Reich Training Gamp) Freisach, or at St Cloud near Paris. The training consists of courses in Nazi indoctrination, and in the handling of AA guns and searchlight batteries, and small arms such as the MG (machine-gun) and the MP (automatic pistol). Even after the completion of their schooling and between duty assignments, the SK has to follow a daily routine practice in the use of these weapons. The SK is divided into units as follows:

a) SK-Kameradschaft. A unit of about eight to twelve men under a Kameradschaftsführer with the rank of from SK-Rottenführer to SK-Truppführer. The unit is given the narne of its Kameradschaftsführer.

b) SK-Zug. Composed of three to six Kameradschaften or of about thirty-five to sixty men under a Zugführer with the rank of from SK-Truppführer to SK-Hauptruppführer. The platoons are numbered consecutively within each Bereitschaft. (See below.)

c) SK-Bereitaohaft. Composed of two to three SK-Züge or of about 120–150 men under a Bereitschaftsführer with the rank of from Frontführer to OT Oberfrontführer. The Bereitschaft receives a number of men chosen by the Abteilungsführer – see d) below – and is usually attached to an OT sector on OBL level. Some Bereitschaften include, according to need, a Nachrichtenkameradschaft (Communications Unit) composed of a Funker (Radio Man), Blinker, (Light Signals Operator), Fernsprecher (Telephonist), Meldehund (Messenger Dog) and Brieftaube (Carrier Pigeon).

d) SK-Abteilunff. A unit under the leadership of an Abteilungsführer with the rank of from OT Hauptfrontführer to OT Stabsfrontführer. It is attached to an Einsatzgruppe, and it consists of as many Bereitschaften as are needed in the Einsatzgruppe. In some areas, such as in Southern Russia, more than one SK-Abteilung was attached to an Einsatzgruppe. SK-Abt. 11 was attached to Einsatzgruppe West or SK-Abt. 21 to EG Wiking. In Southern Russia SK-Abt. 72 was attached to EG Russland-Süd. Enlarging the example, SK-Bereitschaft 11/5 stands for the 5th Bereitschaft of the 11th Abt. This particular Bereitschaft was working for the Einsatz (formerly OBL) Rouen in 1944, and superseded, in that sector, the 24th Hundertschaft of the Schutzkorps, evidently an older organisation which has been dissolved towards the end of 1943.

The Schutzkommandoführung which forms part of the Frontführung at OTZ (now Amt Bau-OTZ) Berlin is the highest SK authority. The Schutzkommandoführer is also head of the Ersatzabt (SK Replacement Unit), Wachabt (Special Guard Duty Unit), Berlin, and Transport-SK, employed in Germany.

SK units are billeted, fed and paid by the OBL HQ to which they are attached. Weapons are received directly from the Schutzkommandoführung in Berlin; munitions and personnel equipment are, however, distributed by the various Einsatzgruppen.

Two other special units (Sonderkommandos), which belong to the Security Service, were organised out of the existing Schutzkommando for particular tasks. They are known as the Ordnungskommando and the Streifenkommando.

The Ordnungskommando was composed of men of the regular SK and created in German-occupied territory for the task of helping the Feldgendarmerie (Military Police) of the local Feldkommandanturen (Military District Commands) in apprehending fugitive foreign workers. These men do not form permanent units but are picked for what the Germans call 'Razzien' (raiding parties) when the occasion arises. The Ordnungskommando may include Germans, Dutch, Flemings, Danes or Frenchmen; men of any one nationality, however, are not sent out against their own countrymen. The leader of the Ordnungskommando invariably is a German. The fugitives so recaptured are temporarily held in an Anhaltlager; strongly fended off and well guarded by a reinforced guard, called SK-Wachnannschaft and picked from the local Schutzkommando.

The Streifendienst employing SK-Streifenkommandos was introduced in EGW after the Allied invasion, for the same purpose of apprehending fugitive workers as the Ordnungskonmando, except that it acted also against German deserters.

Latest reports indicate that the SK has been redesignated Schutzkommando Speer, and that recruiting for it is actively being carried on by the SS.

SS-Verbindungsführung (SS-OT Liaison)

The third type of security service is that provided by the SS-Verbindungsführung (SS-OT Liaison). This office is found on all levels from OTZ in Berlin down to a Bauleitung (below OBL level it becomes an Aussensteille or Branch Office) and forms an integral part of OT administration. It is a section of the same standing as, for example, Frontführung, Technik, or Verwaltung, staffed by members of the SS under the head of an SS-Verbindungsführer. (SS Liaison officer). The members of this section retain their old SS ranks but also obtain OT ranks, usually – but not necessarily – of a corresponding grade. Originally the SS-Verbindungsführung was attached to OT units for the purpose of field security or elementary counter-intelligence work. The SS-Verbindungsführung at the OBL Cherbourg for example, lists its tasks as follows:

(i) Counter-intelligence, sabotage, political transgressions and crimes, check-up on German and foreign OT members.
(ii) Identification papers for German and foreign members permitting the entry to construction sites.
(iii) Dossier of all OT members in OBL Cherbourg.
(iv) Capture of fugitive workers.

The SS-Verbindungsführung is also known to have arbitrated differences between the German contractors and French subcontractors, investigated black market activities, supervised much of the activity between the OT and offices, firms and individuals of the occupied countries. The SS-Verbindungsführung in France worked hand in hand with the Disziplinarstelle, SK, Feldgendarmerie and the local French police. At the present time, the SS-OT liaison through its assignment of political police, may be said to control every phase of OT activity. This subject is discussed also in the section Liaison below.

Feldgendarmerie (Military Police)

The fourth type of security service – in occupied territory – is that of the Feldgendarmerie (Military Police). In France, for example, units of the Feldgendanaerie were attached to the Feldkommandanturen for the purpose of police supervision of the local population. In this connection, they also did the actual tracking down of OT deserters, after having been furnished with data by the SS-Verbindungsführer. The Feldgendarmerie moreover worked in co-operation with the SK.

SS-Polizei Regiment Todt (SS-Police Regiment Todt)

The fifth type of security service is, or rather was, provided by SS-Polizei Regiment Todt. Nothing much is known about the activities OT of this unit.

Two independent sources mention a Kdo (Kommando) of the 1st Bn of Pol. Regt. Todt at Cherbourg under a Leutnant der Schutzpolizei und Kdo-Führer Dittmer. Another less reliable source reports a Bn. of the 28th Regt. Polizei Todt stationed at Annecy in April 1944 (coming from Yugoslavia) and composed of personnel of Polish, Austrian, Yugoslav and Czech nationality. Its continued function at the present time in the service of the OT is problematical.

Technische Nothilfe (Technical Emergency Corps)

The sixth type of security service of which the OT may avail itself at the proper place and time is the Technische Nothilfe (Teno: Technical Emergency Corps). This type of security service will be discussed in Liaison section, as far as OT-SK liaison is concerned.

Sicherheitsdienst (SD: Security Service)

Finally, the Sicherheitsdienst (SD: Security Service) enters into the activities of the OT, mainly because of the masses of foreign manpower employed by the latter. Normally the help of the SD in this respect is enlisted only on special occasions when manpower raids of major proportions are made in occupied territory, or in cases of the suspected presence of subversive elements within the OT. SD-OT liaison is normally established through the SS-OT Verbindungsführer at the proper level. The SD is discussed from the point of view of political liaison, in IIGc94.

G. Liaison

Note: As may be seen below, the OT, even though it is considered as belonging to the Wehrmacht, has established liaison with government and Nazi Party agencies without recourse to Army, Navy or Air Force channels. OT liaison with outside agencies will be studied under four headings:

a) Military
b) Economic
c) Political
d) Operational

The need for OT liaison with military authorities, particularly the Army, is obvious. The need for economic liaison arose from the fact that the OT is classified as an essential industry within the comprehensive scheme of priority allotments of supplies as administered by the Reichsministerium für Rüstung und Kriegsproduktion (Ministry for Armament and War Production), and priority allotments of manpower as administered by the Generalbevollmächtigte für den Arbeitseinsatz (Plenipotentiary-General for Manpower Allocation). The need for political liaison arose from the fact that for four years practically all of OT's assignments were outside of the Reich, in either occupied territory or in satellite or protected countries, and involved the employment of vast masses of foreign labour. Another important aspect was counter-intelligence which in the case of the OT was political rather than military. The need for operational liaison arose from the fact that OT co-operated directly with such organisations as NSKK and Teno, for example. The economic, political and operational liaison has been further subdivided into two types: German and foreign collaborationist agencies.

a) Military Liaison

Wehrmacht-OT (Germany) Liaison

At the present time all the construction facilities of the Wehrmacht have been put at the disposal of the OT. The working arrangements are discussed in detail in sections below.

The link between Amt Bau-OTZ and the OKW is established through the Rüstungsamt des Reichsministeriums für Rüstung und Kriegsproduktion. (Armament Bureau of the Ministry for Armament and War Production) also called the Speer Ministry. (The newly created Rüstungsstab (Armament Staff) in the same Ministry enters into liaison with Amt Bau-OTZ only in case of operational difficulties). The Armament Bureau was created in May 1942 to act as a co-ordinating agency between the civilian Speer Ministry and the now dissolved War Economy Bureau of the Armed Forces Command (Wehrwirtschaftsamt des OKW).

The Armament Bureau which started out as an agency of a military character, under the same command as the War Economy Bureau, General der Infanterie Thomas, later succeeded by Generalleutnant Wager, and finally by General Stapf, has since been made part of the Zentralamt (Central Bureau) of the Ministry, and has lost much of its original military character as far as the composition of its personnel is concerned. The present head of the Bureau is likewise reported to be a civilian. Much the same may be said of the regional offices of the Armament Bureau which are called Rüstungsinspektionen (Armament Inspectorate). It is these Inspectorates which are responsible for continued efficiency in armament and war production in their individual regions of control. These inspectorates controlled regions which, originally based on Wehrkreis boundaries, were recently modified to roughly comprise the area covered by two Gaue.

The regional production programme and problems involving priority of manpower and material are discussed and decisions made at sittings of

Rüstungskommissionen (Armament Conmissions), the composition of which contains regional key officials, both civilian (Gau and Land) and military (Wehrkreis officials), and includes OT representatives. The military personnel is divided into three representative groups: Army, Navy and Air Force. Originally only one Armament Commission was set up within the region of each Armament Inspectorate to iron out the various regional problems arising from the shortage in manpower and machine replacement parts, the destruction of factories and transport systems by Allied air raids and so forth. After the boundaries of the Armament Inspectorates (which incidentally coincide with the boundaries of the various OT Einsätze) were modified, however, to conform roughly with the boundaries of two Party Gaue, a sub-commission was established (August 1944 for each Armament Commission, called Rüstungsunterinspektion – Armament Sub-Commission).

At the present time, therefore, there sits in each of the two Gaue which together make up an Armament Inspectorate area, either an Armament Commission or an Armament Sub-Commission, the latter being controlled by the former. Each OT Einsatzgruppenleiter (OT Chief of Einsatzgruppe) is the appointed OT member of the various Armament Commissions in the area covered by his Einsatzgruppe. The Chief of Einsatzgruppe normally accredits his subordinate Chiefs of Einsatz as his representatives to the appropriate Armament Commissions. Each Chief of Einsatz is in turn the appointed OT member of the Armament Sub-Commission in the area of his Einsatz. He, like the Chief of Einsatzgruppe, normally delegates someone to take his place, this time at the sittings of the Sub-Commission, the delegate usually being one of the four OT Construction Deputies (Einsatz level; accredited to the Reichsverteidigungskommissar (Reich Defence Commissioner) of the competent Gau. The subject of OT regional liaison with the Armament Inspectorate, Armament Commissions and Sub-Commissions, and the Reich Defence Commissions has also been discussed earlier. It should be added here, however, that recently OT liaison has been carried down below OT Einsatz-Armament Inspectorate level, that is to say, liaison has now also been established (January 1945) between the OT Oberbauleitung and the Rüstungskommando (Armament Headquarters).

Army-OT Administrative Channels of Liaison

(i) EGW area as of summer 1944

The chief administrative army officials in the one-time Einsatzgruppe West were the military commanders, or rather administrators, of France (Stülpnagel) of Belgium and NW France (v. Falkenhausen) and of Holland (Christiansen). Their main concern with the OT consisted in circulating and supervising regulations which had already been laid down by existing government agencies. The most common object of concern was with OT manpower. OT manpower, even though it is termed Wehrmacht Auxiliary, is basically subject to manpower distribution control by German Labour authorities as represented at the top by Fritz Sauckel. When the military commander therefore circulates, for example, a regulation forbidding unsanctioned transfers of manpower from one OT-Firm to another, he does it on the basis of the existing regulations on the subject already laid down by OT Labour Trustee Schmelter who represents the OT on Saukel's staff.

Similarly, regulations circulated by military commanders on the price tariff for the requisitioning of construction equipment originally emanate from the offices of the Reichskommisar für Preisbildung (Reich Commissioner for Price Control).

The supervision of these regulations was left to the local Feldkommandanturen, the geographical sphere of authority of which in France roughly corresponded with the French Departements (France is divided into thirty-five Departements). The Feldkommandant's disciplinary authority in regard to OT personnel extended to all but serious court-martial offenses which came under the competence of the divisional canmanding general stationed in the corresponding sector. Nor did the Feldkommandant encroach on OT's own disciplinary powers which consisted essentially of sending refractory workers to disciplinary camps such as Erziehungs, or Schulungslager (Disciplinary Camps). The Feldkommandantur was the army administrative echelon in that it co-operated directly with the OBL administratively, just as the Festungsbau Pionierstab co-operated directly with the OBL operationally. Moreover the Feldkommandantur in France by controlling the French Département provided the OBL with channels to the French civilian population living within its sector. Consequently the Feldkommandantur was the local military agency involved in the tracking down of OT deserters in France.

(ii) Current Channels, Germany

Outside of disciplinary jurisdiction of regional and local military commanders over OT personnel stationed in their area, Army-OT administrative channels are bound up with Wehrmacht-OT channels to such an extent, that to discuss them would be equivalent to repeating the information given earlier. Reference is therefore made to that paragraph.

Army-OT Operational Channels of Liaison

(i) EGW area as of summer 1944

Operational liaison at the top between the Army and OT is established through the Vertreter des Leiters der Amt Bau-OTZ beim Generalstab des Heeres (Representative of the Chief of Amt Bau-OTZ to the Army General Staff). Liaison at the next lower echelon is maintained between Einsatzgruppe (abbreviated EG) and the Army or Army Group occupying the corresponding area. The nature of the liaison between EG and Army or Army Group depended mainly on the tactical situation and on the political status of the occupied territory. The Chief of EG West, (France, Belgium and Holland) for example, Oberbaudirektor Weiss, was at the same time Rundstedt's Chief Engineer; consequently he represented the OT on Rundstedt's staff. In Italy, OT liaison with the Army is established at the top through the OT-Verbindungsführer (Liaison Officer) to Oberbefehlshaber Südwest. In the Balkans, liaison was established through the Beauftragter der OT (OT Representative) to the General Engineer of the Commander in Chief South-Eastern Theatre with HQ at Sofia. Similarly, in Russia, OT had established liaison through the several Beauftragtender OT to the corresponding Generals of Engineers on the various Army Group staffs in North, Central and Southern Russia.

(ii) Current Channels, Germany

Since Germany has become a Kriegsgebiet (Theatre of Operations), the Chief of the Hauptabteilung Technik (Technical Bureau) at OTZ, Berlin, has had operational liaison with OKH through the Beauftragter der OT beim General der Pioniere und Festungen.

In regards to OT's functional status in the Army, two general observations may be made: 1) OT formations are not designed for any type of combat or assault engineer assignment. 2) In the immediate zone of operations, OT units are formed into special mobile units and, as such, come under the direction of the particular Army or Wehrmacht authorities most immediately concerned. In the wake of German troops on the offensive, it is their primary task to assure an uninterrupted flow of supplies by restoring the transport and communications systems destroyed by the retreating enemy. In this type of assignment, even though the execution of the task is itself under the supervision of OT engineers, the work is sometimes specified on the spot by Army officers (engineer or transport officers) down to divisional level, but more often by Corps and especially Army, in contact with the OT through OT liaison at Corps or Army HQ.

OT's task in defensive operations is somewhat more complicated. For one thing, OT personnel has been known to remain with German troops in isolated defense positions, especially those which call for skill in the construction of fortifications. Examples are the besieged German garrisons at La Rochelle, St Nazaire, Lorient and in the Channel Isles, especially Alderney. In all the above garrisons, OT personnel is detailed to the local Festungspionierstab (Fortress Engineer Staff). OT work details have occasionally been also assigned to dig trenches, lay minefields and prepare demolition charges for blowing up bridges and other key points of conmunications under orders of the Army engineers, from division upwards. The primary defensive tasks of the OT, however, are skilled construction and salvage work in the rear zone or at most in the rear lines of the front zone.

The basic and most common contact with OT in the construction of defence work is made by the Fortress Construction Engineer Staff competent in the particular sector where the OT personnel is at work. If the area is sufficiently stable to allow an OT administrative HQ, such as an OBL, to be set up, the execution of the task is supervised by the OT-Firm executive and his supervisory staff to whom the specific piece of construction has been assigned. The equipment used is likewise owned or at least rented by the firm. An overwhelming majority of individual workers in rear zone construction has up to recently been composed of foreigners, and indications are that the Germans have even now very considerable foreign assistance – willing or otherwise – at its disposal. The Fortress Construction Engineer Staff controls the proper carrying out of specifications. If, on the other hand, the area is considered too dangerous for stabilisation, firm equipment is transported to the rear along with most foreign personnel, and all German females and males are either directly detailed to the Fortress Construction Engineer staffs or are split up into mobile units attached to Division, Corps or Army (Engineers, or Transport, or Services of Supply) depending on the fluidity of the situation and local factors. In such cases, the OT formations, devoid as they are of the greater part of foreign OT elements, are termed Bautrupps (Construction Detachments).

OT's facilities were increasingly employed in France in emergency and even permanent repair of air-raid damage to transport and communication systems, to power plants and other sources of supply essential to a military machine. The best-qualified personnel in the organisation, amounting to about 10%, of the total number, was assigned in May 1944 to a manpower pool for air-raid emergency repair. After D-Day, OT's entire remaining facilities in France were used for this purpose.

Air Force Liaison

The Luftwaffe, until June/July 1944, was operationally in close liaison with the OT, but retained control over its own construction agencies. For example, the construction corporation Strassenbau Aktien Gesellschaft (trade name Strabag), which is said to be controlled by the Göring-interests, devoted practically its entire facilities to repair and construction work for the German Air Force in France and the Low Countries until the spring of 1942. Strabag and similar construction firms were administratively controlled by the Luftwaffe Feldbauamt (Air Force Field Construction Bureau) competent in the particular sector where such construction activity was going on. The Luftwaffe Feldbauamt furthermore had authority to sign building contracts directly with private firms, provided the basic terms such as pay scales and the tariff for hiring equipment conformed with existing governmental regulations. The Luftwaffe Feldbauamt was in turn controlled by a higher echelon the Bezirksbauleitung. This was the highest GAF organisation specially set up to supervise construction locally. Beyond the Bezirksbauleitung, regional construction was administered by control staffs i.e. Luftgaukomnando (Air District HQ) Verwaltung/B (abbreviation for Bau or Construction) under command of the Luftgauintendantur. Disciplinary orders were handed down from the Luftgaukommando through the Feldluftgaukommando (Field Air District HQ), the Flughafenbezirke (Air Port Area) and the Flughafenkommandanturen (Air Port Regional Command) acting as administrative channels respectively for the Bezirksbauleitung and the Feldbauamt. Around April 1942, when the OT administration was becoming both centralised and stabilised in the West, Strabag and other firms, which by that time had completed the bulk of the GAF programme, transferred the largest part of their personnel and equipment to the OT. Summarising, therefore, the GAF construction agencies, while in close liaison with the OT, were independent agencies.

As Allied air raids on targets in Germany increased in scope and effectiveness, the tasks of the OT became increasingly identified with air-raid protection and hence under the direction of the GAF. The first step toward reversing the chain of command and placing GAF's construction agencies and facilities under control of the OT was a decree issued by Reichsmarschall Göring on 21 May 1944 ordering the transfer of operational direction of the Bauwesen der Luftwaffe (GAF Construction Branch) from its Chief to the Chief of Amt Bau-OTZ, i.e. Ministerialdirektor Dorsch. The Chief (GAF) remains, however, in control of GAF construction policy and as GAF-OT liaison to Göring. Inasmuch as the GAF Construction Branch HQ were in the Speer Ministry (Armament and War Production) – as Amt Bau-OTZ is at present – this transfer of functions amounted, at the top, to not much more than an interdepartmental transfer within the Speer Ministry. Control of GAF Construction agencies reverts to the GAF at the end of the war. Furthermore the OT is to use GAF construction facilities within their existing framework, but is not to modify the internal structure of the GAF construction organisation. In short, GAF construction agencies were operationally, if not administratively, attached to the OT.

The relative spheres of authority of the OT and the GAF in regard to control of the regional construction agencies of the GAF within Germany are defined in Speer's decree of October 1944, given in summary below:

(i) The organisation of two GAF construction HQ, the first on a level with OT Einsatzgruppe HQ, that is to say, Luftgaukommando, Verwaltung/B; the second, on a level with OT Oberbauleitung HQ, that is to say, Luftwaffe Feldbauamt.

(ii) Changes in chain of command made by GAF authorities in regard to GAF construction agencies as a result of their operation henceforth under OT direction.

(i) (a) Organisation of the HQ of Luftgaukommando, Verwaltung/Bau (Luftgau HQ Section Administration Subsection Construction)

(The Organisation is very similar to that of the first two sections in an OT Einsatzgruppe HQ and is here consequently given in summary form only.)

Verwaltungsgruppe B (i.e. Bau) (Administrative subsection Construction).

Professional governmental rank of Chief; Regierungsoberbaurat.

Referat (Sub Unit) BI

1: Baueinsatz, Sonderbauvorhaben (Construction Commitment, Special Construction Projects).
2: Arbeitseinsatz (Manpower allocation).
3: Bauwirtschaft: Bau Firmen, Baugeräteinsatz (Construction Management: Allocation of Construction firms and equipment).
4: Vertrage, Baumaterialkontingente (Contracts, Quotas of construction materials).
5: Feld-und-Nachschub Bauanlagen für Flughafenkommandanturen (Ground and Supply Installations for subordinate Airport Regional Commands).
6: Flak Anlagen (AA, Anti-Aircraft, Construction).
7: Baupröfung (Construction Inspections).

Referat (Sub Unit) BII:

1. Hochbau, Bauplanung (Above Ground or Surface Planning and Construction).
2: Tarnung (Camouflage).
3: Luftwaffe Nachrichten Anlagen (GAP Signals Communication Construction).

Referat (Sub Unit) B III:

1. Tiefbau (subterranean construction).
2: Ingenieurbau (Engineering).
3: Wasserbau (Waterworks: supply, irrigation, drainage).

Referat (Sub Unit) BIV:

1. Elektrotechnik (Electro-Teohnics).
2. Maschinentechnik (Techno-Mechanics).
3. Wärmetechnik: Heitung, Luftung (Thermo-dynamics: Heating, Ventilation).
4: Energie Versorgung (Power Supply).

Referat (sub Unit) BV:

1–3: Vermessung, Plankamer und Planverwaltung (Surveying, Plan Drafting and Safe-keeping).

(i) (b) Organisation of the HQ of a Luftwaffe Feldbauamt (GAP Ground Construction Office).

(This HQ, like the preceding, is given in summary form only. Professional-governmental rank of chief: Regierungsbaurat.)

Referat (Section) 1:

Baueinsatz, Personal, Abrechnungen, Tarnung, Feuer und Luftschutz. (Construction Commitment, Personnel, Accounting, Camouflage, Fire and Air-Raid Protection).

Referat (Section) 2:

Hochbau, Nachrichtenanlagen, Flak Anlagen, Bauplanung und Ingenieurbau. (Above Ground or Surface Construction, Signal Communications Installations, AA Construction, Planning and Engineering).

Referat (Section) 3:

Tiefbau, Flugangar, Werkstatte, Flugplätze, Be- und Entwässerung. (Subterranean Construction, Hangars, Workshops, Landing Fields, Irrigation and Drainage).

Referat (Section) 4:

Electrotechnik, Maschinentechnik, Transport. (Electro-Technics, Techno-Mechanics, Transport).

Referat (Section) 5:

Vermessung. (Surveying).

(ii) Changes in chain of Command of GAF construction agencies, resulting from the assumption of their operational control by the OT.

(The changes are given in the form of a summary translation of a decree by Göring (20 June 1944), effective 15 July.)

(i) All GAF construction agencies, establishments, depots, facilities, equipment and building supplies, with the exception of Betriebsdienststellen (Administrative offices) and Vermessungsdienststellen (Survey offices) have been removed from the jurisdiction of the Luftgaukommando HQ and (through the Chief of the GAF Construction Branch) put at the disposal of the Chief of Amt Bau-OTZ.

(ii) Personnel administration of GAF construction personnel (rations, clothing, billeting, pay, allowances, bonus, allotments). Excepted are: special task officers of the Truppensonderdienst (Special Service), Wehrmacht officers and Wehrmachtsgefolge (Wehrmacht Auxiliary). These will remain under GAF personnel administration.

The above arrangements remain, however, flexible; if found advantageous, feeding, clothing, and so forth of individual GAF construction A personnel and units will, on occasions, be provided by local GAF administrations.

(iii) All personnel barracks and buildings permanently assigned for use by GAF construction personnel are to be placed under OT administration. At the present time, the Luftwaffe Bau Batl and Luftwaffe Bau Ersatz-Batl (GAF Construction Bn and Replacements Bn) have been broken up to serve as replacements for combat personnel, and their places taken by OT personnel.

Navy Liaison

Abbreviations:

CNC   (Chief of Navy Construction: Dorsch)
CND   (Chief of Naval Defences; Watzecha)
INC   (Inspector of Naval Construction)
BNC   (Bureau of Navy Construction)

Administrative relations between the Luftwaffe and the OT as described above generally held good also for relations between the Kriegsmarine and the OT provided the Marinebauamt is substituted for the Luftwaffe Feldbauamt, and similar substitutions are made on other levels. (The installation of coastal guns, however, provided an exception to the above. In that case, the Marinebauleitung (technical staff of Marinebauamt) would turn the blueprints over to the Festungsbaupionierstab which would supervise the actual work of emplacement and installation as performed by the OT).

On 20 July 1944 a decree issued by Gross-Admiral Dönitz, similar to the Luftwaffe decree issued by Göring on 20 June, placed the Kriegsmarine construction agencies and equipment under the OT. Ministerialdirektor Dorsch, in his capacity of Chef des Amtes Bau-OTZ (Chief of the Bureau of Construction – OT Central HQ) in the Reich Ministry for Armament and War Production, thus became more or less automatically also Chef des Marinebauwesens (Chief of Navy Construction). The following is a translated summary of the decree:

High Command

1. The Chief of Amt Bau-OTZ (Bureau of Construction – OT Central HQs) in the Ministry of Aimament and War Production as Chief of Navy Construction takes over all Marinebaudienststellen (Navy Construction Agencies), equipment, etc.

2. Although the agencies are subordinated to the above-mentioned OT Chief, they remain Navy agencies; they do not become administratively incorporated into the OT.

Published in *Fritz Todt, der Mensch, der Ingenieur, der Nationalist*, the caption for these photographs states, 'An der Westkuste Frankreichs baut die Organisation Todt – meist im Schutze gewaltiger fangedamme – ein System Flottenstutzpunkte'. On the west coast of France and built by the Organisation Todt, a new system of massive shelters protects the fleet. The U-boat pens were some of the largest reinforced-concrete structures constructed by the OT. See also page 101 and colour section.

Above: Interior of a submarine pen at St Nazaire, with a U-boat being overhauled. The post-war British publication in which this photograph appeared stated, 'heavy charges will be needed to destroy these bomb-proof structures'. *(CMcC)* Below: Fritz Todt leads a party of artists and architects across a construction site 'in the West'. The arts, including poetry and architecture, were frequently linked with engineering projects, especially in publications such as *Bauen und Kampfen* which consists of poems and illustrations concerning the OT. Some of the illustrations from it are reproduced in the colour section of this book.

3. The Chief of Navy Construction (abbreviated CNC) is responsible to the Commander-in-Chief of the Navy. (Note: This places a dual responsibility upon Dorsch, inasmuch as he is responsible to Speer for administration of the OT as a construction organisation).

4. The CNC may use outside agencies for Navy construction work, if necessary in the interests of efficiency; he may likewise use Navy agencies for non-naval construction, if necessary for the defence of the country. The programme as laid down by the C-in-C of the Navy must not, however, be in any way affected.

5. The C-in-C of the Navy retains control and ownership over construction. In his dealings with CNC he is represented by the Chef Kriegsmarine Wehr (Chief of Naval Defences, abbreviated CND). The CD is represented on the regional level by the Oberbefehlshaber MOK (Commanders on the Navy High Command) or their subordinate Oberbefehlshaber Marinegruppen Kdos (Commanders of Navy Group Commands) and the Kommandierend Admirale (Admirals Comma nding). (See Supplement at the end of this Decree.)

6. The CNC's liaison officer at OKM (Navy High Command K represented by the CND is designated Inspekteur des Marinebauwesens, inspector of Naval Construction, abbreviated INC). The INC in agreement with the CND conmandeers construction officials and their personnel for the establishment of higher Engineer Liaison offices and Liaison Engineer offices on a regional level (see Supplement 2 at the end of this Decree).

7. The decree of 16 February 1943, regulating the construction tasks assigned to the Navy through the former Amt Marinebauwesens (Bureau of Navy Construction) as distinct from those assigned to the Army through the Antsgruppe Pioniere und Festungen (Pioneers and Fortifications Branch), remain in force.

CNC Organisation

1. All personnel of the former Bureau of Navy Construction (BNC) and its subordinate agencies, except the personnel commandeered to the Abteilung Betrieb (Admin. Section, see Supplement at the end of this Decree) are placed under the-CNC.

2. Likewise soldiers, insofar as they were detailed to construction posts as draughtsmen, motor vehicle drivers, etc., on or before 1 July 1944. (Special regulations will be drafted to apply to future construction detachments for which provision has been made by the Navy.)

3. All trucks (lorries) hitherto allotted to Navy construction agencies will be placed at the disposal of the CNC; additional trucks will be placed at his disposal only for the duration of their specific task, as will all personnel carriers essential for personnel transport.

4. All construction machinery, separate pieces of equipment, derricks, tugboats, etc., already at the disposal of the BNC will be placed at the disposal of the CNC. Tugboats serving river traffic may not be diverted to other work, particularly those employed on the Jade River.

5. The above regulations apply also to immobile facilities (administrative and service quarters, building yards, etc.).

Service Status of Navy Officials and Auxiliary Personnel (Gefolgschaftsmitglieder)

1. All Navy officials and auxiliary personnel as outlined in CNC organisation remain members of the Kriegsmarine and will be cared for as such.

2. Appointments, promotions, discharges of Navy officials are recommended by the CNC through Navy channels.

3. Appointments, promotions, discharges of Gefolgschaftsmitglieder (Navy auxiliary personnel) are granted on the authority of the CNC.

4. Basic pay of the above personnel is that of the Navy; additional bonuses may however be granted for efficiency, etc., according to OT pay scales.

5. Soldiers on detached service to the OT may wear the OT uniform.

6. The disciplinary authority of the CNC is that vested in him by virtue of article 24 para. 1 & 2, No. 1 of the RD St O (Reichs Disziplinar Strafordnung or Reich Penal Code) and D article 18 of the WD St O (Wehrmacht Disziplinar Strafordnung or Armed Forces Penal Code) and as personnel administrator in the sense of BDO of the Kriegamarine.

7. Leaves and Service travel are regulated according to Navy regulations.

Replacements
1. The CNC decides on the TO/WE of construction establishments and may dissolve or activate individual agencies.

2. The CNC appoints technical replacements. The Navy High Command appoints administrative replacements.

3. Replacements of motor vehicle parts, etc., will be furnished by the Navy in lump deliveries.

Communications
1. Communication services of the Navy, including the installation of new lines, will be extended to OT agencies working far the Navy.

Construction Programme Channels
1. The ND informs the INC of the construction requirements on the basis of military urgency. The latter draws up a construction programme after collaboration with the competent office (see Supplement at the end of this Decree) in regard to the technical and economic practicability of the projected programme. Having obtained the approval of the CND, he then recommends the execution of the programme. The Commanders of the Navy High Command put in their individual requirements through the competent offices, within the limits of the entire allotment.

2. The CND will in the future receive his regular quotas directly from the Wehrmacht without going through Navy channels. Special quotas, such as poured iron and non-ferrous metals hitherto provided from Navy contingents, will, in the future, also be provided in quarterly Wehrmacht allotments.

Emergency Measures
1. In case of imminent danger, military commanders in occupied territory down to Seekommandant, and in Reich territory down to Küstenbefehlshaber, are empowered to issue directives in connection with the execution of emergency measures approved by the CND.

Billeting, Messing, etc.
1. The Navy will continue to provide quarters, rations, pay, clothing, medical care, etc., for personnel in the Navy construction agencies placed under the CND.

Financial Accounting
1. The administrative agencies under the CND keep their own account records and are solely responsible for expenditures.

Supplementary Decree
Any questions which arise will be clarified in the form of supplementary decisions made by a Commission on which the Navy High Command and the CNC will each

be represented by one representative. The commission will sit on 23 July 1944.
  Signed by Dorsch for OT
  and Warzecha (Chief of Naval Defences) for the Navy

Supplement: Scope of Function and Organisation of the Administrative Offices remaining under Military (Navy) Chain of Command

1. Untere Instanz (Lower Level)
(a) Marine Betriebs Abteilungen and Marine Betriebs Dienststellen (Navy Administrative Sections and Offices) will have as assignments the continued performance of Navy Construction business and the maintenance of existing facilities in this respect. Navy administrative sections will be established at Wilhelmshaven, Kiel, Gotenhafen and Pillau; Navy administrative offices will replace the rest of the former Marine Oberbauämter and Bauämter (Navy Construction Bureaux).

Specifically the tasks of the administrative sections and offices will be as follows:
(i) Operation and maintenance of the electrical current, heat and steam of Navy installations and shipyards, insofar as they have hitherto been administered by the Bureau of Navy Construction (BNC).
(ii) Operation of Navy waterworks, water and gas conduits.
(iii) Crane operation in Gotenhafen.
(iv) Navy railway operation in the ports, ordnance sites and oil depots.
(v) The functions of power and safety engineers.
(vi) Running of the experimental hydro construction station in Whilelmshaven.
(vii) Maintenance of Navy facilities and estimates of the current requirements of construction detachments.

2. Mittlers Instanz (Regional Level)
(a) The Navy administrative sections are on a regional level in relation to the Navy administrative offices within their sphere of competence. They are subordinated to the CND who represents the Zentral Instanz (central level, see below). They receive their directives in regard to current construction troop requirements from the competent higher Liaison Engineer and Liaison Engineer on a Regional (MOK) level.

3. Zentrale Instanz (Central Level)
The central level will be a separate administrative section in the Navy High Command, subordinate to the CDN and directed by the INC. In addition to its routing functions in regard to administrative sections and offices, the following are tasks also assigned to the central level:
 (i) Final accounting of previous undertakings in armament construction.

(ii) Professional consultation in matters of construction with Section FEP (meaning of abbreviation unknown) in regard to patents.

(iv) Care of Navy Construction personnel insofar as it has not been performed by the CNC.

SS Liaison

Construction agencies and facilities of the SS have, like those of the GAF and the Navy, been at the disposal of the OT since the summer of 1944. No official documents similar to those regulating the relationship between GAF construction agencies and the OT (see above), or that between German Navy construction agencies and the OT (see above), have so far been uncovered, dealing with SS and OT working agreements. The subject has however been dealt with from the standpoint of the OT, in Part II.

b) Economic Liaison

German Agencies

Economic liaison in regard to allotments of raw material was established between Amt Bau-OTZ (Bureau Construction – OT Central HQ in the Ministry for Armament and War Production) and the Rüstungsamt (Armament Bureau). Inasmuch as the channels are those of theWehrmacht, the subject has been covered in the preceding section (Military Liaison).

The interests of the OT firms as an eoonomic group of the Reich are taken care of by liaison with the Wirtschaftsgruppe Bauindustrie (Economic Group: Construction Industry) and the Reichsinnungsverband des Bauhandwerks (National Guild of Building Craftsmen). This subject has been covered earlier. Since the zone of operations has come to include Germany, however, the OT as an agency of the Ministry for Armament and War Production has taken over not only the construction facilities of the Wehrmacht, but also all government agencies administrating construction in Germany (see Speer's decree of 16 October 1944). Consequently it must be assumed that the influence of the Construction Industry as an economic force has been reduced to a minimum where private commercial interests are involved.

The Deutsche Arbeitsfront (German Labour Front), commonly abbreviated DAF, has been treated as a political rather than as an economic organisation in section c) Political Liaison, below.

Collaborationist Agencies

There were basically two types of collaborationist organisations economically allied to OT. One type, such as was set up in France, was patterned after the German Building Industry. The purpose behind a collaborationist organisation of this type was to make it serve as a responsible and subservient agent through which the German authorities could exploit French manpower, equipment and resources. For example, the Comité d'Organisation de Bâtiment et des Travaux Publicques (Committee for the Organisation of Construction and Public Works) was nothing more than a uniform price fixing and labour recruitment agency for the EGW. COBTP (as it was commonly abbreviated) had no direct channels to EGW headquarters in Paris, but was obliged to resort to its German counterpart the Wirtachaftsgruppe Bauindustrie as an intermediary. (This subject has likewise been touched upon in Part II.)

The other type of foreign economic collaboration is exemplified by the working arrangement which existed between the OT and the various satellite Balkan governments. The Derubau (Deutsch Rumänische Baugesellschaft) for example, was a German-Rumanian Building Association entrusted with the development of roads and laying of oil pipes. The OT's part in the arrangements consisted in beginning the program and allowing it to continue under Rumania technical supervision, as soon as it was functioning smoothly. Bulgaria concluded an agreement (June 1942), whereby the OT under a five-year plan would complete 900 miles of asphalt roads between 1942 and 1946. A building programme was inaugurated in Slovakia (1939) by the Inspector General of German Roadways (Fritz Todt) whereby the OT would begin a network of roads, the completion of which would be left to Slovakia.

c) Political Liaison

German Agencies
(i) DAF and NSDAP
Die Deutsche Arbeitsfront (DAF: German Labour Front) was formally established toward the end of 1933 when it took over all pre-existing Labour Unions. In German official language it was founded by the Führer in order to educate all 'racial' Germans economically employed, in National Socialism, on the basis of social unity. The DAF claimed a membership of over 25 million in September 1942 including all OT workers (except forced labour). Individual weekly dues range from RM 0.55 to RM 1.10. A stamp to be pasted in the DAF-Beitragsnachweiskarte (membership card) is given in receipt of dues paid, and a record of membership payments is kept in the DAF-Mitgliedsbuch (DAF Membership Book). In the case of OT workers this record is to be replaced by an insertion in the OT Dienstbuch (Pay and Identity book).

The DAF may with some justification be termed the Labour Morale and Indoctrination Service of the NSDAP. By the same token, the basic emphasis remains on its functions as a political rather than as an economic organ. Dues were automatically deducted from each German OT man's pay for the

Gefolgschaftsbetreuung (OT Membership Welfare) as administered by the Frontführung, acting for the DAF. Thus every German OT man automatically became a member of the DAF. Foreign OT workers who belonged to collaborationist labour organisations at home, such as were set up by the DAF Auslandsorganisation in the various occupied and satellite countries, when transferred to Germany, of necessity became DAF members. Other foreign OT workers in Germany except Poles, Russians, Czechs and small national minorities, are organised in special national groups and are represented in the Central Department of the DAF by liaison officers, one to each nationality.

The DAF functions in connection with the OT are administratively expressed through the Frontführung, as was remarked above. The subject Frontführung will be covered in Part III. An overall view of DAF-OT liaison, as given below, is intended to complete the picture.

The Chief of Frontführung Amt Bau-OTZ is at the same time Generalinspekteur für die OT bei der Zentralinspektion für die Betreuung der ausländischen Arbeitskräfte der DAF (OT Inspector General of DAF Central Inspectorate, Welfare and Indoctrination of non-German DAF Members). While his DAF rank is not known, he may be assumed to be on the DAF Central Staff.

The Chief of Frontführung of an OT Einsatzgruppe in Germany is an ex-officio member of the staff of the DAF Gauobmann of the Gau in which the Einsatzgruppe is situated. If the area of an Einsatzgruppe cuts across two or more Gaue (as it invariably does), the OT Frontführer (Einsatzgruppe level) is appointed to the staff of one of the Gauobmänner by common agreement. He is at the same time OT Inspector for his area for the DAF Central Inspectorate, Welfare and Indoctrination of non-German DAF Members. His DAF rank is that of Gruppenbetriebsobmann. This rank is an adaptation of the basic DAF rank: Betriebsobmann, which is roughly translatable as (DAF) Leader of Factory (or Firm) Personnel. A Gruppenbetriebsobmann consequently is the (DAF) Leader of all OT firms situated in an Einsatzgruppe, and in that capacity he is also the 'Beauftragte der NSDAP' (NSDAP Deputy) for the Einsatzgruppe.

The Chief of Frontführung of an OT-Einsatz in Germany has the DAF rank of Einsatzbetriebsobmann and is correspondingly charged with representing NSDAP interests within his Einsatz area. The Einsatz HQ at present in Germany is a control staff mainly concerned with the technical aspects of the priority programme in the area under its control. Consequently an Einsatz does not normally contain a Frontführung staff; when it does, the latter's activities are confined to propaganda, training, security and special assignments, without provisions for the messing and billeting of personnel.

The Chief of an OBL Frontführung has the DAF rank of Oberbauleitungs-btriebsobmann (abbreviated OBL Betriebsobmann) and is an ex-officio member on the staff of the DAF Kreisobmann of the Party Kreis (District) in which the

A party of high-ranking officers, most probably including Fritz Todt himself, speaks to the workers during the construction of the Westwall as they excavate a trench to receive the dragon's teeth anti-tank defences. Note the narrow gauge rails for the many tipper trucks used to move the waste. Several of the workmen are wearing 'Org. Todt' brassards or armbands. In the lower image the rows of newly cast concrete teeth can be seen in the background, and the railway track curves upwards to the spoil heap on the right.

OBL is situated. If the area of the OBL cuts across two or more Kreise, the OT-Frontführer (OBL level) is appointed to the staff of one of the Kreisobmänner by common agreement. As OBL Betriebsobmann, he is the (DAF) Leader of all OT-Firms situated in an OBL, and in that capacity he is also the 'Beauftragte der NSDAP', Deputy for the OBL. In addition, he is OT Inspector for his area, of the DAF Central Inspectorate, Welfare and Indoctrination of non-German DAF Members.

The OT administration of Frontführung ceases at OBL level. Frontführung of Bauleitungen, Abschnittsbauleitungen, and individual firms is entrusted to a Frontführung staff composed mainly of OT-Firm personnel, and headed by a Frontführer with the DAF rank of Betriebsobmann.

(ii) SS, SA and SD

Basic SS-OT liaison operated at OBL level in France, as it does at the present day in Germany, provided conditions there are sufficiently stable to allow the establishment of OBL administrative HQ. An official outline of the functions of an SS-OT Verbindungsführer (SS Liaison Officer) attached to an OBL is given in the following:

1. Apprehension of political offenders.

2. Responsibility for internal-external security and the prevention of sabotage.

3. Control of and issue of personal passes, identification cards, etc.

4. Responsibility for the safe keeping of classified documents.

5. Responsibility for the safe keeping of explosives.

6. Preferring of charges in cases of embezzlement.

7. Preferring of charges in cases of corruption.

8. Setting in motion the procedure for the apprehension of deserters.

9. Acting as liaison between the OT and Police authorities, SD (Security Service) etc.

The above functions are limited in practice to routine police duties. For example, a fearless and conscientious SS-OT Liaison Officer could, in theory, go to the length of bringing charges of 'running a local black market' against some influential party member in a highly placed OT post. What is more likey to happen, however, is that the SS officer will turn over evidence placed in his hands to the SD Aussenstelle in his sector. It follows, therefore, that he is not usually expected to uproot irregularities of the above type, nor has he normally the necessary agents-provocateurs at his disposal. Likewise it is the SD's functions rather than those of SS to discover enemy agents or covert inimical elements amongst workers, especially foreign OT workers. This is done by the classic procedure of planting an SD Vertrauensmann (Confidential or Undercover agent or Agent-Provocateur – commonly abbreviated V-Mann) among worker groups. In this connection French agents working for SD and Abwehr (Counter Intelligence) were exempted from French Labour conscription. To make such exemptions inconspicuous, French agents were ostensibly given OT besonderes Vorhaben (OT Special Building Projects, V-sites etc.) labour assigrments. The German Feldkommandanturen (Military District Conmanders) in France, Belgium and the Netherlands kept records of all such identity cards.

It is as guardian of Nazi Party doctrine and authority that the OT-SS Liaison Officer reigns supreme. In fact he is the OT-NSFO (National Sozialistischer Führungs Offizier or National Socialist Indoctrination Officer) in all but name, and has been such since the founding of the OT in 1938.

In France friction developed not infrequently between SS Liaison Officers with a tendency towards officiousness, and OT Frontführer ready to make concessions to foreign workers in the interests of efficiency. The clashes arose mainly over matters of procedure, after the recovery of OT deserters. At the present time, however, there is a likelihood that most Frontführung staffs are composed of SS and SA man.

Basic SA-OT liaison operated like SS-OT liaison – at OBL level. Its functions essentially were to protect the interests of the SA and of SA men in the OT. The latter are considered as a rule to be Party men with connections sufficiently influential to obtain jobs in the OT. Such jobs are usually in supervisory positions, in connection with discipline and training, and were for the most part assigned to Frontführung. The present Chief of Frontführung in Amt Bau-OTZ (Schneider) is an SA man. The following captured document, here given in translation, illustrates the early stages of formal SS and SA incorporation into the OT, which by the present time has resulted in political control of OT by the SS:

Org. Todt, Einsatzgruppe West
P (Personal)   In the field, 5 May 1944.

To all Einsätze and Oberbauleitungen in Einsatzgruppe West.

Subject: Procedure for the transfer to the new rank-system of the OT, of those SA and SS Leaders delegated by the SA High Command and Reichsführer SS (Himmler) into the OT.

Below I reproduce an extract from a General Order of the OT Zentrale and request your attention to it.

A number of SA and SS leaders were detached to the OT by the SA High Command and by the Reichsführer SS who, by reason of an assurance given by the OT, have been permitted up to the present to wear the rank insignia appertaining to the rank held by them within their own organisations. Inasmuch as the transfer of these leaders into the OT must be carried out according to the actual service status of their present employment in the OT, it will not be possible, in many cases, to grant them the rank in the OT corresponding to the previous appointment they held therein; on the contrary, it will frequently, be the case that these leaders will now be granted a rank which is lower than that held by them within their own party organisation. In order to be able to inform the SA High Command and the Reichsführer SS of the grounds for such incorporation, the reason for demotion in OT grade of SA or SS personnel just be determined in every case involving an appointment to a different rank. Controversy arising from such cases must be communicated to the Personnel Branch of the OT-Zentrale, Abt PI. The Personnel Branch will forward information based on this controversy through the liaison officers of the party organisations to the SA High Command and the Reichsführer SS.

While on this subject, it is appropriate to point out that in future, in cases of substantial punishment or the dismissal of Party members, the attention of the Personnel Branch of HQ Einsatzgruppe will be drawn to the fact that the person concerned is a member of the formation, in order that this officer can forward the necessary information to the OT-Zentrale.

Heil Hitler
Verified : Blume. By Order Mangold

Collaborationist Agencies

Political liaison between the OT and satellite, puppet and protectorate governments through the medium of political parties, labour and special organisations, governmental and semi-official agencies and so forth, is not only a complex subject, entailing lengthy separate study but also somewhat outside the immediate purpose of this handbook. A list of collaborationist liaison of the above type has therefore been considered adequate.

d) Operational Liaison.

German Agencies.

Only operational liaison other than Army, Air Force or Navy is discussed in this section. For liaison with the Wehrmacht see above.

A public parade of the Reichsarbeitdienst (RAD), the Reich Labour Service. With polished spades held aloft, their distinctive insignia identifies them as RAD Company 1/260. In 1934, RAD divided into RAD/Männer, for men, and RAD/wJ, der weibliche Jugend, for women.

The flag of RAD, which, as the ears of wheat indicate, was not confined to construction work. Originating in 1925 as a non-military organisation permitted under the Treaty of Versailles, it later became the RAD as part of a programme to create employment in Germany. From 1935, all non-Jewish men aged 18–25 had to complete six months in the RAD before their military service. The poster, right, proclaims, 'Before: Unemployment, loss of hope, demoralisation, strikes and lock-outs. Today: Work, joy, culture, comraderie.' *(Wolfsonian-Florida International University)*

(i) NSKK (Nationalsozialistisches Kraftfahr Korps – SK National Socialist Motor Corps.)

The working arrangement between the NSKK and the OT as expressed by the incorporation of NSKK transportation units into OT, first under the designation of Kraftwagenleitung West (Motor Vehicle Command West), then respectively under the designations of NSKK – (Motor) Transportstandarte Todt, NSKK (Motor) Transportbrigade Todt, NSKK (Motor) Transportgruppe Todt or simply NSKK-Gruppe Todt are fully discussed earlier. (The designations NSKK-Baustab Speer, NSKK (Motor) Transportstandarte Speer, NSKK (Motor) Transportbrigade Speer. Legion Speer, NSKK-Transportbrigade Luft, or NSKK-Motorgruppe Luftwaffe, and Transportflotte Speer are likewise discussed there.) Until recently the transport branch of the OT was very frequently also referred to as NSKK-Transportgruppe Speer, or simply as NSKK-Gruppe Speer. Transportkorps Speer seems to be the latest, and official, designation for the same unit.

For individual OT-NSKK liaison assignments, see Part II.

(ii) RAD (Reichsarbeitsdienst – Reich Labour Service)

Up to the present time no indication has been found linking the RAD to the OT in any other way except that RAD personnel has performed unskilled and possibly semi-skilled labour under the direction of the OT. Thus RAD units have on occasion been detailed to perform excavation work on OT construction sites, especially in connection with the construction of air-raid shelters and AA installations in general. Such RAD units remain however administratively independent, nor can OT control the movements of RAD units beyond putting in a request to the RAD authorities. Inasmuch as the OT rates a very high priority, such requests are not usually refused. The earliest instance of the above OT type of co-operation occurred in 1938 when Todt took over the construction of the Westwall. At that time approximately 100,000 RAD personnel were temporarily detailed to the OT. When OT began to acquire foreign manpower, the RAD reverted to work for the Air Force and Navy and in lesser numbers to the Army mainly in the communications zone. When the OT took over all Wehrmacht construction facilities in the sunmer of 1944, relations between the two organisations evolved into an arrangement whereby the RAD operationally became more and more subordinate to the OT.

At the present tine, the RAD's status is that of an organisation whose personnel has been turned over to Army authorities for the duration of the war, 'for operational training purposes'. Thus it is placed at present under Himmler's command in his capacity of Commander-in-Chief of the Replacement and Training Army. In some measure RAD's former tasks have been taken over by the Hitler Jugend (Hitler Youth Movement, see below) and the Volkssturm.

(iii) HJ (Hitler Jugend – Hitler Youth Movement)

There are so far no indications of any formal link between the HJ and, the OT, and it is very much doubted whether any are contemplated, as long as politically and morally unreliable elements, especially foreign elements, form part of OT personnel. The natural trend seems to be for the HJ to replace, in some measure, RAD personnel in the digging of emergency defence earthworks behind the lines, and similar auxiliary tasks. The possibility that the Nazis may employ HJ formations in conjunction with OT elements in a 'mountain retreat' should at this stage, however, not be discounted without further consideration.

(iv) TENO (Technische Nothilfe – Technical Emergency Corps)

Co-operation between OT and TENO is on a higher operational level than between OT and RAD. By far the most common occasion for co-operation occurs in case of air-raid damage to public utility and power installations in crowded cities. In these cases it is the TENO which provides the technical direction, while OT performs the skilled mechanical labour. It is quite possible that the OT not only repairs but actually operates vital plants, such as synthetic oil plants, under TENO direction.

Since TENO personnel are generally mature men normally employed in key technical positions, they are mostly early Nazi Party members. Beside their functions of technical control, they are invested as part of the Ordnungspolizei (Orpo: Regular police) with authority to control any mass action, containing signs of an incipient uprising. In addition their technical training facilitates discovery of sabotage in connection with complicated installations.

(v) Reichsverteidigungskommissar (Reich Defence Commissioner)

Each Gau in Germany is a Civil Defence District headed by a Gauleiter. The office originated when, in September 1939, Göring appointed sixteen Civil Defence Commissioners for the then existing Wehrkreise on the recommendation of Frick and Hess (formerly Reich Minister of the Interior, and Party Chancery Leader respectively). At the present time each Gauleiter (of whom there are forty-two at present) is Defence Commissioner for the Party Gau in his capacity as executive agent of the Ministerialrat für die Reichsverteidigung (Ministerial Council for Defence of the Reich, or General Staff for Civil Defence and War Economy). The Council's president is Göring – and its members include Himmler, Funk, Speer, Keitel, Bormann and Lammers. The essential tasks of the Gauleiter are the mobilisation of housing and of labour. Their authority in the case of housing problems is derived from their office of Gauwohnungs-kommissar (Commissioner for Housing in the Party Gau); the exercise of their manpower authority is facilitated by the fact that for purposes of defence they have at their disposal Sauckel's manpower control organisation as represented in each Gau by the Reichstreuhänder für die Arbeit (Reich Trustee for Manpower). Specifically they have the authority to close shops and enterprises in the course of total mobilisation, to issue orders, to make available vacant accommodation, to improve on existing accommodations, to allocate accommodations to certain groups of the population, and so forth. They are especially active in air raid target areas, where they look after the billeting of bombed-out people, repair of

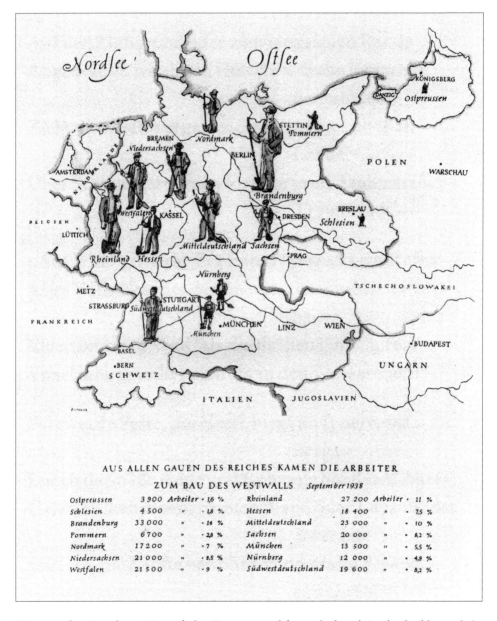

AUS ALLEN GAUEN DES REICHES KAMEN DIE ARBEITER

ZUM BAU DES WESTWALLS *September 1938*

Ostpreussen	3 900	Arbeiter · 1,6 %	Rheinland	27 200	Arbeiter ·	11 %
Schlesien	4 500	" · 1,8 %	Hessen	18 400	" ·	7,5 %
Brandenburg	33 000	" · 14 %	Mitteldeutschland	23 000	" ·	10 %
Pommern	6 700	" · 2,8 %	Sachsen	20 000	" ·	8,2 %
Nordmark	17 200	" · 7 %	München	13 500	" ·	5,5 %
Niedersachsen	21 000	" · 8,5 %	Nürnberg	12 000	" ·	4,9 %
Westfalen	21 500	" · 9 %	Südwestdeutschland	19 600	" ·	8,2 %

Diagram showing the origins of the German workforce deployed in the building of the Westwall. Published in *Bauen und Kämpfen*.

damage, reconstruction and provision of materials and special rations for the population.

When, to the above description of the functions of the Defence Conmissioner, is added the fact that in general their task is to unify and co-ordinate civil defence and all administrative branches connected with civil defence, except the railway, postal aid finance systems, it will be obvious that the Defence Conmissioner must be in close liaison with the OT for the efficient execution of his tasks.

OT control staffs on Einsatz level, have as one of their main functions the task of correlating civilian demands on the OT, as expressed through the Reich Defence Conmissioners, with military demands as expressed through the Rüstungs-kommissionen and Rüstungsunterkommissionen (Armament Commissions and Sub-Commissions). This subject has been discussed in detail, from the point of view of OT operational methods, in Part II; from the point of view of OT's status within the comprehensive system for war production as set up by the Speer Ministry is also in Part II. One aspect of the Reich Defence Commissioner's sphere of authority as against that of the OT, which has not yet been stressed is the fact that the latter has priority over manpower, even in the face of the emergency powers with which the Defence Commissioners have been vested. Thus there have been complaints by several Commissioners to the effect that the OT has conscripted manpower in their districts, with detrimental results to the output of factories and agriculture. While complaints of this sort may have had some effect on the OT's manpower authority in rear areas, there is little likelihood that OT front zones (i.e. Front OT) have been in any way affected.

(vi) Volkssturm

There is no indication of formal liaison between the Volkssturm and the OT. On the other hand there is no reason for doubting that co-operation, in both rear and forward areas, has on occasion taken place between the two organisations. Normally such co-operation in rear areas would be regulated on the part of the Volkssturm (in this case, the Stand-Bataillone), by army authorities of the Replacement and Training Army, viz. the various Wehrkreis Commanders, or, as their second in command, the Höhere SS und Polizei Führer (HSSPf: Superior SS and Police Commanders). The nature of such co-operation would be in the nature of military and political security. As such, the subject has already been dealt with. Co-operation in forward areas would, on the part of the Volkssturm (in this case, the Einsatz-Bataillone) be regulated by army operational authorities. The Volkssturm's part in such co-operation would consist of tasks, similar to those formerly assigned, on occasion, to the RAD: doing the spade work on OT jobs, under the direction of the OT.

Adolf Hitler addresses a group of awe-struck workers during the construction of the Westwall. As usual, Fritz Todt is there just behind him. Below: Map from the 1945 Handbook showing the extent of the OT Einsatzgruppen in the autumn of 1944.

PART III

Personnel

A. Composition of Personnel

Early Period 1933–39 (Westwall Arbeiter/Frontarbeiter)
(The purpose of IIIA is to review in broad outline the composition of OT personnel from the early stages of formation up to the present time. For a more detailed study of OT personnel, IIIB should be consulted. For a detailed study of manpower, see Part IV.)

The building organisation, which Fritz Todt evolved for the specific task of rushing the Westwall to completion and which was so successful in that task that it became the construction arm of the Armed Forces, has retained the basic characteristic of co-operation between the German construction industry and the government to this day. The Construction Industry made the investment in the form of individual firms with their equipment and clerical and technical staffs, including their executives. The German Government, through the Wehrmacht, invested the manpower and the building material, as well as the administrative staffs controlling the entire OT personnel including firms and affiliated services, such as the NSKK-OT. This personnel carried (and still carries) a Dienstbuch (Pay and Identity book) and was permitted to carry arms when the OT was put on a war footing in September 1939.

When Fritz Todt took over the task of completing the Siegfried Line from the Army engineers in June 1938, he developed, in the space of somewhat over two months, a building organisation of a half-million men. This organisation consisted, in round figures, of 350,000 German workers, 100,000 RAD (Reichsarbeitsdienst or Reich Labour Service) personnel and 100,000 Army Festungspionier (Fortress Engineer) personnel. Generally speaking, the RAD personnel performed the unskilled labour tasks, while supervisory tasks and the skilled construction work were entrusted to OT personnel. Most of the workers consisted of the same personnel which had previously worked on the Reichsautobahn (Reich Highway System).

The OT and RAD personnel were popularly known as 'Westwall Arbeiter' (West Wall Workers). Such material comforts as were deemed over and above those essential for existence were provided for them by the DAF (Deutsche Arbeitsfront or German Labour Front).

In September 1939 the entire OT was put on a war footing. It was attached to the Wehrmacht as 'Wehrmachtsgefolge' (Armed Forces Auxiliary). The administrative control continued to be exercised by the General Inspektor für das deutsche Strassenwesen (Inspectorate General for German Roadways) until some time in 1941 when OT-Zentrale (OTZ) Berlin took over that function. With the outbreak of war, the term Frontarbeiter (Front Zone Worker) was substituted for the earlier designation Westwall Arbeiter. The significance of this new designation was twofold:

1) It prescribed the possession of a Dienstbuch (Pay and Identity book) by the designee and his right to carry arms for personal defence.

2) It entitled the designee to Frontarbeitersold or Wehrsold (Front line duty allowance). When OT began to employ foreign labour en masse, the designation 'Frontarbeiter' was extended to include Volksdeutsche (Racial Germans) and Nordic volunteers.

DAF/Frontführung

The DAF's Social Service was absorbed at the outbreak of war by a newly created department in the OT, the Frontführung (Front Area Personnel Section). Its leader, the Frontführer, however, continued to represent in his person the DAF's interests in the OT, inasmuch as he remained an official in the former organisation.

'Mobile' Period 1940–42 (Inclusion of Foreign, at the Expense of German, Elements)

The personnel of this early OT organisation were gradually absorbed into the German Armed Forces during 1941/42. Only those remained who did not meet physical or mental requirements, or were deferred because of essential occupations, such as OT-Firm executives, technicians and administrative chiefs. The German worker personnel with physical shortcomings became a supervisory cadre over foreign worker units, as soon as the latter became available en masse after the campaigns of 1939/1941.

'Mobile' Period 1940–42 (OT-Firms, Bautrupps, Services, SK, OBL HQ Personnel)

When the West Wall was completed at the end of 1940, the OT personnel moved out of Germany following the German armies in Poland, the West and the Balkans. (OT did not engage in construction work, to any large extent, in Norway until the winter of 1940/41.) Their first tasks were the restoring of communications of all types and assuring the safe flow of army supplies to the various fronts. In fact, up to well into 1941, OT personnel executed its tasks more in the mobile manner of rear echelon army engineers than in that of a separate organisation with a centralised administration of its own. The firms constructing the Channel defences along the North Sea coast in 1940/41, for example, insofar as they were controlled from Berlin, were administered by the semi-autonomous Construction Industry through large building corporations such as Strabag, rather than through the 'mother' administration, the General Inspektor für des deutsche Strassenwesen (inspectorate General for German Roadways).

In relation to the OT, therefore, the picture which generally held until about mid-year 1941 in Poland, Norway, the Balkans and even to some extent in the West was one of construction firms in the form of comparatively small units specialising in bridge construction, harbour construction, road and canal construction and so forth. These firms worked in close liaison with the army. They were mobile within the limits of their own operational sector and consisted of the firm executive and his clerical and technical staff. The firm executive was, at the same time, the OT Construction Executive with a corresponding OT rank, normally that of a 2nd or 1st Lieutenant. His staff likewise were members of the OT but moved with their employer from job to job. His sphere as supervisor of construction included the supervision of all OT workers within his Baustelle (construction site). As already stated, most of the Facharbeiter (skilled labourers) in the beginning were still German. They were divided into 'Bautrupps' (Construction detachments) approximately 100–150 men, with Hilfsarbeiter (auxiliary labourers) drawn from foreign personnel. Such construction detachments were classified as OT organic personnel. Their movements were controlled by the OT authorities of higher echelons (Einsatz HQ and upward) on the basis of a construction programme as agreed upon between the OT and Army or Army Group HQ. The number of such personnel on any one construction site depended on the size of the job. (The term Bautrupps fell into gradual disuse, due to the mass influx of foreign workers into the OT after the German victories of 1940/41, but it was revived shortly before D-Day.)

Unskilled manpower was provided in the form of either prisoners of war, locally hired or impressed, or occasionally RAD personnel. Mention is made in secondary sources of Stellungsbau, Tiefbau, Feldbahn and Strassenbahn Bataillone (Construction battalions specialising in the building of fortified positions, tunnels, highways and railways). No documentary evidence has been found testifying to the existence of such units in the OT, however, and it is believed that the units involved were army construction units and RAD units working with the OT. Not much is known of the early organisation of the services such as transport, medical and so forth. It may be safely assumed that they were both mobile and, to some extent, improvised to meet changing requirements. Protection to installations and personnel, particularly in Russia and the Balkans, was afforded by the Schutzkommando (SK: Security Guard) composed of very small mobile contingents, so disposed as to be capable of quickly forming larger defence units. Liaison was also maintained with Army and SS line of communications regiments in case of emergency.

Local sectors, consisting of one or more construction sites and hence of one or more construction firms, were controlled by the local sector OT HQ – usually an OBL. In the early days of the OT, the control of firms and firm personnel was much looser than at present. The main reason lay in the economic protection afforded OT-Firms by the powerful German Construction Industry as contrasted with the comparatively lax administration by the General Inspektor des Deutsche Strassenwesen (Inspectorate General of German Roadways). The period from mid-year 1941 to mid-year 1942 was a period of transition in respect to composition of personnel. The Balkan campaign and the first phase of the Russian campaign resulted in the employment by the OT of a vast number of Russians and a proportional number of Serbs, Greeks, and so forth; in addition Hungarian and Rumanian Engineer, or more aptly, Labour battalions, provided another source of manpower in Russia. When Speer took over control of the OT upon Todt's death in February 1942, he incorporated his Baustab Speer with a strength of 100,000 into the OT in the Crimea. (The Baustab had been building aerodromes for the German Air Force. Subsequently it had moved into the Crimea to perform tasks similar to those of the OT.) The NSKK-Transportbrigade Todt was also activated in order to take OT care of transport. The entire OT manpower strength in March 1942 is estimated at approximately one million men.

'Stable' Period, 1942–44 (Foreign Labour, Kolonnen, Hundertschaften or Bereitschaften and Abteilungen)

About the middle of 1942 a defensive policy became evident in German military strategy. Fortifications on a vast scale began to be built in Russia, Norway and Western Europe. OT Zentrale (OTZ: OT Central HQ) in Berlin, which had begun to make its central control felt especially in the West by establishing operational sectors there on a 'permanent' basis, began systematically to co-ordinate all phases of OT operation. At the same time, the OT began to recruit manpower in earnest in the occupied territories. In the West and in Norway, manpower, much of it skilled or semi-skilled was recruited locally and put to work on the massive fortifications. This was augmented by mass transfers of unskilled workers, mostly Poles and Russians, from the East.

Contractual relations between the OT and OT-Firms were stabilised, and uniform regulations were issued on a comprehensive scale which the firms were expected to follow. By this time the proportion of Germans to foreigners had dropped to less than 10%, and a uniform pay tariff, applicable to all OT personnel except Zwangsarbeiter (Forced Labour), was issued in June 1942, to become effective January 1943. The status of OT personnel as militia was more strongly established than it had been heretofore around 1 January 1923 by substituting the phrase 'Wehrmachtangehörige' (member of the Wehrmacht) for the term 'Wehmachtsgefolge' in the Dienstbücher (Pay and Identity Books).

If all the manpower which worked for the OT directly or indirectly in the early part of 1943 is calculated, the figure may well reach the neighbourhood of two million, mostly located outside the Reich. In the winter of 1941/45, before the current Allied advances into Germany, it is estimated to have dropped to about one million, mostly inside the Reich. A further step in regimenting manpower was taken in March 1944 when all foreign labour was partitioned into units of twenty men called 'Kolonnen', units of about 125 called 'Hundertschaften' or 'Bereitschaften', and – sometimes – into units of 250 called 'Abteilungen'. These formed the vast bulk of OT labour and included the Zwangsarbeiter (Forced Labour), mostly Russians and Jews. The term Bautrupps which had ceased to exist after the dissolution of the early German construction detachments, was revived some weeks before D-Day.

Current Developments (Front-OT, OT Legionare, Special Brigades, Russian Units)

When the OT evacuated occupied territory and withdrew into Germany in the simmer and autumn of 1944, some of its personnel lost their standing as Frontarbeiter (Front zone workers) insofar as their new location took them into an interior zone in Germany. On the other hand the term Front-OT was created to designate a forward area in which OT personnel retained their standing as Frontarbeiter (or OT Legionare in the case of foreign collaborationists). Simultaneously with the creation of the 'Front-OT', special OT units were activated and formed along military lines, i.e., Brigades, Regiments, Battalions and Companies. Two OT regiments have so far been identified, but it is doubtful whether the entire formation, planned at 80,000 highly skilled men with sufficient equipment for three times that number, has been activated. This development has been more fully discussed earlier. Another current development of similar nature is the incorporation into the OT of the Russian military units recruited by General Vlasov. This step seems to have been taken in March 1945.

Composition of OT Personnel, with the Exception of Manual Labourers, in an OBL Sector

The staff of a basic construction sector (OBL) can be broken down as follows:

OT-eigenes Personal (OT organic Personnel):

(1)   Poliere (foremen over labour gangs of varying size)

(2)   Schutzkommando (Security Guards)

(3)   Transport and services personnel

(4)   Lagerführer (camp supervisors)

(5)   Administrative personnel of a clerical nature

(6)   Administrative personnel of a technical nature

(7)   Chiefs of operational sectors.

Firmenangehörige (firm personnel):

(8)   Clerical staffs

(9)   Technical staffs

(10) Construction supervisors

(11) Construction site supervisors (OT-Firm executives).

The administrative staff of an OBL at present possibly numbers less than 2% of the total OBL manpower; thus an OBL HQ controlling 15,000 men consists of approximately 300 men and women.

By D-Day the shortage of OT personnel had become such that, with the exception of (1) and (7) (see above), foreign personnel, notably Dutch, Flemish, Danish and Frenchmen, were entrusted with the other assignments, as enumerated above, in the following proportions respectively: (2) almost exclusively; (3) to a very large extent; (4) to a great extent as assistant or deputy in charge; (5) mostly confined to female clerks; (6) very small proportions; (8) mostly confined to female clerks; (9) in a somewhat larger proportion than (6); (10) in a very small proportion, if any. The signals communication systems are run by detachments of exclusively German OT Nachrichtenmädels (Communication girls). Higher administrative echelons naturally were exclusively German as was OT liaison personnel – always conceding the presence of the foreign element in clerical staffs. Indications are that the great majority of Hilfspoliere (male collaborationist labour gang leaders) were evacuated into Germany.

A class of OT personnel, confined perhaps to the West, Norway and Denmark, is 'local' OT labour. This category, living near the construction site, is allowed to sleep and eat at home. Finally, too, there is the occasional day labour composed of female cleaning and kitchen help in labour camps. This category worked for the OT on a short-term basis but was not contracted to the organisation.

Other Special Units in the OT
Besides the Baustab Speer which was mentioned earlier, there are the following
other units in the OT to which special functions are assigned:

1) Bergmannkompanie (Miner Company).
2) Bergungsregiment Speer (Rescue and Salvage Regiment Speer).
3) Polizei Regt. Todt SS (SS Police Regiment Todt).
4) NSKK Transportbrigade Todt (Transport Korps Speer).
5) Legion Speer.
6) Transport Flotte Speer.

B. Classification of Personnel

a) General Classification
Classification of OT Personnel
OT personnel can be considered from several points of view. Basically they may
be looked upon as forming an auxiliary to the armed forces. From the point of
view of internal administration, however, they are classified as follows:

OT Eigenes Personal (OT Organic Personnel)
OT organic personnel is subdivided into seven functional groups:
(1) Supervisory personnel in the operational sector (OBL), such as for instance
the Lagerführer (Camp Supervisors);
(2) Service Personnel, mostly administered by the OBL, although supply and
communication personnel, for instance, are found also in higher echelons;
(3) Administrative Personnel in the Construction Sector, such as the heads and
staffs, including female clerks, of the various departments in OBL HQ, or the
Oberbauleiter himself;
(4) Area Control Staffs and Central HQ, such as the heads of the various
departments in EG (Einsatzgruppe) HQ and in Amt Bau-OTZ, up to the Chief
of Amt Bau-OTZ;
(5) The Regiearbeiter (government monopoly employee), a comparatively
small group, employed as OT mail and railway clerks and so forth;
(6) The Frontarbeiter (Personnel so classified is normally given supervisory
assignments with corresponding rank; in fact it is the expressed wish of the
OT administration that no German should grade occupationally below Polier
(Foreman). Retarded mentality or political unreliability may account for the
presence of German personnel with ordinary worker assignments); and finally
the lowest group;

(7) The Einsatzarbeiter. This term is a consolation prize for a comparatively select group of non-Nordics who, because of their race or nationality, cannot become Frontarbeiter, and is bestowed on OT volunteers of a collaborationist complexion after a three-month trial period. Czechs, Poles, Jews and Comnunists cannot become Einsatzarbeiter. At present the Einsatzarbeiter in forward areas in Germany and elsewhere have been given the designation of OT Legionäre.

2) Firmenangehörige (Firm Personnel)
Administratively, firm personnel is divided into two classes;
   (1) Stamm Personal and (2) the rest of the employees such as foreign clerical assistants, including females. Functionally, firm personnel is also divided into two groups; (1) Supervisory personnel; and (2) office (clerical and technical personnel including females).

3) Abgeordnete and Beamte (Delegates and Government Officials)
This group includes a comparatively small body of officials assigned mostly to technical and administrative supervision and control.

4) Ausländische Arbeiter (Foreign Workers)
This term is commonly restricted to manual labourers and does not include service personnel and collaborationist leaders and supervisors. The foreign workers compose the OT labour army which performs the actual work on OT construction projects, and comprise about 8% of all OT personnel. From the standpoint of OT administration, they are not properly speaking 'OT personnel'; they merely 'work for the OT' and accordingly wear an armband with the inscription 'Arbeitet für OT'. Moreover they are bound to the OT in various forms, ranging from local labour contracted to the OT on a voluntary basis and permitted to go home nightly, to forced labour permanently restricted to their own camp and not entitled even to a day of rest. A number of Russian women classified by the Germans as partisans and communists, amounting it is estimated to a few thousand, was included in the latter group. Inasmuch as it is onerous, in many instances, to make the distinction referred to above, the term 'OT personnel', for the purposes of this handbook, can be presumed also to include the category Ausländische Arbeiter.

5) Women
OT female personnel have been listed in the appropriate functional groups Nachrichtenhelferinnen (Telephone, telegraph, teletype operators, messengers, etc.); female clerks in OT administrative offices and in firm offices; female menial help in kitchen, camps, etc. Those in the last group were natives, mostly local, whose relationship to the OT is somewhat tenuous. Certainly no disciplinary

measures were taken against those who took informal leave. Special quarters for women were, however, available in OT camps and centres.

b) Construction Personnel and Camps

i) Supervisory Field Staffs

Under Normal Conditions
The conditions in the West are taken as standard, and most references in this section are made to EGW (Einsatzgruppe West).

The NCO runs the OT just as much as, if not more than, he may be said to run the regular army. However, in the process of becoming 8% foreign in respect to its personnel (as opposed to the virtually 100% German composition in May 1938), the composition of the NCO cadre underwent a similar change in nationality, although to a much smaller proportion than the rest of the organisation. Before the shortage of manpower upset its plans, Amt Bau-OTZ planned to control the daily routine of its manual labour by placing all or as much control as possible in the hands of Germans. (This statement should not be interpreted as implying that, had Germany ended the war victoriously, the OT would not have effected a working arrangement in occupied territory which would have delegated a measure of control to collaborationist elements. What is meant is that in being confronted with what was believed to be a temporary military situation, the OT had no definite political or social policy, except to get as much work performed in as short a period as possible. The policy adopted during the first two years in occupied territories (1940–42) when supervision and security was predominately in German hands, was, on the whole, brutal; later when German personnel was withdrawn and the need for foreign manpower became imperative, attempts were made at pacification and appeasement. By spring 1944, official regulations for the treatment of foreign workers had assumed some humane characteristics. How effectively these regulations were carried out by petty officials in charge is another story.)

Control during working hours – under normal conditions – was placed in the hands of the technical staff of the OT-Firm, composed of (1) the firm executive, in charge of construction in the entire area in which the firm was active; (2) the latter's assistants in charge of the individual pieces of construction; (3) their foremen, for the greater part skilled in excavation and underground construction, which is the basic type of work done by the OT. The two former carried OT officer rank. The last two mentioned carried NCO rank, their assignment consisting of the supervision of section gangs on the construction job, They brought with them into the OT from civilian life their trade guild occupational grade, such as Polier (and/or Schachtmeister) (roughly translatable as 'excavation and tunnelling foremen', or 'pit or shaft overseer'). Their OT rank could be any from Obermeister to Obertruppführer (corporal to staff sergeant).

This dual classification of both occupational grade and military rank is given to firm employees who at the same time have supervisory assignments over OT organic personnel, such as foreign worker detachments. Consequently the grade of Polier and Schachtmeister in the OT is not restricted to those in charge of excavation work, but is given to all firm employees with comparably responsible assignments (see below). Moreover a Polier or a Schachtmeister can be promoted to Oberpolier or Oberschachtmeister while working for the OT, if he is considered as having satisfied the trade guild requirements in this respect. Such promotion in occupational grade does not, however, automatically involve a corresponding promotion in OT rank. German personnel in lower occupational grades could, in like manner, be promoted to Polier or Schachtmeister.

Control in the camp and to and from work was placed in the hands of OT-eigenes Personal (organic personnel) of appropriate NCO rank such as Truppführer (Sergeant). Their assignment was normally that of either Fronttruppführer or Obertruppführer. Supervision of 'Zwangsarbeiter' (forced labour) was largely entrusted to the SK (Schutzkommando or Security Guard). On the construction job the duties of the Front- and Obertruppführer were subordinated to those of the Poliere and Schachtmeister in that the former were to help the latter keep discipline amongst their men, convoy additional manpower needed in the course of the day, be alert for signs of sabotage, and so forth. At the end of the working day, it became the duty of the Polier to send his men into the proper formations, ready to leave for camp. The duties of the Polier and the Schachtmeister thus ended with the working day, and the OT-eigenes Personal (OT organic personnel) took charge of the men until time for work the next day. Overall control rested in the Frontführung of the OBL and its staff. A check was kept on the morale amongst foreign workers through the employment of collaborationist agents who mixed with their countrymen as co-workers or 'social service' agents. These agents were the eyes and ears of the Frontführer and the SS-Verbindungsführer (SS-Liaison Officer).

Modifications in Supervisory Field Staffs due to shortage of German Personnel
As implied above, supervisory assignments in the Personallager (Camp), usually called simply 'Lager', gradually became entrusted to foreigners. An effort was made to stabilise this situation by issuing a series of new regulations (contradictory in some instances) during the spring of 1944. The reorganisation which resulted may be summarised as follows:

i. The Poliere and Schachtmeister became, during the working hours, the nucleus of the irreducible minimum of German NCO supervisory personnel over foreign manpower. Control during working hours, therefore, remained entirely German. The problem of obtaining sufficient German Poliere was met by lowering the requirement standards to the point where the designation 'Polier' no longer guaranteed a minimum of skill and experience; by the selection of elderly men including septuagenarians; by giving the Poliere assistants in the form of foreign 'Hilfspoliere' (Assistant Foremen), see below. The Polier, in turn, was also called upon to assume some responsibilities in camp in addition to his normal responsibility on the construction Job.

ii. Foreigners were deputised to positions of trust and responsibility in the camp, usually over groups of their own countrymen. Final control, however, rested with German personnel. Lagerführer (camp supervisors), for example, formed the nucleus of German control in the Camp. Even in their case, though rarely, collaborationists came to be entrusted in 1944 with the running of camps. Those instances, relatively few in number, came about through the insistence of Amt Bau-OTZ, which, in its efforts to obtain effective foreign collaboration in occupied Europe, had embarked on a conciliatory policy. This policy generally met opposition from local OT officials and in the last analysis was effectively sabotaged by German personnel in the various camps. Hilfslagerführer (Assistant Camp Supervisors), on the other hand, were all foreigners. Incidentally, many of the Hilfslagerführer also acted as Assistant Foremen during working hours on the construction job.

iii. Inasmuch as the main part of the above-mentioned reorganisation (March 1944) in personnel administration, involved the transfer of a good deal of responsibility B in this respect from the Frontführung to the individual OT-Firms operating within the OBL sector, a new post was created within each OT-Firm to take this responsibility. The post is that of Mannschaftsführer (OT-Firm personnel officer), and is discussed below.

The New Chain of Command in the Supervision of Labour

The effect of the rearrangement of personnel administration in the spring of 1944 was to make the OT-Firm, for all practical purposes, a self-contained operational unit, and as such a lower echelon of the OBL. The OT-Firm remained essentially static within the limits of its operational sector (at least such was the hope of the higher administration). Yet inasmuch as relations between firm personnel and worker detachments had become closely integrated, the OT-Firm was capable of reverting to a mobile status on start order. The characteristic of the new arrangement was the investment of one individual with dual and even triple functions with correspondingly dual or even triple responsibility, a characteristic already familiar to us in German political and military organisations as a whole. The new chain of command in the supervision of labour, as a result of these modifications in the spring of 1944, is as follows:

i. The Einheitsführer (Firm Executive) is responsible to the Oberbauleiter and to the Frontführer, to the first in matters concerning construction, to the second in matters concerning personnel.

ii. Betriebsführer (Firm Manager). Now that the firm has a personnel administration of its own, it has become in effect a lower echelon of the OBL administration. The need, therefore, arose for a commanding officer responsible in this respect to the OBL HQ. The Firm Manager, a post usually filled by the Firm Executive himself, was consequently invested with this new responsibility. Under this arrangement, the Mannschaftsführer (see iii. below) is personnel administrator, but final responsibility rests with tha Betriebsführer.

iii. Einheitsmannschaftsführer or Mannschaftsführer (OT-Firm Personnel Officer). The Mannschaftsführer is the Frontführer of the firm. He is especially concerned with the German personnel, care of the foreign workers being entrusted to the Kilfspoliere (see vi.). He is either assigned to the firm by the OBL or selected by the firm from among its own personnel. In the latter case, he undergoes schooling in respect to Frontführung duties (see IIIC130) before being accepted by the OBL. In the former case he is made a member of the 'Stammannschaft' of the firm, although his service status remains that of OT-organic personnel. As a Frontführer he also has the rank of Betriebsobmann in the Deutsche Arbeitsfront (DAF: German Labour Front) and as such represents the DAF's interests in the OT. His office is located on the construction site rather than in the camp. Computation of expenses incurred by him for the welfare of the men in his charge is made according to instructions issued by the Vertragsabteilung (Contracts Section) of the EG. His principal duties include the education of the Frontarbeiter in respect to Nazi ideology, to discipline, fellowship, air-raids, gas and fire-protection, guard duty and functions of the SK; advice on questions of pay, tariffs, furlough; control of Dienstbuch (Pay and Identity Book) and identification discs; aid in case of accident, death, personal problems; improvement of billeting accommodations; distribution of rations and supervision of their preparation; rationing of canteen articles; maintenance of equipment; assignment of details and regulation of leisure time; library administration, distribution of newspapers and magazines; indoctrination of German personnel in the proper employment of foreign workers according to OT regulations in respect to race and nationality discrimination. The routine duties of his office are divided amongst (1) the Poliere, in regard to German personnel with the exception of the clerical staff, 2) the Senior Clerk, in regard to the clerical staff, (3) the Hilfspoliere, in regard to the foreign workers.

iv. Oberpoliere (and Oberschachtmeister). The Oberpolier is a senior foreman on Jobs employing two or more foremen and reports directly to the Bauleiter

(Construction Supervisor) much the same as a ranking NCO in the army reports to his CO.

v. Polier (and Schachtmeister) (Foremen; only the personnel administration assignment of Polier and Schachmeister is discussed here. Their assignment as labour gang foremen is discussed below.) The Polier (and Schachtmeister) is deputised to perform basic administrative duties of the Mannschaftsführer. In effect, the Polier and Hilfspolier (see vi.) between them take over most of the routine administration from the Mannschaftsführer, and leave to the latter only the function of supervision, except for such special duties as occur in cases of accident, death and so forth. The Polier, like the Mannschaftsführer, is concerned primarily with the German personnel in his charge (as far as personnel administration is concerned).

The Hilfspoliere, as already stated, are foreigners and concern themselves with worker detachments made up of their own countrymen. Specifically the duties of the Poliere (and Schachtmeister) are (1) on the construction job: to march their men to cover in case of enemy attack, to set out gas masks and steel helmets in proper order ready for use, to demonstrate the proper use of the equipment and of firearms, to distribute noonday rations and to render advice on personal problems; (2) in camp: to assist the Lagerführer (see vii) in the capacity of a company sergeant, to make inspections of clothing and equipment. At all times they are to 'set an example to their men'.

vi. Hilfspolier (Bereitschaftsführer – Hilfslagerführer). (Assistant Foreman – Worker Detachment Leader – Assistant Camp Supervisor, the Hilfspolier is discussed here principally in his assignment as Hilfslagerführer. His other two assignments are discussed below.) The Hilfslagerführer-Hilfspolier-Bereitschaftsführer is a collaborationist of the type on whom the Germans put a great deal of dependence. He was to have been 'the type out of whom the modern European labour leader' was to be developed (OT Directive, 15 May 1944). He is, naturally enough, of the same nationality as the men who compose the Bereitschaft (Worker detachment) in his charge. He is an NCO, wears an OT uniform, has undergone Frontführung schooling and is part of OT-organic personnel. He is paid by the OT and attached to a firm, where he is active in the interests of the Mannschaftsführer. Hilfspolier is the occupational grade (although he is not a member of the German trade guild) according to which he is paid and which is given him solely in order to subordinate him to the Polier inasmuch as his main function is to assist the latter on the construction job (see para, 119 below). The designation Bereitschaftsführer indicates his assignment as leader of a marching formation of 100–150 foreign workers. The designation Hilfslagerführer indicates his assignment in camp as a subordinate of the Lagerführer. The Hilfspolier's administrative duties towards his men are similar to those of the Polier and Mannschaftsführer towards the German personnel. These are specifically: to call reveille in the morning, take roll call, keep order, investigate unauthorised absence, enforce hygienic regulations, keep personnel strength and casualty reports, look after the social routine, distribute mail, distribute rations and keep order during mess, investigate irregularities in the pay of his men, advise his men on personal problems, family matters, insurance, allotments and on furlough regulations, check personal equipment, convey his men to cover during air raids, render first aid, report recalcitrant workers in his charge (who were then put in specially guarded formations: Bewachte Bereitschaft). Furthermore he has to keep his men properly indoctrinated, and above all, keep the number of absentees from work, for any case whatsoever, to an absolute minimum. In short, all his functions point to one objective, that of getting the most out of the men, as far as work is concerned. In the performance of his duties he combines the functions of an American mess sergeant, mail orderly, supply sergeant, medical orderly, company sergeant, morale officer and company commander. In any matter concerning the personnel administration of his men or improvements in billeting accommodations he is to put his requests before the Mannschaftsführer, to whom he is also to take any complaints made by his men. If his requests prove fruitless or if he believes himself injustly treated by the Mannschaftsführer, he can take recourse to the OBL Frontführer. Supervision over his actions is exercised by the Betreuungsführer (Morale and Welfare Officer) of the OBL to whom he is accountable in the form of monthly reports. He goes along with his men in case they are transferred to another firm.

vii. Lagerführer (Camp Supervisor). The Lagerführer is like the Polier and Schachtimeister, part of the irreducible minimum of German supervisory personnel. Even so, efforts were being initiated in the spring of 1944, despite some opposition by local Frontführer, to substitute collaborationists for German supervisors over foreign worker camps. The reason in this case was not so much a shortage of German personnel (there were in all some 400-odd camps in the west), as to stabilise the political relationship between the Germans and the peoples of Occupied Europe. The OT, in its own words, was to be 'the trail-blazer, not only in respect to construction projects of a strategic and economic nature, but also to the creation of a politically united Europe', in effect, a number of Hilfslagerführer (Assistant Camp Supervisors), especially Dutch, were in charge of camps in the capacity of 'acting' Lagerführer.

Under the new administrative arrangements (March 1944), the Lagerführer were transferred from the control of the OBL Frontführer to that of the firm Mannschaftsführer. As already indicated, the Lagerführer is assisted by the Hilfspoliere insofar as the foreign personnel is concerned, and by the Poliere who act as Company Sergeants over the entire camp personnel. The Lagerführer's specific duties consist of the supervision of the issue of rations, canteen articles, personal items of clothing; of the daily routine in respect to hygiene and sanitation, and barracks discipline. He supervises regulations governing the differences in rations between Germans and foreigners. Although OT authorities made attempts recently to institute more humane treatment for the bulk of foreign workers, differences in rations, which were left to the discretion of the chief cooks and the Lagerführer, are the main cause of petty intrigue and friction in the daily camp routine.

viii. Hilfslagerführer (Asstistant Camp Supervisor), Polier, vi. above.

ix. Bereitschaftsführer (Leader of a foreign worker detachment). His assignments are discussed below. (See also Hilfspolier, vi. above).

x. Abteilungsführer (Worker Detachnent Leader). Leader of a foreign worker formation composed of three Bereitschaften. This formation is used only on special occasions when large masses of manpower are required on a particular construction job.

xi. Vorarbeiter (Senior Worker). His assignments are discussed below.

ii) Worker Detachments and Units

The Arbeitsbereitschaft

The Arbeitsbereitschaft, or Bereitschaft as it is more commonly called, is the march-formation of a body of foreign workers on their way to and from work. It comprises 100–150 men and is composed of four to six Kolonnen (squads) of twenty to twenty-five men, depending on the manpower requirements of the individual construction jobs. The men in a Bereitschaft are all of the same nationality but of mixed age. They are billeted and mess together. They wear working clothes with an armband, 'Arbeitet für OT' (Works for the OT). The various trades, such as mason and bricklayer, are represented in fairly equal proportions, the squads generally containing workers of the same trade.

Each Arbeitsbereitschaft was to have been numbered consecutively (from the number 1 upward) by EG HQ, but this part of the worker regimentation plan is either not consistently adhered to or was abandoned altogether. The composition of the Bereitschaft as to squads and hence as to trade, is made up each morning according to daily requirements of the construction job. After roll-call, the Bereitschaft marches or is transported to work, depending on the distance from camp, led by the Bereitschaftsführer (Detachment Leader). As already stated, this is an assignment, like that of squad leader, and not a rank. Each Kolonne or squad is led by a Kolonnenführer (squad leader) selected from amongst the men by the Bereitschaftsführer. On the construction job, this squad leader's grade becomes that of Vorarbeiter (senior worker). Arriving at the job, the Bereitschaftsführer theoretically reports to the Bauleiter (construction supervisor), but actually he reports to the Oberpolier (senior foreman or Polier foreman). The Bereitschaft then falls out by squads under guidance of the squad leaders, and reform into labour gangs under the supervision of a Polier.

The size and composition of the labour gangs are naturally determined by the nature and size of the job. The Polier takes roll-call of his gang, whereupon work is begin. As soon as work starts, the Bereitschaftsführer assumes his assignment as Hilfspolier which consists of smoothing out any difficulties, linguistic or otherwise, which may arise during working hours between the men belonging to his Bereitschaft and the Poliere amongst whom they are split up. In addition he performs for his men the same services, such as distributing noonday rations, as the Polier performs for the German personnel. Generally he keeps an eye on his men in regard to discipline and morale.

Specially Guarded Formations

Specially guarded formations, Bewachte Bereitschaften, are formations of Zwangsarbeiter consisting of Communist and partisan Russian men and women, Loyalist Spaniards (so-called Rotspanier), Jews and penal detachments composed of political prisoners and recalcitrant workers. Such formations are guarded and convoyed by SK men.

Hundertschaft and Abteilung

The term Hundertschaft (Century) is sometimes substituted for the term Bereitschaft, especially in the case of Zwangsarbeiter. In order to facilitate keeping a check on the amount of Zwangsarbeiter employed in an Einsatzgruppe, the Hundertschaften were supposed to be numbered consecutively. For instance, Hunderschaft 33 means that at least 3,300 of these men are at the time located in the particular EG. Numbered worker detachments are, however, very rarely identified in captured documents, and systematic records are apparently kept not below EG level, if kept at all.

A larger formation called Arbeitsabteilung and composed of three Bereitschaften (or Hundertschaften), led by an Abteilungsführer, is used only on special occasions, when large masses of manpower are required on a particular construction job.

Bautrupps (Construction Detachments) and Arbeitstrupps (Labour Petachnents)

The term Trupps (detachments) in the OT is reserved for worker detachments which stand high in the classification of OT personnel according to race and nationality. Accordingly the term Bautrupps is the earliest unit designation in the OT: it can be traced back to the OT worker units employed on the West Wall in 1939/40, when they were predominantly German.

The term itself was taken from the designation given to army GHQ construction units, which in due time were entirely replaced by the OT worker detachments. The term fell into gradual disuse, with the absorption of foreign elements into OT worker formations, including Zwangsarbeiter. It was revived (but still restricted to Nordics and 'reliable' volunteers) when special emergency detachments were activated in France to repair air-raid damage. Other, presumably less skilled, personnel were attached to the various components of Army Group West, in anticipation of the Allied landings in France. The designation Arbeitstrupps (Labour detachments) was given to these latter detachments, whose functions at the time were to assist the army service units.

At the present time, the designation Bautrupps is also given to the Front-OT companies activated in the autumn and winter of 1944/45 (see below). The designation Arbeitstrupps is now given to temporary formations of OT Service personnel detailed to function as auxiliaries to local Bautrupps in case of serious air raid damage in the vicinity. Such auxiliary formations are responsible for assistance in the case of air-raid damage within a radius of twelve miles of their station.

Front-OT Brigades, Regiments, Battalions and Companies

The formation of picked OT personnel into Front-OT Brigades, Regiments, Battalions and Companies is the last stage in the development of OT emergency detachments activated for the purpose of coping with the task of restoring communications in forward areas, damaged by Allied air raids. The original order for their activation, signed by Hitler on 13 October 1944, disclosed that eight Brigades were planned in all, consisting of about 10,000 men each.

Each company (or Bautrupp, see para. above) was to have at its disposal enough equipment to enable it, in case of necessity, to control personnel three times its own strength. Units were activated in the autumn and winter of 1944/45, but it is doubtful whether total effective strength at any time approximated the total projected strength. Eleven battalions have so far been identified belonging to three separate Regiments, and to possibly two or three separate Brigades. (Units identified; Bns 250, 251, 252, 353 of Regt 20; Bns 260, 261, 262, 263, 264 of Regt 22; Bn 220 of Regt (?); Bn 462 of Regt 103 of Brig 4.)

The strength of the companies, and hence of the higher formations, varies widely. Given below are summary details as to composition and function. (Foreign personnel is, according to regulations, not to exceed three-quarters of the total composition of a unit.) On the basis of the five battalions identified, four companies to the battalion and four battalions to the regiment seem to be the rule in practice. Although the TO/WE provides for not more than five companies, one battalion has been identified, containing six companies. Not enough is known about the composition of the brigade in respect to regiments, to warrant a similar statement in its case. The individual complements of the sixteen companies of one identified regiment range from 58 to 159 men. The smallest proportion of foreigners to Germans in any one company is nil foreigners to 128 Germans; the largest proportion is sixty-eight foreigners to ninety-one Germans. The normal TO/WE apparently provides for two companies specialising in the repair of railway tracks, two companies specialising in the repair of bridges, and one Compaq for road maintenance. In practice, this composition was modified to suit local requirements. Each company is commanded by an OT-Firm executive, who is also responsible for personnel administration. The company commander's rank is normally that of Bauführer (equivalent to that of Lieutenant). The company sector is called Strecke Kommando (Str.Kdo: Area control) and is estimated to cover an area, with a three mile radius.

The strength of the individual battalions ranges from 532 to 358 men. The smallest proportion of foreigners to Germans found in any one battalion is nil foreigners to 452 Germans; the largest proportion is 145 foreigners to 319 Germans. The rank of Battalion commander is normally that of Bauleiter (equivalent to Major). The composition of the regiment fully identified is 1,562 Germans and 244 foreigners. The rank of the commander is probably that of a Lt.-Col. or Col.; his second in command carries a Major's rank. Liaison on Company and Battalion level with the Army is established through the Army Ortskommandantur (Local Commander). Direct contact is also established with the Festungspionierstab (Fortress Engineer Staff) in each Abschnitt (sector).

iii) Camps

Personallager (Camps)

Personallager (Camps) or Lager, as they are commonly called, are situated as near to construction sites as is found practicable, the furthest distance on record in the West being twenty miles. Efforts are made to keep men of the same nationality together. Thus barracks housing men of one nationality form 'centres', e.g., Centre français, in charge of a Hilfslagerführer. Worker detachments assigned to a particular OT-Firm are similarly billeted together as far as possible. This dual arrangement does not ordinarily involve complications, inasmuch as foreign worker detachments are assigned to particular firms not only on the basis of their occupational skill and speciality (or lack of either) but also on the basis of race and nationality. Thus, for example, certain firms are considered to be peculiarly equipped to employ Jewish workers. The barracks are standardised in several types and contain accommodations for from 78 to about 150 men. The average camp contains accommodations for about 500 men. Camps holding more than 2,000 are considered impractical.

In the autumn of 1944, co-operation between the OT Frontführung and the

Deutsche Arbeitsfront (DAF: German Labour Front) became closer than it had ever been before in respect to the control of OT worker camps. It is not known, however, to what extent the DAF put the facilities of their Gemeinschaftslager (Group Personnel Camps) at the disposal of the OT.

c) Administrative Personnel

i) Basic Construction Sector (OBL)
Referat Frontführung (Front Area Personnel Section), Definition, Origin and Development

The sections Frontführung and Technik constitute between them the essential administration of the OBL and are its two most important branches. Inasmuch as the Frontführung deals with all phases of personnel management in the construction sector, the Frontführer, as its head, is therefore the Oberbauleiter's representative in all questions involving the human factor. Consequently the Frontführer is responsible for the individual capability of OT personnel in respect to output of work, affected as it might be by ill-health, worry, recalcitrant or contumacious attitudes, or just plain laziness. Responsibility for the collective work output rests with the Oberbauleiter as part of his responsibility for the entire building programme of his sector. A captured document, translated in summary below, defines the Frontführer's sphere of responsibility both in respect to his duties on the construction site and during leisure hours at camp, as follows:

> The basic duty of the Frontführer is to facilitate the construction of defensive installations insofar as the human element is concerned. The Frontführung is created in agreement with the DAF as an instrument of National Socialist leadership of men at work, according to the experience gained in front zone activity. It is the task of the Frontführung to ensure high, productivity on the part of the Frontarbeiter (Front zone workers), even in the face of enemy activity. The post comprises, moreover, the functions of the Betriebsobmann (see below), it is the Frontführer's goal to create a contented and disciplined following, whose honour it is to work and produce on behalf of Germany. The Frontführer supervises the regulations concerning the discipline, deportment and fellowship in the OT. OT personnel is subject to its own disciplinary regulations as well as to those of the Wehrmacht and to the international rules of warfare.

It will be seen from the above that the functional sphere of personnel administration in the OT as represented by the Frontführung is far broader than that of personnel administration in either the British or the American Army. The term Frontführung originated when the OT was put on a war footing in

September 1939, while it was working on the West Wall. Before that time, the Deutsche Arbeitsfront (DAF: German Labour Front) had ministered to the welfare of the OT labour army from the material and the intellectual, or rather ideological, standpoint, along the same lines as the DAF Betriebsobmann. (DAF personnel administrator in German factories).

With the advent of war, the OT administration took over all of the routine duties of Baustellenbetreuung (routine duties at the construction site, such as for example supervising distribution of hot soup at lunch time), while the DAF confined its activities to Lagerbetreuung (camp routine) and Sozialbetreuung (social welfare). These three spheres of personnel administration were presently merged into one, and the Frontführung was established to take charge of the new arrangement.

Frontführer agreeable to the local administration (OBL) were appointed by Amt Bau-OTZ to the various sectors. The DAF retained its interests, in the person of the Frontführer inasmuch as he carries, in addition to his OT rank, the DAF rank of Hauptbetriebsobmann. Most of the Frontführer appointed came from the ranks of DAF personnel already assigned to the OT; some of them also belonged to the SA and the SS. For them the appointment merely meant continuing their old functions under a new name, after having completed a six-week course at a Frontführer school.

The Frontführer in the operational sector, as it was stabilised in the West, is normally associated with the section Frontführung on OBL level. Important Bauleitungen (sub-sectors) may, however, have a Frontführer of their own, accountable to the Frontführer. A case in point is Bauleitung Adolf (Alderney Isle) which, although a sub-sector of OBL Chebourg, had its own administrative staff, the personnel of which is individually responsible to its higher echelon at Cherbourg. In the event that the operational sector happens to be on a fluid front (on mobile status), the Frontführung is relieved of the administration of rations and billets. These functions are then taken over by the OT-Firms.

As can be noted from the above, personnel administration in the OT is intended to be an extension into conquered and annexed territory of the DAF functions in German plants and factories. As such it was adjusted to the needs of the German worker in occupied Europe with family connections in Germany. To give an extreme example of the opposite sort, the Russian OT worker, transported to the West, even under favourable circumstances, was lucky if he was adequately fed, not to mention family benefits, insurance, and so forth. No attempt was made for a time to set up a similar organisation to remedy, or at least to investigate, family problems of foreign workers. (An exception were 'Nordics', especially of Dutch and Danish origin, whose status and treatment differed little from that of German personnel). It is true that each nationality in camp had, from the beginning, its own Betreuungsführer (Morale and Welfare Officer). He, however, was a German Frontführung appointee who had proved his trustworthiness to the Germans, and was expected to justify his appointment by reporting to the Frontführer any conversations leading to the disclosure of refractory elements amongst his men, and by doing general spying of a similar nature.

In the latter part of 1942, however, the status of the foreign worker was made uniform within the framework of Nazi racial and political discrimination by a series of regulations passed by Amt Bau-OTZ. It was not until about one year later, however, that a French Frontführung organisation was set up, comparable to the German Frontführung in its basic functions of feeding, clothing and billeting personnel. Its status, however, remained purely that of an advisory body to the German Frontführung. It was called the Service Social de Chantiers de Travaux (Social Service at Work Sites), and was represented at the various OBLs by a French liaison man to the German Frontführung. He offered suggestions and gave advice on the basis of reports received from his 'worker delegates'. The new agreement officially did away with the French Betreuungsführer mentioned above. The German Frontführer, however, never relied entirely on his French liaison man, but retained confidential channels of his own.

The Flemish, Dutch, Danish and Italian personnel also were ultimately represented by their own Frontführung. Less favoured nationalities like the Russians had to remain contented with the representation furnished by their Betreuungsführer who was nothing more or less than a collaborationist agent.

The assignment Sozialbeauftragung in the OBL was created in November 1943 simultaneously with the organisation of all foreign manpower into Hundertschaften or Bereitschaften. The Sozialbeauftragter was selected by the Frontführer from Frontführung staff personnel and was expected to perform his new functions in addition to his old assignments. His new task consisted of supervising the administration of the newly created Hundertschaften (or Bereitschaften as they were later more commonly called) until this new arrangement should begin to function smoothly under the guidance (in EGW) of the Hilfspoliere (Assistant Foremen) and the French Frontführer. This was expected to take several months. A document issued in March 1944 contains an indication that the task was usually entrusted to the OBL Betreuungsführer (Morale and Welfare officer). The term Sozialbeauftragter in itself is, however, an indefinite one, merely designating someone who is performing a temporary task of a social nature.

Referat Frontführung. Present Organisation and Functions

The organisation and functions of the Frontführung were simplified in the spring of 1944 by making the OT-Firm responsible for the duties involved in personnel administration of firm employees as well as of OT manpower assigned to the firm. The old and the new arrangements have already been discussed in, with particular emphasis on the Mannschaftsführer (OT-Firm Personnel Officer).

Responsible as he is for the smoothness of OT operation in his sector, the Frontführer's competence is measured in terms of his Betreuung (Morale and Welfare) personnel. His own Betreuungsführer (Morale and Welfare Officer) co-ordinates the various reports arriving daily at OBL HQ, from the various sub-ordinate Bauleitung Frontführer or their Betreuungsführer, or directly from the Mannschaftsführer assigned to the firms, from the Hilfspoliere attached to firms to take charge of their foreign workmen, and from the Flemish Frontführer, the Dutch Frontführer, Italian Frontführer, French Frontführer and so forth, as well as from the Russian Betreuungsführer, Polish Betreuungsführer, and so forth.

The paper work of Betreuung, especially soziale Betreuung (Social Welfare, i.e., that which involves correspondence with higher echelons, administrative authorities in Germany, or outside agencies) is carried on in the Gefolgschaftsstelle (Personnel Services Office). It is in connection with his functions of soziale Betreuung that the Betreuungsführer's office is located in the Gefolgschaftsstelle. Frontführer are, as a matter of procedure, kept informed of the current building programme by the Chief of OBL. In case of disagreement between the two, the former can argue his case, and if disapproved can appeal to a higher echelon Frontführung. In matters of vital importance they are duty bound to turn in a report of any disagreements arising.

Some indication of the type of German personnel employed in the Frontführung in the West, shortly before the Allied liberation of this territory, is reflected in an arrangement which Wehrmacht authorities concluded with the OT in July 1944. By this arrangement 500 OT men born after 1899 and classified as fit for combat duty were exchanged for 2,500 incapacitated officers and enlisted men, for assignments under the various OBL Frontführungen.

In the matter of discipline and counter-intelligence, the sphere of the Frontführer overlaps with that of the SS Verbindungsführer (SS-OT Liaison Officer). The basic cause for friction between the two – when friction does develop – is usually shortage of manpower, differences arising over competence in the recovery of deserters and in dealing with individual irregularities. The Frontführer will often overlook infractions of discipline, while the SS Liaison Officer will insist on punishment in dealing with the same case. Much depends, in this respect, on the personalities of the Frontführer and the Verbindungsführer and on whether or not the former is an SS, SA or active NSDAP man.

At the present time, however, most, if not all, Frontführer may be presumed to be SS men.

Referat Technik (Technical Section)
The technical section in an OBL HQ, which deals with all technical and engineering problems, is subdivided into a number of subsections.
ii) Administrative Personnel above OBL level.
Einsatz, Einsatzgruppe and Amt Bau-OTZ (Area Control Staff, Army Level; Area Control Staff, Army Group Level; Bureau Construction OT Central HQ)
An important function of the OT control staff on Einsatz level is that of OT liaison with military and civilian authorities on regional level. Consequently, the Einsatz HQ is staffed with construction officials dealing with OT activities on three different levels: (1) controlling the construction programme of subordinate Oberbauleitungen; (2) acting as liaison between the OT and the Armament Commission and the Reich Defence Commissioner; (3) sending reports of estimated requirements in materials and manpower to higher level (Einsatzgruppe), on the basis of previous consultations with the military and civilian authorities mentioned in (2).

The OT control staff on Einsatzgruppe level distributes allotments of materials and manpower to its subordinate OBLs on the following basis: firstly according to the general directives from Amt Bau-OTZ, secondly according to the large-scale operational requirements of the German Army, Navy and Air Force, thirdly according to strategic requirements (e.g. repair of armament factories), and fourthly according to vital civilian requirements. Estimates of requirements in the last two cases mentioned are based on reports sent in by the subordinate Einsatz staffs; estimates of large-scale operational requirements are based on consultation (on EG level) with Hauptbedarfsträger (Principal Consumers: Army, Navy, Air Force, the SS and so forth).

C. Training

Military Training
Regulations issued by the Wehrmacht through the OT provided for basic military training of all German personnel (both Reich and 'racial' Germans) and for 'reliable' elements of foreign personnel. In actual practice, however, these regulations were carried out spasmodically at best. In theory the training procedure was as follows: a German employee of an OT-Firm was, upon enrolment in the OT, issued a uniform and given military training. The latter consisted of rifle drill and practice, and a certain amount of combat training. It was carried out under Wehrmacht supervision and usually took place on Sundays or after work, although sometimes a group of workers was taken from their jobs to partake in these military exercises. In case of invasion, these men were to assist the armed forces.

When in January 1944, the danger of an invasion seemed to have become more imminent, the Frontführung West (EGW) issued an order that every firm should form a training and combat unit of its own. This regulation obviated the necessity for constant Wehrmacht assistance in this respect. These units were armed, mostly with captured weapons of various makes, but an attempt was made at uniformity by restricting the equipment of each firm to one type of rifle. For every German, the official issue was one rifle and 198 rounds of ammunition. Thirty rounds were to be carried on the construction site, the remaining ammunition was to be stored in a place easily accessible in case of alarm. Pistols were only issued to OT officers and to NCOs from the rank of Obermeister up. It was laid down that, in case of alarm, the armed German OT personnel was to guide the foreign workers to their respective camps and post a guard over them.

Just how this plan was to work out does not seem to have been very clear even to the OT leaders themselves. In certain areas training was started under Wehrmacht NCOs detached to the OT for this purpose, but this practice does not seem to have proved generally successful. Reports tell of complaints being lodged against these NCOs for their brutality towards elderly men. Others tell of men who left their rifles, usually obsolete French models, lying around, having never been given instructions on how to use them.

The GAF seems, on the whole, to have done better in training OT men in the use of anti-aircraft weapons for their own protection and that of the construction sites. In case of danger, OT personnel was to man these guns entirely without military, i.e. GAF, supervision.

Schools for Leadership Training and Other Schools

In order to train selected men and promote them to advanced positions in the OT, picked personnel is sent to so-called Führerschulen (Leader Training Schools). In the early days when OT personnel was still being recruited from Germany, a so-called 'Haus der Kameradschaft' (Fellowship House) was created in connection with the Haupterfassungslager (Main Induction Camp) in Berlin. Workers in responsible positions such as Poliere (foremen) and other supervisory personnel were trained there for the specialised task of OT leadership. Their training included certain fundamental military subjects such as the use of firearms, besides indoctrination in Frontführung (Front Area Personnel direction) and construction supervision.

The earliest and best-known school of this type, however, is situated at Plassenburg near Kulmbach, and is now called OT Reichsschule Plassenburg. It was established in the twenties as an SS ideological centre and was used by Nazi members of the Nationalsozialistischer Bund deutscher Technik (Nazi League of German Technicians). The League was founded by Fritz Todt, and the school, beautifully situated as it is, in Bavaria, rapidly became a Nazi retreat, to which flocked high-ranking Nazi engineers and other technicians to discuss ways and means of putting into practical operation the strategic and economic plans of what was to become the Third Reich.

The other Führerschulen, this time under the supervision of an SA leader, are located respectively in the other two OT Main Induction Camps: Neu Isenburg, near Frankfurt, and Inowodz, in Poland. Here the prospective OT Leaders underwent a four-week course in all phases of instruction having to do with service in the OT. Another school of this type in German-controlled territory is reported to have been located at Poseu.

A sixth school was located at The Hague, in Holland (Nieuwe Parklaan 28–30). The course given here is described simply as 'Lagerwesen' (Camp Administration). Again an SA Leader (SA Sturmbannführer Aidinger) is in charge. The instructors were NCOs in the OT and included a number of Dutchmen. This school graduates about thirty men a month.

Beside the general Führerschulen there are training schools for specific assignments. The most important of these is the Frontführerschule (Training School for Front Area Personnel Officers). Candidates were mostly selected from among senior workers and other supervisory personnel. In France men of the rank of Truppführer (equivalent to Sergeant) and higher were selected to take a course at the Frontführer at Pontivy. This course lasted twenty-seven days, and was followed by an eight-day course at the Schutzkommando (SK: Security Guard) West at Pontivy, where a school had been founded in 1942, controlled by the SS. This eight-day course served to familiarise the future Frontführer with the functions of the SK. After this, the candidate was returned to Pont Callec for a final ten days. Most Oberbauleitungen were urged to send as many as six men from their sector at one time to take the course.

The OT also conducts Lehrlager der Frontführung (Front Area Personnel Training Camps). Frontführer candidates in need of a refresher or preparatory course attend classes there for a month in such subjects as Nazi ideology, Order and Discipline, Comradeship, Soldierly Conduct, Obedience, Gas-, Fire- and Air-raid Protection, Guard Duties and the Duties of the SK. OT Reichslehrlager Friesack (Brandenburg) is one such training camp.

Besides the above-mentioned Lehrlager, the OT operated Erziehungs-und Schulungslager (Disciplinary Camps). These are not so much training as disciplinary establishments for recalcitrant and delinquent workers. They are run by OT-SA and SS personnel.

Frontführung personnel was mainly of German nationality until well into 1942. The growing manpower shortage, the vast increase in foreign personnel, and ensuing difficulties owing to language differences and foreign customs resulted in the selection of reliable foreign OT men with leadership ability for NCO training.

After having attended an NCO training school, this type of collaborationist personnel could be promoted up to the rank of Obertruppführer. Most trusted among these various foreign elements were at the beginning the 'Nordics', Norwegians, Danes, Dutch, Flemings and Walloons; later, Frenchmen, Italians and anti-Soviet Russians also received this training. To cite an example, a report discloses that captured Soviet officers with a technical background, and ideologically tractable, were given a five-week course and entrusted with supervisory positions, such as construction supervisors, draftsmen and foreman technicians, in the Crimea and the Donets Basin.

To improve standards of work and keep up morale, the various Oberbauleitungen have Lagerschulen (Camp Schools) of their own. Lagerführer (Camp supervisors) and their Hilfslagerführer (Assistants), head cooks, and foremen of all types have to attend these courses. If it is not possible for all those enrolled to take these courses at the same time, the OBL establishes several weekend courses. These extend over four weekends and include training in weapons (pistol, rifle, handgrenades and machine guns), marching, gas mask drill, care of equipment and clothes, political indoctrination, hygiene and OT problems in general.

Special Unit Training (Schutzkommando)
Of all the special units in any way connected with the OT, only the Schutzkommando (SK: Security Guard) can be termed an organic OT organisation. It is a police organisation the duty of which is to round up deserters, maintain order and discipline on the construction sites, act as guards on convoys, and so forth. It also takes part in the training of OT leaders (see para. above). Its German personnel is, for the most part, composed of men with army experience but incapacitated for combat service. It is, for example, not uncommon to find an SK man with only one arm. For the most part, however, its ranks are filled by trusted foreigners. The subject is mentioned here because SK training is an OT function, unlike, for instance, NSKK-OT training which is undertaken by the NSKK.

Trade Training in OT
The problem of recruiting an adequate number of skilled and trained manpower, always present, became acute in the fourth year of the war and has remained so ever since. In the beginning all the skilled workers were Germans who had learned their trade at home in civilian life. In order to bolster their thinning ranks and to prepare men for the special requirements of OT work, elementary courses were given to selected workers in specific trades. These courses, for German and foreign personnel alike, usually ran for from four to six weeks. For semi-skilled workers there were shorter courses which enabled them to become foremen and supervisors in their own trade. Most of these schools in the EGW

were in the vicinity of Paris, and every type, from cooking schools to schools for administrative and communication personnel, is found there.

While the various Einsatzgruppen in occupied territories ran their own schools and courses, the OT within the Reich maintains additional schools to teach OT methods of construction and operation. Elementary courses are given at the Main Induction Camps and the Lehrlager (Training Camps) mentioned in the previous paragraphs. German mechanical and technical schools are made available to OT personnel for more advanced training.

D. Uniforms, Insignia, Personal Equipment

and Decorations

Uniforms

The OT-Dienst Uniform (OT Basic Uniform) is worn by all members of the OT who are permitted to carry a Dienstbuch (Pay and Identity Book).

These men, both Führer (Officers and NCOs) and Frontarbeiter (Front Zone Workers) receive their clothing and equipment at an OT Ausrüstungslager (Equipment Depot) from the OT Ausrüstungsstelle (Equipment Headquarters) which is part of Amt Bau-OTZ in Berlin. On discharge from the OT, OT members return their clothes and equipment to an Entlassungslager (Discharge Camp). This procedure applies equally to OT officers, NCOs, workers, and employees of firms on contract to OT. If, in case of discharge, the civilian clothes of an OT man are not immediately available, he receives a Marschanzug (travelling suit) which is then turned in when he reaches home.

OT members up to and including the rank of Truppführer (equivalent to Sergeant) receive their entire clothing and equipment free of charge. Nor are they charged for repairs. Truppführer to Haupttruppführer (Sergeant to Sergeant Major) and officer candidates receive their uniform free of charge and an allowance of RM 150 – for the purchase of underwear, shoes, socks and so forth. Officers, on the other hand, receive an outright allowance of RM 500 for the purchase of a uniform and other items of clothing. All clothing and equipment, whether issued or sold by the OT, is recorded in the OT member's Pay and Identity Book.

Regulations further state that the uniform must be worn at all times, on and off duty and on leave. Only in cases of special assignments, such as counter-intelligence, can an OT member wear civilian clothes, and then only with the permission of the OBL or higher echelon, for the duration of his specific mission.

On the construction site, German OT members generally wear either an old uniform or an Arbeitskluft (fatigues or overalls). Foreigners more often than not,simply wear their own clothes, with an armband in the nature of an insignia of distinguishing mark. Insofar as they are permitted to wear any uniform at all they must buy all items of clothing and equipment. In this respect of course collaborationist elements fare best of all. The lower the status of the worker, the less care he receives, and Zwangsarbeiter (Forced Labourers), once their own clothes wear out, generally are compelled to employ what may be picturesquely described as makeshift methods.

In case a member of a firm is on liaison duty between the home office of his firm in the Reich and his OT Construction Site, he is allowed to wear an OT uniform with a rank commensurate with the importance of his mission.

Active Army officers on attached duty with OT may wear Army uniform. Reserve officers now in the OT must wear OT uniform.

A small proportion of the women in OT wear a uniform. Most of them simply wear an OT brassard over their civilian clothes. Nachrichtenmüdel (Signal communications girls) wear blue uniforms to distinguish them from other female employees.

All OT Frontarbeiter (Front Zone Workers) wearing the Swastika brassard, salute with the Hitlergruss or German Nazi salute. Foreigners of Einsatzarbeiter

A photograph from the 1945 Handbook showing an NCO of the Organisation Todt in full 'Dienst' uniform with backpack, and wearing the 'Overseas' cap. This gentleman, with his fine up-turned moustache, seems to confirm that the organisation relied on men who were too old to fight in order to meet its requirements for German NCOs.

status may use the salute of their own country. They must, however, salute all officers and NCOs in the OT, the Wehrmacht and the Nazi Party. Officers in cars with mounted flags are also saluted.

Insignia

In the OT, as in the Wehrmacht, the uniforms for both officers and enlisted men (other ranks) are of the same cut and colour, the only distinguishing feature being the insignia. On this subject a certain amount of confusion has existed, mainly because so many changes in OT insignia have taken place that it is difficult to state definitely just which directive is being followed at the present time. It is in fact highly probable that many variations in OT insignia are being worn by OT members in different sectors. For instance, the question of 'shoulder straps'. The latest directives on the wearing of OT insignia make no mention of them; however, OT members taken prisoner were found wearing them.

The replacing of the 'Swastika brassard' by a Wehrmacht Hoheitsabzeichen, is another point that has remained unclarified. This change in insignia has been referred to in directives and in entries in the OT-Dienstbuch, but so far no photographic proof that this change has actually taken place has been received. The most recent regulations on this subject are orders to those in uniform to cover the Swastika armband with a grey cloth in the event of contact with the enemy; those in civilian clothes are to substitute a yellow armband with the lettering: Wehrmacht.

Personal Equipment

A record of clothing and equipment issued to an OT member upon his induction is entered in the Dienstbuch (Pay and Identity Book) in a column headed 'Leihweise von der Org. Todt erhalten' (Received on loan from the Org. Todt). Certain issues of the Dienstbuch however, have a slightly different wording, i.e. 'Leihweise in Lager durch die DAF erhalten'. (Received in camp on loan from the DAF: Deutscher Arbeits Front or German Labour Front). The following are lists of clothing and equipment issued to OT members upon their induction.

NCOs up to the rank of Truppführer (Sergeant) and all other German Frontarbeiter (Front Zone workers) are issued the following items:

1	cap
1	jacket
1	pair of trousers
1	Swastika brassard
1	'Org. Todt' brassard
1	belt (for SK men only)
1	pair of working shoes

1	pair of leggings
2	pairs of under drawers
2	undershirts
3	pairs of socks
2	working shirts
2	handkerchiefs
1	tent shelter (to be used as raincoat)
1	pair of overalls
1	bread bag
1	field pack
1	water bottle
1	cup
1	mess kit (with knife, fork and spoon)

In winter the following items were added:

1	overcoat
1	pullover
1	pair of gloves
1	Swastika brassard
1	'Org Todt' brassard

In special cases arctic or tropical clothing is also issued.
NCOs from the rank of Truppführer and upwards received the following:

1	cap
1	jacket
1	pair of trousers
1	belt
2	Swastika brassards
2	'Org. Todt' brassards
1	overcoat (in winter only)

In operational zone Front-OT, they furthermore receive:

1	field pack
1	bread bag
1	water bottle
1	mess-kit (with knife, fork and spoon)

In special cases arctic and tropical clothing is also issued.

All the above-listed clothing and equipment have to be turned in on discharge from the OT. Additional items of clothing, such as extra underclothing and socks, are to be bought by the OT member himself.

The individual camps issue blankets and in some cases also mess-kits which have to turned in when a man is moved. As of February 1943, every man in EGW had to have a gas mask and a steel helmet.

Every German OT member and those collaborationists who are permitted to carry a Dienstbuch (Schutzkommando or Security Guard men for the most part) are armed. The arms come from Wehrmacht depots and are for the greater part Beuteware (captured or requisitioned equipment). Thus, in January 1944, an order was issued that German nationals in Cherbourg should be given a French rifle, 196 rounds of ammunition, a cartridge belt and rifle cleaning equipment. Later, in May 1944, a rifle was issued to every 'Frontarbeiter'. In addition, from the rank of Obermeister (Corporal), upwards, each man was issued a pistol. From Bauführer or Frontführer (Lieutenant) upwards, a machine pistol was issued. Trusted collaborationists are likewise issued arms.

2 June 1943, Adolf Hitler presents Albert Speer with the Fritz Todt Ring at a ceremony in Berlin. The ring was of the signet type decorated with a large 'T' on the face and had several swastika emblems around its body. *(CMcC)*

Decorations

Members of the OT may be awarded Wehrmacht decorations. The following medals are listed in the OT Dienstbuch (Pay and Identity Book):

1. Schutzwallehrenzeichen — German Defence Westwall Medal Wound Badge
2. Verwundetenabzeichen — Wound Badge
3. Eisernes Kreuz I & II Klasse — Iron Cross I & II class
4. Spange zum Eisernen Kreuz — Bar to Iron Cross
5. Rettungsmedaille am Bande — Life Saving Medal with Ribbon
6. Ostmedaille — Eastern Front Medal
7. Kriegsverdienstkreuz I & II Klasse mit & ohne Schwerter — War Service of Merit Cross I & II class with and without swords
8. Kriegsverdienstmedaille — War Service of Merit Medal

Established by a Hitler decree of February 1944, the Dr Fritz Todt Preis is awarded to scientists, inventors, and engineers for OT outstanding contributions in the field of weapons, ammunitions, and military equipment, and for inventions and processes resulting in a saving of manpower, raw materials, and electro-power in the production of war materials. The prize is awarded in three grades:

Dr Fritz Todt Ehrennadel in Gold (Gold honour pin)
Dr Fritz Todt Ehrennadel in Silber (Silver honour pin)
Dr Fritz Todt Ehrenadel in Stahl (Steel honour pin)
with an additional cash bonus and certificate.

Ordinarily the award is made on 4 September 4 (Todt's birthday) or on 8 February (the date of his death).

Professor Albert Speer was decorated with the Fritz Todt Ring in 1943. [See opposite, although the date does not correspond with those given above.]

Decorations for women in the OT are recommended, if they have been on duty for more than two years outside of Germany proper.

Women can receive the following decorations:

Kriegsverdienstmedaille — War Service of Merit Medal
Kriesverdienstkreuz II Klasse mit & ohne Schwerter — War Service of Merit Cross II class with and without swords.

E. Pay, Allowances, Allotments, Insurance, Benefits, Deductions

(a) Introduction

General Pay Principles

In the course of any discussion of OT pay, it must become apparent that the Organisation Todt is not a uniform organisation such as the armed forces, wherein rank is the chief factor in determining pay. It should not, therefore, be expected that its pay and allowances can be computed from one uniform chart and according to a central system. Indeed, there are as many different categories and schemes of pay, as there are classes of personnel, and even within these groups there is a number of important variations according to nationality, nature of employment, status within the OT and so forth. As an overall division of OT personnel, from the point of view of pay, the following classifications can be made:

> OT organic personnel (OT-eigenes Personal)
> Todt-firm personnel (Firmenangehörige or Firmenangestellte)
> Forced labour (foreigners) (Zugewiesene Ausländer)

OT-eigenes Personal comprises all employees regardless of nationality, including officials (Beamte and Abgeordnete) who are directly employed by the OT. Such personnel form the nucleus of the OT, and the officials are members of the higher administration of the organisation. Firmenangehörige comprises all employees, German and foreign who are employed by the OT-Firms, including executives. Such personnel are again subdivided into regular and permanent employees (Stammarbeiter) and those who have been detailed to specific firms for the execution of OT contracts (Dienstverpflichtete). Zugewiesene Ausländer are foreign personnel in occupied territories who are detailed to the OT but who cannot be regarded as either OT-eigenes Personal or Firmenangehörige. As previously stated, all foreigners, regardless of which of the above mentioned groups they belong to, are again classified according to their nationality, and their pay may vary considerably. Indeed, in many instances, such remuneration seems to be merely a theoretical one designed to cover up the actual exploitation of foreigners for slave-labour. A definite rate of pay may be set down for such groups, but only a small allowance is in fact paid to these workers.

In addition to the above listed general divisions of OT personnel, all members of that organisation are classified according to the type of functions they fulfill.

These classifications are, at the same time, the basic pay classifications:

Beamte and Abgeordnete (officials)
Angestelilte (employees)
Technische Angestellte (technical employees)
Lohnempfänger (wage earners)

Technically all pay and allowances of OT personnel are also divided into Frontbezüge (front pay) and Heimatbezüge (home pay) in a manner similar to the pay of the German Armed Forces. Frontbezüge include:

OT Sold (regular OT pay) – apparently the same as the equivalent Army pay
Frontzulage (front line allowance)
Allowance for quarters and subsistence

It should be noted, however, that a regulation of December 1944, published in Nr. 35/36 of the Reichsarbeitsblatt, established a definite rate of pay for the so-called Front-OT. While it is not quite clear whether that new regulation affects all OT members including the OT-eigenes Personal, it seems certain that the majority of OT personnel, in particular all employees and wage-earners, are now receiving their remuneration under that plan. The old system of OT pay plus Frontzulage may thereby have been rendered obsolete, except possibly in the case of the comparatively small nucleus of OT-eigenes Personal. In the succeeding paragraphs an attempt is made to present a selection of the most important pay regulations and charts without any claim to completeness in a subject which is in no way clearly defined in the conventional manner of pay computation. Since at this time the vast majority of OT personnel must be regarded as Front-OT, particular emphasis will be placed on what information is available on their pay.

Under the general classification of Heimatbezüge, OT personnel may get the following:

Base pay
Premiums
Allowances
Social welfare benefits

While the Frontbezüge are paid out to OT personnel in the field, the Heimatbezüge are transferred to an account in Germany which the German employee may designate or, in the case of foreigners, to collective accounts.

OT-Führer (commissioned officers) receive a monthly salary and a flat rate for overtime. Pay of all other personnel is based on hourly wages (Stundenlohn), plus any of the additions in the form of allowances and benefits. This procedure is now completely in effect and supersedes any previously existing arrangement.

In this discussion of pay it should always be clear that the term Sold does not at any time mean base pay or tariff. Sold is an addition to any wage, salary, or tariff and is derived from the German armed forces 'Sold' which is a special straight payment to compensate the soldier for the hardships suffered. It is an allowance to cover the man's personal needs in the field. To avoid any error on this score, this explanation will be repeated whenever necessary in the succeeding pages.

(b) OT-Eigenes Personal (OT Organic Personnel)

General Principles of Pay
As in most other German organisations, regular members in the OT administration can be classified as either Beamte (officials) or Angestellte (employees). Personnel in those categories are paid according to two tariffs, Tarifordnung A and B (TOA and TOB – tariff code A and B). Tarifordnung A für Gefolgschaftsmitglieder im öffentlichen Dienst covers mainly the clerical occupations. Tarifordnung B für Gefolgschaftsmitglieder im öffentlichen Dienst takes in all those OT-organic personnel not covered under Tariff A. These tariffs are identical with those of the German Civil Service.

A number of special tariffs regulate wages for OT organic personnel employed in the medical, transport, and communication service. The most important of these is the Tarifordnung für die im unmittelbaren Arbeitsverhältnis zur OT stehenden Frontarbeiter (Tariff for Frontarbeiter directly employed by the OT). Payments of such tariffs are made through the Amt Bau-OTZ.

In general it can be said that there has been an increasing tendency to equalise OT and Armed Forces pay. To a certain extent this has been accomplished, but there are still many instances of wide discrepancies since the pay of OT workers must necessarily be based on hourly wages and tariffs. In this connection it is important to remember that pay according to accomplished work rather than fixed rates tends to provide an incentive for greater output.

Pay Scales

All OT-eigenes Personal receives armed forces pay (Wehrsold) corresponding to their equivalent rank in the OT. In addition they are given hourly wages based on a standard pay scale which progresses according to rank in the OT. While authentic documents on the tariffs are not available, a reliable report lists the following wage scales as of May 1944:

Rank	*Hourly Wage Wage RM (Reichsmark)*	*Wehrsold (monthly) RM*	*Monthly Clothing Allowance*
OT Mann		Up to 18 yrs: 36 above 18 yrs: 43.20	
Hilfsarbeiter	.60		Clothing issued
Facharbeiter	.80		Clothing issued
Vorarbeiter			
Hilfsarbeiter	.70	50.40	Clothing issued
Facharbeiter	.80	50.40	Clothing issued
Meister			
Hilfsarbeiter	.90	54.-	Clothing issued
Facharbeiter	.99	54.-	Clothing issued
Obermeister			
Hilfsarbeiter	1.-	58.20	Clothing issued
Facharbeiter	1.10	58.20	Clothing issued

Monthly Salary:

Truppführer	260.-	66.-	22.50
Obertruppführer	310.-	86.10	30.00
Haupttruppführer	500.-	128.40	30.00
Frontführer	580.-	128.40	30.00
Bauleiter	580.-	128.40	30.00
Frontführer	580.-	128.40	30.00

(c) Firmenangehörige (OT-Firm Personnel)

Pay Classifications

Originally the relations between most firms and the OT were regulated by the Selbstkostenerstattungsvertrag (Cost Reimbursement Contract). Under this contract, each firm was allowed a fair amount of latitude in determining its own labour policies. This resulted in a number of discrepancies in labour conditions between various firms in the same area. Consequently, the Oberbauleitungen was swamped with inquiries by firms, and circulars and decrees had to be published rendering decisions on labour policy in an attempt to create some workable system out of the general confusion. In May 1942 Dr Schmetler was appointed Sondertreuhänder der Arbeit für die Organisation Todt (Special Labour Commissioner for the OT). He established a number of tariffs creating more uniform wage conditions for all workers.

Eventually most pay for Firmenangehörige (or Firmenangestellte) came to be regulated by the following tariffs (Tarifordnungen) issued by the Reichstreuhänder der Arbeit (Reich Commissioner of Labour) and the Sondertreuhänder der Arbeit der Organisation Todt (Special Labour Commissioner for the OT) for Reichsdeutsche (Germans) or by the Militärbefehlshaber (Military Commander) for workers of occupied countries:

(i) Reichstarifordnung für den Leistungslohn im Baugewerbe covers German construction workers inside the Reich. It is modified by a number of Bezirkstarifordnungen (District Tariffs), each making allowances for regional labour conditions. There are altogether some 600 occupations in the building and construction industries, each of which is covered under the different tariffs issued by the Reichstreuhänder der Arbeit (Reich Commissioner of Labour).

(ii) The Tarifordnung für die reichsdeutschen Gefolgschaftsmitglieder der OT – OT Frontarbeitertarif, effective 20 January 1943, covers German workers employed outside the Reich.

(iii) The Anordnung zur Regelung der Arbeitsverhältnisse der bei der OT eingesetzten Betriebe des Baugewerbes und der Baunebengewerbe – OT Firmenangestelltentarif of 20 Jan 1943 originally dealt with commercial and technical employees of the OT serving outside Germany and classified all such personnel as Frontarbeiter.

(iv) Among the most important tariffs is the OT Firmenangestelltentarif of 26 February 1943. While some pay regulations were revised in the provisions of the Front-OT Tarif (No. (v) below), the important outlines have remained the same.

(v) In December 1944, however, all Front-OT Firmenangestellte (Firm employees), German and foreign, were covered by the new Tarifordnung für die zur Front-OT gehörenden reichsdeutschen und ausländischen Angestellten der Organisation Todt. It seems improbable that since the time this tariff went into effect much of a distinction between front lines and rear echelons could have been made. Consequently, it may safely be asumed that aside from OT-eigenes Personal and certain categories of slave labour practically all OT personnel are by now paid according to that tariff. Special stress will therefore be placed on its regulations and mention of any other previously existing regulations will be made only where it may be of aid in rounding out the historical picture. Not covered by the new regulation are native workers in occupied territories, OT-eigene Angestellte who are paid according to Tarifordnung A, employees who are visiting the Front-OT installations only temporarily for purposes of liaison, Vorstandsmitglieder (members of the executive board), Poles and Eastern workers. Under this regulation all German employees are classified as OT-Frontarbeiter and all foreigners as OT-Legionäre.

Under this scale OT employees are paid monthly, but salaries are not handed over to the workers. They are sent to the address designated by the payee or, in the case of some foreign personnel, to a so-called Sammelkonto (collective account).

During the course of the OT's rather varied functions a number of other Tarifordnungen have, at one time or other, regulated the pay of the OT personnel in various occupied territories. In addition, special regulations govern the pay of certain other nationalities such as North Africans, Ostarbeiter, and other categories of Zwangsarbeiter (forced labour), as well as of Jews. No official tariffs for these workers have been published, but regulations were issued from time to time in the form of circular letters (Rundschreiben).

In the succeeding pages some of the special regulations will again come up for discussion. However, such instances should only be regarded as partial illustrations of a field which cannot be dealt with exhaustively, for it must be remembered that the OT has constantly been permitted to mushroom out in any manner which seemed expedient for the handling of vast contingents of foreign slaves.

Firmenangestellte Wage Scales
The following pay regulations, based on the proceeding tariffs above, are valid for all OT stations outside Germany proper, but including the General Gouvernement; for all German employees (Reichsdeutsche Angestellte) residing in Germany; and for employees of all firms which are within the effective limits of the Reichstarifordnung (National tariff regulations) for the construction industry, of November 1941. It may, however, be assumed that by this time the same regulations cover all OT employees within Germany as well.

OT Firmenangestellte are divided into the following wage groups:

Group J1: Commercial and technical employees under twenty years and without a completed professional education.

Group J2: Commercial and technical employees under twenty years with a completed education and apprenticeship.

Group K1: Employees with a mechanical or schematic (schematische) occupation, such as correspondents, file clerks, mimeograph experts, wage computators, and trained office machine experts.

Group K2: Employees with a simple occupation, such as typists, assistant accountants, assistant cashiers, etc.

Group K3: Employees handling difficult jobs with own responsibility, such as wage accountants, statisticians, store room administrators, etc.

Group K4: Leading employees with wide professional and practical knowledge, who independently manage their sections, such as chief accountants and cashiers, etc.

Group Tl: Technical employees with a predominant mechanical or schematic occupation, such as plans and drawings, classifiers, assistant overlay experts, etc.

Group T2: Employees in simple technical and drawing occupations, working under supervision, such as elementary statisticians, estimators, supervisors of simple constructions, etc.

Group T3: Employees handling difficult jobs on their own responsibility, such as draftsmen.

Group T4: Leading employees with wide professional and practical knowledge, who independently manage their sections, such as construction chiefs, who compute constructional data, on their own responsibility and independently negotiate with the contractors and public authorities, engineers and chiefs of large construction posts, etc.

Group M: 'Poliere' and excavation foremen and other experts, such as construction machine foremen.

Group MO: 'Oberpoliere', 'Oberschachtmeister' (excavation foremen) and other expert craftsmen.

Tariffs for Firmenangehörige in France

As previously pointed out, tariffs vary according to the various countries in which the OT was employed. It is, of course, far beyond the scope of this book to illustrate the pay scales of all those territories.

All employment and wages were regulated by a decree of the Military Commander which became effective on 15 April 1944, and concerned itself especially with the Building and Construction Industry. Its rulings applied to all German firms of the industry in France and to all non-German firms under contract to a German firm. It covered all workers whose residence was in France, with the exception of drivers, and included also workers from Belgium and Holland. French territory was divided into regions as follows:

Region I.	Paris and similar localities. Cities of more than 500,000 population
Region II	Cities of more than 100,000 population
Region III	Cities of more than 20,000 population
Region IV	Cities of more than 5,000 population
Region V	Cities of less than 5,000 population

The actual wages paid vary according to those six regional classifications.

Tariffs for Frontarbeiter

Up to this point OT tariffs affecting the Firmenangestellten only have been discussed. A somewhat different wage scale exists for OT-Frontarbeiter and OT-Legionäre, most of whom are Firmenangehörige.

Miscellaneous Tariffs

The Tarifordnung für die reichsdeutschen invalidenversicherungspflichtigen Gefölgschaftsmitglieder der OT im Einsatz Ruhrgebiet-OT-Frontarbeitertarif Ruhrgebiet of Sept 1943 was a special tariff. It gave giving all OT workers in the Ruhr front-line status and gave these workers extra money in the form of Frontzulage. For married workers from North Africa, Algiers, Morocco and Spain (Rotspanier) whose families did not have residence in France, the Ausländer-Bautarif West is applicable, but 8% of their gross wages had to be transferred to the Familienausgleichskasse (Family Settlement Section of the Pay Office for Foreign Workers) in Paris.

Jewish workers are paid according to the circular, published by EWG.

Wages for Jewish workers may be granted according to the 'Arbeitsbedingungen des Militärbefehlhabers' (Terms for labour set down by the Military Commander). They may be employed in line witn the output principle whereby their efficiency rating must be severely considered. Only wages for work actually performed are to be granted. No claims can be made for continuance of payments in case of illness. Extra pay for overtime, night work, work on Sundays or holidays is not authorised. Donations in form of premiums of any description are prohibited. Lodging in closed camps and messing are free, but 12 francs per day are retained for costs of messing. In addition 5% of the wages are retained as taxes. Family allowances are not authorised. Social insurances of any kind are not in effect for Jewish workers, but private insurance is permissible. For the defrayal of personal needs, pocket money of 20 francs per day is deducted from the wages and paid out in cash. In case of inferior output of work, deduction of pocket money from the wages may be denied. The balance of the wages is transferred by the firm to the family of the Jewish worker.

15% of the gross wages of Jewish workers are retained for the so-called Judenabgabe (special tax on Jews).

(d) Zugewiesene Ausländer (Forced Foreign Labour)

Pay for Forced Labor

All foreign workers – unless they have been given status of OT-eigenes or Firmenangeörige-are classified as Forced Labour (Sonstige-zugewiesene Ausländer). This includes Forced Labour which is broken down into two types, Hilfswillige ('Volunteers') and Zwangsarbeiter (Forced workers). The basic hourly wages listed for these workers show little difference from those of the German tariffs. The 'Einsatz Pay' of married workers for the defrayal of the personal needs of the foreign worker corresponds roughly in amount to the Army Sold of the German Frontarbeiter.

Foreign workers are not covered by the Social Welfare Benefits provided through the German Government, but they belong to private insurance institutions. Medical care is provided through certain foreign Krankenkassen (hospital insurance) which are controlled by the OT.

Foreign personnel are chiefly employed as manual labourers, with some classified as skilled workers (Facharbeiter). No foreigner may be a commissioned officer (Führer) in the OT. The highest assignments he may attain are Hilfspoliere and Fachvorarbeiter. While the 'Einsatz Sold' was paid to the foreign workers in cash in France, all other wages, which supposedly were to go to his family, actually went to the Ausländerlohnzahlstelle (Pay Office for Foreign Workers) in Paris.

Russians, Ukranians, White Russians, Lithuanians, etc. are grouped together under the term 'Ostarbeiter' (Eastern workers). While working in France they received pay on the basis of French workers' gross wages. Additional output pay was the same for both French and Ostarbeiter. The Ostarbeiter, however, is paid only for work actually performed. He is not entitled to overtime pay. For such time as he is unable to work because of illness or injury, the Ostarbeiter is given merely rations and quarters. Contractors employing Ostarbeiter must remit an Ostarbeiter-Abgabe (levy), but no taxes or social insurance fees are paid by the worker.

A daily deduction for rations and quarters of RM 1.50 is made. This amount may be reduced down to RM 0.50 if the worker conducts himself exceptionally well. In outstanding cases rations may be free.

All Ostarbeiter are divided into four efficiency groups as follows:

Group I	Free rations and quarters are granted when work is excellent
Group II	RM 1.- is deducted when his work is good
Group III	RM 0.50 is deducted when his work is satisfactory
Group IV	The average Russian worker without any noticeable willingness to work. RM 1.50 is deducted for his rations and quarters.

Ostarbeiter, who distinguish themselves in their loyalty and good work receive upon completion of their first year of employment a bonus of 20%, after two years 3% and after three years 50% of their wages.

Pay for forced labour cannot, of course, be expected to have been adhered to by the Germans, As previously pointed out, such arrangements were often merely made on paper in order to preserve the semblance of legality. Some instances are, furthermore, available in which completely insufficient wages have been paid to forced labourers. One German document, for example, lists the following weekly wages paid to Russian forced labour:

2.00 RM for ordinary workers

3.00 RM for especially good workers

3.00 RM for Kolonnenführer

4.00 RM for Bereitschaftsführer

5.00 RM for Abteilungsführer

e) Special Regulations Affecting OT Pay

List of Pay Additions

The actual pay received by OT employees is affected by a number of special regulations concerning compensations, extra pay, allowances and deductions. Aside from taxes and penalties for work of inferior quality (Minderleistung) or for work not performed (Lohnausfall), most of the regulations affecting the basic pay are additions. The most frequent factors of this kind:

OT-Sold or Wehrsold

Frontzulage (Front-line allowance)

Leistungslohn (Pay for output)

Mehrarbeit (Overtime)

Erschwerniszulage (Allowance for dangerous work)

Lohnausfallentschädigung (Compensation for time lost other than through worker's fault)

Leistungszulage (Special premiums)

Lohnnebenkosten (Allowances)

OT 'Sold' for Employees

Sold, whether in the armed forces or in the OT, must not be confused with basic pay. It is strictly a wartime addition to compensate for various hardships and sacrifices. At the same time Sold is designed to serve the soldier or, in the case of the OT, the worker as his personal allowance in the field.

OT Sold is not paid to foreign workers who receive Einsatzgeld (pay for front-line duty) for the defrayal of their personal expenses in foreign countries. In discussing OT pay in general and Sold in particular, it is important to know that the ranks and rank insignia of OT-eigenes Personnel also apply to Firmengestellen. There are three rank scales for each pay scale. New employees are placed in the lowest rank scale and into the corresponding Sold group. While no increase of wages is connected with promotions, the OT Sold group changes.

OT-Sold for Workers

All OT-Frontarbeiter receive Sold corresponding to the armed forces Sold in the particular locality.

Frontzulage (Front-line Allowance) and Leistungslohn (Pay for Output)

Frontzulage is granted as compensation for living under field conditions. The amount is RM 1.- daily for all ranks and is authorised by the Chief of the Armed Forces High Command. A circular letter issued by the EGW, dated 31 March 1942, states that according to an order of OKW the front-line allowance was to be discontinued for EGW, with effect from 1 April 1944.

At the beginning of 1944 a new regulation went into effect establishing a new wage system called the Leistungslohn (pay for output). It is a revival of the old piece work principle (Akkordarbeit). A mean hourly wage (Mittellohn) of RM 0.90 for German and RM 0.70 for French workers was used as a basis for the computation of the actual pay. The whole system of computing the Leistungslohn seems to be very complicated, and there is much room for discrepancies as to the various methods in calculating the Leistungslohn by the individual firm.

Overtime

The regular working hours for Angestellte is calculated on a weekly basis of forty-six hours, and for workers on a daily basis of eight hours. Exceptions to these rules are the following: the regular working time for Maschinisten, Heizer, Kraftfahrer, Befahrer, and Kutscher is ten hours, and for guard personnel, barracks orderlies, and cooks twelve hours per day. Certain classifications of mechanics may have to work a regular week of sixty hours.

In the case of all Angestellte who work on the basis of the forty-eight hour week, overtime is to be paid only if increased working hours have been ordered for a period of more than a month and exceeding fifty-two hours per week. Overtime is paid in the form of a lump sum and does not take into consideration hourly excess work.

No overtime allowances are granted to Jews and forced labour.

Erschwerniszulage (Allowance for Dangerous Work)

This was originally paid only in especially endangered areas, where an addition of 20% of base pay was frequently granted. That allowance could be increased to 30% for work performed under aerial bombardment, and a special addition of 50 francs per day is known to have been given to workers employed on some French sites containing unexploded bombs. In this connection it should be noted that full payment is made for work not performed because of enemy bombing.

Lohnausfallentschädigung (Compensation for Time Lost Other than Through Worker's Fault)

The following conditions permit a Lohnausfallentschädigung, i.e. compensation for time lost for reasons other than the worker's fault or negligence:

   time lost because of adverse weather conditions
   time lost because of enemy action
   time spent by worker on leave

In such instances the worker is entitled to payment of hourly tariff for eight hours per day, even if he was able to work only for part of that time.

In all instances of inability to work because of accident, injuries or illness sustained in the line of duty, payment of salary or wages is continued for a period of up to twenty-three weeks. If inability for a period exceeding thirteen weeks is to be expected, an immediate report is to be made to Amt Bau-OTZ, Abt. Sozialversorgung. In special instances that bureau may order payments for a period exceeding the thirteen weeks. Similarly payment of salary and wages continues if the worker or employee has been ordered to undergo a special medical cure or treatment or if he has been sent on sick-leave.

Leistungszulage (Special Premiums)

Special premiums may be granted to OT personnel for extraordinary work performed by them, provided that they are not working under the regulations of the output principle. Such premiums may be granted up to 10% of the tariff. Only in special instances designated by the Reichs- oder Sondertreuhänder der Arbeit or in cases where personnel have received such premiums regularly since before 16 October 1939, may the 10% be exceeded.

Lohnnebenkosten (Allowances)

The following Lohnnebenkosten (allowances) are listed under the Leistungsvertrag (Efficiency Output Contract).

Trennungszulage – Allowance on travel or non-travel status when subsistence and quarters are not, or only partly, furnished.

Lohnausfallentschädigung bei Erkrankung – Compensation in case of illness.

Frontzulage – Front-line addition, see above.

Wegegelder – Travel allowance between residence and place of work.

Entfernungszulage – Allowance for workers whose residence is distant from place of work.

Anu. Rückreisekosten – Travel money on leaves and furloughs.

Verpflegungszuschlüsse bei Nichtteilnahme an der Gemeinschaftsverpflegung – Subsistence allowance when OT messing facilities are not available.

Miscellaneous Deductions and Allotments

Deductions from OT pay may be made for various social insurance purposes, such as ordinary insurance (Versicherung), hospitalisation and health insurance (Krankenkasse) and forced saving (Eisernes Sparen). The amounts of these deductions are not listed in the various tariffs. They differ with each individual case according to the status of the worker and his family and dependants.

German legislation provides for an elaborate system of nationalised social welfare designed to assist the worker upon discharge from his organisation, as well as to alleviate his and his family's hardships while he is still on active service. The Reichsversicherung (national insurance) is an informal term under which various welfare institutions, including the Krankenkassen, are grouped together. All workers in the Reich and all OT-eigenes Personal are members of the Reichsversicherung. While OT regulations and directives call for free medical care for all personnel, those benefits are actually provided and financed through the various social insurance and hospitalisation institutions of the Reich. Workers therefore are subject to the regulations and by-laws of the various Krankenkassen.

OT-eigenes Personal are members of the Betriebskrankenkasse des Reichs, Zweigstelle OT, Berlin – Siemensstadt. All German OT Gefolgschaftsmitglieder are members of the Deutsche Krankenkasse. While serving within the Reich, German Gefolgschaftsmitglieder receive their benefits through the Ortskrankenkassen (local Krankenkassen). French Gefolgschaftsmitglieder were members of the equivalent French agency, the Service Régional Des Assurances Sociales, or if married, the Caisse d'Allocations Familiales. Belgian workers employed in France received benefits through the Deutsche Zentralkrankenkasse in Belgium, with the main office at Brussels and branches at Antwerp, Liège, Ghent, and Bruges.

Many OT workers, especially in the Building and Construction industries, received higher incomes before they became subject to OT tariffs. In all such instances the worker may apply for a family allowance. Applications are directed to the OT Amt Bau-Zentrale, Hauptabteilung Arbeitseinsatz und Sozialpolitik. After the family allowance has been approved, it is sent direct to the family of the worker. An allowance of this kind is called Familienbeihilfe. Poles, Ostarbeiter, and forced labour are excluded from any such privileges. If a worker is killed or missing in action, his family receive Hinterbliebenen und Vermisstenbezüge. The following is an illustrative extract from a decree by Reichsminister Speer, dated 21 December 1942. (Soziale Betreuung der Frontarbeiter der OT).

Surviving dependants of OT Frontarbeiter, killed by accident or in action or otherwise deceased, will be granted allowances equivalent to the wages of the current month and three months thereafter. The same payments will continue beyond that period until such time as the dependents claim of benefits (Versorgungsverfahren) is settled. The maximum amount payable is RM 500.

In case of death not proven to have occurred in line of duty no payments are to be made beyond a period of three months.

If a Frontarbeiter is captured or missing in action, wages are sent to his family retroactive to his disappearance.

Upon discharge from service in the OT, the worker is given Entlassungsbeihilfe (Discharge Allowance) provided that he has been on active service with the OT for a minimum of ninety days, that he is honorably discharged, and is in possession of an OT-Dienstbuch (Pay and Identity book). The Entlassungsbeihilfe amounts to 10 RM for every month of service with the OT, but does not exceed a maximum of 50 RM.

Eisernes Sparen (forced or frozen savings) is a commonly adopted form of deduction of savings from salaries and wages. It is carried out and supervised by the Reich authorities. Only German employees who are subject to Lohnsteuer (tax on wages) are included in the system of Eisernes Sparen.

The credit institution at which the particular savings account is to be opened may be selected by the employer. Discounts on forced savings accounts are determined by the Reichsaufsichtsamt für das Kreditwesen (Reich Bureau for the Control of Credit Institutions).

Rations, Lodging and Clothing Allowances

Food and lodging are, as a rule, provided for OT personnel without charge. Whenever regular billets and messing facilities are not provided for, a per diem allowance is paid in lieu of subsistence and quarters. Clothing, too, is furnished free in most instances. When that is not possible, a daily clothing allowance is paid. All commissioned officers must furnish their own uniforms, but they receive an allowance up to RM 150. Officer candidates (Führeranwärter) are issued with their uniform, but must furnish their own shoes and underwear. To cover their expenses, they receive, however, an allowance of RM 150.

OT uniforms are issued by the OT-Ausrüstungsstelle (OT-equipment depot). The uniform remains the property of the OT, and every issue is recorded in the Dienstbuch. Female OT-Firmenangestellte receive a uniform allowance of 10% of the value of the uniforms issued to male employees.

OT employees who for some special reason are not issued with any uniforms receive an allowance in the amount of the uniform set down on the official price list.

Urlaub (Leaves)

Every OT employee is entitled to leave. The number of days granted depends on the local rulings in the various territories within and outside the Reich. New members of the Front-OT may get their first leave after six months of uninterrupted service. After that leaves may be given after three months of field service. Time and duration of leaves are determined by the local OT-Bauleiter. For the duration of leaves and travelling time salaries continue to be paid. Travel from OT station to the worker's home is free.

Sonderurlaub (special leaves) may be granted in case of death or serious illness of parents, wife, or children of the OT worker or employee. Such special or compassionate leaves may be given for a total of seven days per year, not counting any possible travel time.

PART IV

HILFSWILLIGE BEI DER OT

Aufnahmen:
OT-Kriegsberichter Hanns Neumann

Frauen
suchen schwere Arbeit

Es ist eine dem russischen Wesen eigentümliche Erscheinung, daß die Frau dort ebenso wie der Mann und manchmal noch offensichtlicher die schwersten körperlichen Arbeiten leistet. Der Deutsche ist anfangs erstaunt, wenn er sieht, wie diese jungen Frauen zupacken können und so wie hier im Dienste der OT beim Ausladen von Steinmaterial für den Straßenbau mit mehrzentnerschweren Felsbrocken hantieren. Selbstverständlich ist diese Arbeit durchaus freiwillig, und es ist bezeichnend, daß die Frauen sich geradezu nach ihr drängen, weil sie gut entlohnt wird. Dabei sind sie trotz ihrer schweren Arbeit immer vergnügt und zufrieden.

Pflastersteine aus Holz

Mit Holz pflastert man Straßen schon seit langer Zeit, und in holzreichen Ländern ist das auch durchaus kein Problem. Besonders beim Straßenbelag von Brücken verwendete man früher das sogenannte „russische" Holzpflaster aus prismatisch geformten Holzstücken. Daß die OT es im Kriege auch viel einfacher kann, zeigen unsere Aufnahmen. Hier wird Rundholz, das in gleich lange Stücke zerteilt ist, als Ersatz für Pflastersteine verwendet. Dieses Verfahren hat sich in der Praxis bereits gut bewährt, und es wird überall dort angewandt, wo Steine schwer zu beschaffen sind. Bei dieser Arbeit werden vornehmlich russische Hilfswillige beschäftigt, unter ihnen findet man viele recht tüchtige Fachleute auf diesem Gebiet.

A page from an edition of the OT's own magazine, *Der Frontarbeiter*, published in February 1944. It features Russian 'Hilfwillige', volunteers, smiling happily as they go about their work repairing a road with wooden blocks. 'Women seek hard work', claims the article, 'of course this work was entirely voluntary'.

Manpower

A. General Manpower Statistics and Occupational Percentages

General Statistics

When the OT, under the administration of the Generalinspektion des deutschen Strassenwesens, took over as its first task, the building of the Westwall from the Army Engineers in May 1938, it comprised roughly 350,000 men. The greater part of these, approximately 75% were the old construction hands who had worked on the Reichsautobahn, the remainder was made up of Construction Firm employees consisting of technicians, skilled workers, and clerical assistants. In order to hurry things along, with prospects of war imminent, the OT had been lent additional help by the temporary attachment of about 100,000 RAD personnel, and the Army Engineers who had begun the original construction in 1936. The latter amounted likewise to approximately 100,000 men. The above figures, even though taken from German propaganda sources, may be accepted as reasonably accurate. Similar sources place the total OT personnel about the time of its greatest period of expansion, May 1943, at approximately a million and a half men (and women) outside the borders of the Reich. The latter figure, however, is not supported by data compiled from captured German documents, unless it be understood to include (1) industrial labour working for OT indirectly, such as French cement plants and lumber mills; (2) manpower raised for OT by short-term levies for specific tasks; (3) supplementary manpower at one time attached to OT, such as Rumanian and Hungarian Engineer battalions.

German figures for OT personnel in the EGW alone, for example, reach as high as 600,000, but are reduced to less than half on the basis of the documentary sources available. It should, however, be remembered in this connection that manpower working for the OT indirectly, such as was mentioned above, has not been taken into account here. The total OT manpower in the Reich in February

1945 on the other hand, is estimated at approximately one million.

Occupational Percentages

The proportion of Baufacharbeiter (skilled construction workers) to unskilled labour in the EGW was as high as 2:3. In other areas such as, for instance, Russia and the Balkans, it was considerably lower. There were several reasons for this: (1) French construction firms which, by placing themselves under the direction of German contractors, joined OT as subcontractors, brought along their own skilled employees; (2) The skilled workers belonged for the most part to the older generation and consequently had not been captured in 1940 as prisoners of war. Their age and family responsibilities similarly provided a reason against their subsequent deportation to Germany for factory work; (3) Wages for skilled workers in OT coupled with family benefits etc. attracted many applicants; (4) The demands upon training and skill made by the complexity of installations in the West, such as V-sites, were higher than in other sectors; (5) Next to Germany, France was the greatest potential source in Continental Europe of manpower with technical training.

The proportion and composition of skilled OT personnel in Germany until Allied penetration in late winter and early spring of 1945 made all figures valueless. It can be said here in summary that there existed a great dearth of qualified German personnel in responsible jobs, that the proportion of qualified foreigners although lower than in former German occupied territory, remained high, in rear areas especially, and that the picked German personnel was sent to the zone called Front-OT. Even in the latter zone, a proportion of three foreigners to one German was permitted by regulations, although in practice the number of foreigners apparently did not reach this proportion in the late autumn and winter of 1944/45.

Women

Women regularly working for the OT are estimated to form 7% of the Organisation. The proportion of female administrative assistants such as typists, clerks, etc., to the menial help, such as kitchen and cleaning women, is roughly 3:2. The only female OT-eigenes Personal (OT organic personnel) which can be considered as forming a Unit are the Nachrichtenhelferinnen (Signals Communications Assistants) more popularly known as Blitzmädel. They are part of the TO/WE in OT HQs on all levels. The menial help is recruited locally in the vicinity of the OT camps, and their relationship to the OT is tenuous if not informal. In the West approximately half of the clerical assistants were likewise recruited from local areas such as neighbouring towns and cities. Regulations prohibit the employment of German girls under twenty-one in the Fronteinsatz (Front Commitment Area within range of enemy action). The female Zwangsarbeiter (Forced Labour) for the greater part consisted of Polish and Russian women charged with Communist and partisan activities. Their number in the West where the need for manpower was greatest, did not exceed 20,000 and was probably nearer to half that figure.

B. Regional Manpower Recruitment and Allocation

(a) German Manpower

161. In general German personnel in the OT classified as kriegsverwendungsfähig (fit for combat duty) is extremely small even though the organisation still contains individuals deferred from army combat service because of their essential occupations if not through the influence of their political connections. But there is an appreciable number of wounded and incapacitated Germans in administrative positions. In July 1944, for instance, the quota of the EGW for the army was established at 500 men for whom it received in exchange 2,500 Wehrmacht personnel incapacitated for further combat service. In fact OT's efficiency was markedly lowered through the placing of Germans in supervisory assignments whose only qualification is the fact that they are over age or incapacitated.

At the present time the average age of German personnel in the rear zone, except that of the politically, morally unreliable elements (convict soldiers, homosexuals, etc.), is over fifty. In the battle zone the OT has become so closely integrated with the Army Engineers through the Festungspionierstäbe (Fortress Engineers Staffs) that the differentiation between them has practically vanished. Nor can it be said that there are any age limits at this time; juveniles are as acceptable as septuagenarians, as far as their physical condition permits.

Firmenangehörige (OT-Firm Personnel)

The OT had no trouble in the recruitment of German personnel until Army requirements began to make inroads on it. The first task of the OT in 1938 was made attractive enough to induce a sufficient number of construction firms (estimated in some quarters at one-third of Germany's construction capacity) to enroll in the organisation, bringing with them their equipment and employees (the latter are termed Firmenangehörige in contra-distinction to OT-eigenes Personal described below). The outbreak of war resulted in an immediate decrease in civilian construction within the Reich and culminated in a complete stoppage about the time of the attack on Russia. When air-raid damage inside Germany became a serious factor, the OT was gradually called in (viz. Einsatz Ruhrgebiet) until the summer of 1944, when it assumed control of all construction. As a result German construction firms have become completely dependent on the OT.

OT-Eigenes Personal (OT Organic Personnel)

The organising of the OT administrative personnel termed OT-eigenes Personal in contra-distinction to Firmenangehörige did not offer any serious problems, even though there always has existed some resentment in the lower assignments, because of the higher wages received by the Firmenangehörige. The higher administrative (and technical) posts are filled by men whose political connections both with the Nazi Party and the German Construction Industry can be traced back to the early days. Nazi Party doctrine pays great attention to technology, and its 'white-haired boys' include a number of the higher-ranking OT technicians. Another source of supply for administrative posts were the Abgeordnete (civil servants connected with city and regional housing and construction administration and assigned to the OT on detached service). Many of the lower posts are filled by SA and Nazi Party members, classified 'unabkümmlich' (Uk: indispensable) by the Wehrmacht Registration Bureau. The SS is likewise represented in the OT, usually in assignments well adapted for military security and political counter-intelligence work.

Military and Manpower Priority Status of OT German Personnel

The official military status of the OT is quasi-legal and will so remain until it no longer contains within its ranks foreign conscript labour. The status of OT personnel from the standpoint of manpower recruitment, was modified within Germany as a result of OT's withdrawal from France, Belgium, Holland and other areas. Prior to this withdrawal, the OT ranked, in this respect, no higher than any other vital industry, and German OT personnel might be called up for active military service like ordinary civilians working in an essential industry, but not necessarily in indispensable posts. On the other hand the Wehrmacht Meldeamt (Wehrmacht Registration Bureau) could 'reserve' a man for the OT, and the Wehrbezirkskommando (Sub-Area Recruiting HQ) could assign a man to the OT. The former was done arbitrarily in the case of building mechanics or construction workers born in or before 1900. The latter was done for a variety of reasons in the case of individual construction workers born after 1900, and especially in the case of individuals with political connections who preferred to enter the OT rather than the armed forces proper. Both these categories were consequently 'dienstverpflichtet' (conscripted) for the OT, but had no guarantee that they would not eventually be called up for active military service.

The foreign personnel lost to the Germans in occupied territory has been replaced apparently by new levies of foreign workers, such as Hungarian Jews, by members of Hitler Jugend (Hitler Youth Movement) and by German civilians used as emergency stopgaps. OT personnel in occupied territory is called up into the Wehrmacht through the competent Aussenstelle (Branch) of the Wehrbezirkskommando Ausland (District Recruiting HQ for Germans Abroad). The men so called up are, however, to report to their home Wehrbezirkskomnando.

When the OT first withdrew into the Reich in the summer of 1944, its entire personnel retained for a time its status as front area personnel, exposed to enemy action, which it had enjoyed in the occupied West and which entailed special prerogatives and allowances. In the autumn of 1944, however, two separate zones were created, a zone of the interior and a front zone, the latter being called Front-OT. Front-OT personnel retained their special prerogatives, while the rear zone personnel lost the special allowances it had been receiving as well as some of its military character in practice, if not officially.

Defining the respective spheres of jurisdiction between the Reich Regional Manpower authorities (Gau Labour Bureau chiefs and Gauleiter) and the OT Manpower authorities (Dr Schmelter Sondertreuhänder der Arbeit für die OT: Special Labour Trustee for the OT), both of whom derive their authority from Fritz Saukel as Plenipotentiary General for Manpower Allocation, it is not certain whether the latter have the same powers over OT rear zone personnel as over Front-OT personnel, although this is believed to be the case. At any rate, the OT authorities (through the section Arbeitseinsatz und Sozialpolitik in Amt Bau -OTZ) have the authority to transfer their personnel from zone to zone (front and rear), without the consent of the competent Regional Manpower authorities in which these zones are located, although consultation in this connection is normally attempted. For this purpose, there is a Beauftragte (Deputy) of Dr Schmelter in each Einsatzgruppe.

Enlistment Procedure

Until spring 1942, the procedure for enlistment in the OT was no more complicated than the procedure provided for applying for a job in any essential industry. When a construction firm made a contract with the OT, it was automatically placed in the category of war production industry and its employees were accordingly issued Dienstverpflichtungsscheine (Labour Conscription Forms) which forbade the possessor to seek employment elsewhere. These forms were issued by the local Arbeitsämter (Labour Bureaux) competent in the employee's home districts. A firm employee entering the OT on this basis was designated a Stammarbeiter (Permanent Employee) and the firm's entire personnel was designated as Stammpersonal (Permanent Staff).

The firm was processed for operation in occupied terriroty as a unit and travelled as such to its destination along with its equipment. A construction firm already working for the OT in occupied territory could obtain additional personnel from Germany through the medium of its home office and the local Labour Bureau. If the firm was influential enough, it obtained not only volunteer applicants in this manner but also personnel withdrawn by the Arbeitsamt from firms whose work was classified on lower priority. (In this manner a skilled mechanic who would prefer to work near his home for comparatively low wages rather than join the OT, could be put under compulsion.) Personnel recruited in this manner as a rule travelled directly to the location of their new job on travel authorisation permits issued by the competent OBL Frontführung (Front Area Personnel Section). On the other hand, personnel entering the OT directly, whether volunteer or conscripted, was, with some possible exceptions, processed through the OT Haupterfassungslager (Main Induction Camps), in Berlin, Frankfurt, Isenburg and Inowslodz in the general governement.

In the second half of 1942, irregular and surreptitious methods of recruiting for the OT were officially done away with by the establishment of (Branch Labour Bureaux) Nebenstellen Arbeitsamt in those induction centres which henceforth were to process induction papers for all newly recruited OT personnel. (The OT retains the authority to change the status of Firmenangehörige, including Stammpersonal, who have become subject to military service, to OT-eigenes Personal by assigning them to OT administrative positions. However as long as a man has not been formally 'dienstverpflichtet' he remains a 'Freiangestellter' (Free Agent Employee) a status which theoretically allows the possibility of resigning from the OT. At the present time, Dr Schmeleter's priority on German manpower is exceeded only by that of the Wehrmacht proper, see proceeding paragraph.

Processing of Recruits

The OT Haupterfassungslager (Main Induction Camps) did much to make enlistment procedure more uniform, of which the labour recruitment factor touched upon above was only one aspect. The Stammlager Grunewald in Greater Berlin, opened early in 1942, for example, was the replacement pool for the entire West. In this function it contained facilities not only for the induction, processing and training of German personnel, but also for transit of large masses of workers transported for example from Poland to France or vice versa. Grunewald was originally planned for a daily processing capacity of 4,000 men. This camp may have been enlarged since the camp Neu Isenburg near Frankfurt on Main was evacuated because of air-raid damage early in 1944.

Until the withdrawal of the OT into the Reich (summer of 1944) intense competition between firms for manpower however, made OTZs (now Amt Bau-OTZ) regulations for uniform enlistment procedure only as effective as influential firms in collusion with the OBL administration allowed them to be.

Since then the pooling of OT manpower on a national basis within Germany has effectively removed the possibility of such local collusion.

OT processing procedure is as follows:

1. Processing of induction papers at Nebenstelle des Arbeitsamtes.
2. Preliminary medical examination (heart and kidneys) at Nebenstelle des Arbeitsamtes.
3. Medical examination and general assignments as to type of labour (heavy, light), and as to locality.
4. Specific occupational assignment.
5. Issue of Dienstbuch and Erkennungsmarke.
6. Determination of the recruit's pay scale, according to OT tariff differential.
7. Issue of clothing and equipment at Bekleidungskammer (Clothing Office). (Those not entitled to wear uniform received working clothes.)

Discharge and Withdrawal from the OT

Discharge to civilian status can be recommended only by the EG subject to final approval by Amt Bau-OTZ. Up to about mid-year 1942 individual discharges were granted fairly easily in cases considered deserving, such as poor health, after a period of three to four years of service, and in serious cases of family complications. Since then, individual discharges for Dienstverpflichtete (conscripts) have become practically non-existent, except in cases of serious injury. Theoretically, a man of Stammpersonal (Permanent Staff) status will be discharged in the event that his firm withdraws from OT. In practice, however, there is no record of any firm taking such a politically and economically unwise step. Were it to do so, its personnel and equipment would be withdrawn from it, and transferred to other OT firms on the grounds of essential war production. At the present time, with the OT in control of all construction in Germany, the question of withdrawal has become academic.

Discharge from the OT to take up active military service is handled in the same manner as are discharges from any essential industry. Routine requests for Sicherstellung (Deferment) are made by the OT in the case of personnel considered indispensable usually as soon as such personnel are enrolled in the OT. No status whatsoever in OT affords, however, immunity from being eventually called up for active service in the Army.

(b) French Manpower

Integration of French Industry and Manpower into the German System

Inasmuch as, at one time, fully 90% of OT's personnel consisted of foreign manpower, recruiting methods employed by the Germans are discussed below in some detail. The system as set up in France was the most elaborate in German-occupied territory. The problem of French manpower supply was the most complex of its type that the Germans had to tackle in occupied Europe. The need to solve it was essential both from the strategic and tactical standpoint. France was the only large country in Europe which bordered on Germany and possessed great essential industries and industrial resources which could therefore be exploited with a minimum of traffic movement. The German war production authorities (Reichsministerium für Rüstung und Kriegsproduktion), at the head of which is Speer, accordingly geared the French war industries to Germany's war needs and integrated the allotment of French priority materials and distribution of industrial manpower in France within the scheme of total rationalisation of war resources at the disposal of the Reich. Administrative control in France for this purpose was established by setting up German Control Commissions which derived their power from the parent administration in the Reich. Thus the Reichsministerium für Rüstung und Kriegsproduktion set up its delegate staff in France, in Paris, which in turn established liaison with the Wehrmacht economic control commissions (as provided by the terms of the Franco-German Armistice). Similar arrangements were made by separate official bodies with specific missions.

Aktion Frankreich is the German Compulsory Labour Delegation in France representing the Plenipotentiary General for Manpower Allocation of all territories controlled by the Reich government, Fritz Sauckel.

From the tactical standpoint France was an outpost to Germany's inner defences and as such its coastline required adequate fortifications. This task, assigned to the OT, also required manpower running into the hundreds of thousands. It can be said here that in the Nazis' critical hour of need, despite the frantic efforts of Sauckel's staff in France during the latter half of 1943 and the first half of 1944, the French successfully managed to resist Sauckel's efforts at mass impressment of their manpower for war production in Germany and for similarly essential duties, including those of the OT, in France.

Reports which, although based on German sources, are believed to be reasonably accurate, place the French OT personnel in the West at 30% of Todt's total manpower in the EGW in 1944, all but a very minor fraction of which was employed in France, mainly along the Atlantic and Mediterranean coastlines. The backbone of the French skilled and semi-skilled personnel was supplied by French construction firms which had joined the OT.

The number of such firms is estimated at over 1,000, possibly reaching 1,500. There is no figure available for the average number of men employed by the French OT subcontractors; an estimate puts at at no more than twenty-five men per firm.

The age groups of the French OT workers could by and large be divided into two classes, one for those under twenty-one and the other for those over forty years of age. Men between twenty-one and forty were rare. One reason for this is the large number of French prisoners of war in German hands. Another reason was the urgency with which German labour authorities canvassed the French manpower supply for the war plants in Germany.

The subject of industrial manpower recruitment in France – part of which was allotted to the OT – was, as has already been remarked, the most pressing problem of its type facing the German labour authorities in occupied Europe and its study in view of the constant modifications to which regulations were subjected, leads to ramifications of labyrinthian proportions. Not much more than the features essential for a bare understanding of the problem in its entirety is given here. Understanding the labour situation in France will furnish the background necessary for an understanding of strategic labour distribution throughout German controlled Europe, including that of OT.

Regulations Governing Manpower Recruitment in France

The basic laws and regulations through which the Germans claimed to derive their authority to enforce their manpower requisitions were:

(1)   Article 52 of the Hague Convention.
(2)   Article 3 of the Franco-German Armistice Commission.
(3)   Occupation authorities regulation of 31 January 1942.
(4)   Verordnung Nr. 916 (Decree No. 916) of 27 March 1943.
(This decree by the Vichy government made all males eighteen to fifty and all females twenty-one to forty-five subject to compulsory labour. This decree was modified 2 February 1944 by extending the age of males to from sixteen to sixty and of females to from eighteen to forty-five. Males between sixteen and eighteen were exempt from conveyance to Germany, as were females.
(5)   Vichy Decree of 8 December 1943.
(6)   Vichy Decree of 8 Junuary 1944.

Three Phases of German Manpower Policy in France

German manpower policy in France may be divided into three phases.

The first phase lasted from the occupation of Northern France to the summer of 1942, an era of organisation and consolidation as far as the OT was concerned. It culminated in the appointment, in May 1942, of Dr Fritz Schmelter as Controller of OT Manpower and Director of Recruitment for the OT, the latter function by virtue of his membership on Sauckel's staff. Industrial manpower for Germany's war plants rated the highest priority after which came French industries working for Germany's account. All in all, OT's tasks had not acquired the urgency which made its manpower needs imperative, and OT-Firms were allowed, albeit unofficially, to increase their personnel through, their own individual efforts. This they did mainly by subcontracting French construction firms.

Additional labour from distant parts was recruited through the medium of professional 'crimps' which local labour was obtained through local recruiting offices set up both by the OT and by firms through newspaper advertisements and so forth. Minimum manpower requirements for priority projects were supplied by the local OBL administration through contact with the corresponding Feldkommandantur which at that time enjoyed the prestige of an apparently victorious conqueror. The situation consequently had nothing of the grimness in it which characterised the later manpower levies and raids. As a matter of fact, the scarcity of German personnel exceeded that of foreign labour and drove individual firms or even OBL Frontführer into sending recruiting agents into Germany.

Dearth of German OT personnel offered a serious problem inasmuch as firms could not operate unless they had at their disposal a minimum proportion of German supervisory personnel to direct the foreign labour in their employ. A comparatively lax administration in France, however, tolerated the unsanctioned methods of recruiting as described above, until the urgency of the situation no longer permitted such tolerance. In Germany the labour authorities entered a series of complaints, while the establishment of Arbeitsamt Nebenstellen (Branch Labour Bureaux) in OT Induction Centres made such irregular methods of recruiting an exception rather than the rule.

The second phase lasted from June 1942 to about the same time in 1943. At that time a comprehensive construction programme (Atlantikwall in the West, The Ostwall in the East, etc.) was assigned to the OT as part of the general defensive strategy which Germany had adopted in regard to her conquests in Europe. At the same time manpower was needed more than ever for war production in Germany and in France. The needs of the situation resulted in the co-ordination of manpower allotments to the OT with allotments to other essential industries in Germany and in France. In the early spring of 1943 French manpower quotas for the OT were filled on the basis of a priority equal to that given to German essential industries. In practice, however, authorities were unable to furnish the OT with more than a minimum sufficient for tasks which were considered urgent, such as the construction of V-sites, etc. Additional help had to be imported from Poland, Russia, Belgium, and other countries.

The third and last phase was characterised by the effort of the General Plenipotentiary for Manpower Allocation, Sauckel and his henchman, in France, Dr Ritter, (see Aktion Frankreich, below). By mid-year 1943, efforts to raise Germany's war production output had reached a critical stage. In the face of obstinate resistance on the part of the French, the general policy during the second stage had been to force Frenchmen to take essential war jobs in France if they were to avoid deportation to Germany. Such essential industries were classified 'S' industries, 'S' being the abbreviation for Sperrbetriebe (Closed Industries). Employees of an 'S' industry were exempt from removal by Labour Authorities or even the Wehrmacht. Conversely, an employee was subject to severe disciplinary action for unauthorised absence from employment of this type. The OT was classified an 'S' industry on 21 October 1943.

During this third phase, however, a reappraisal was made of the entire manpower supply throughout German-controlled Europe and of means and methods to co-ordinate it once and for all in the light of the critical war production situation in Germany and of a possible Allied invasion of Europe. A compromise was consequently necessary in France between the urgent need of putting to maximum use in France those Frenchmen whom the Germans were unable to transport forcibly to Germany, and the equally urgent need of furnishing German war industries with the maximum amount of foreign manpower and thus not only release Germans for the army but also build up industry where it was safest from enemy action. In this respect the OT was increasingly used in Germany not only on repair of air-raid damage but also in top priority industries such as synthetic plants.

Saukel's staff in France, June 1943 to June 1944 (see Aktion Frankreich, below), attempted to effect a working compromise on the basis of production requirements laid down by the Reichsministenum für Rüstung und Kriegsproduktion, by the following methods:

(1) By reorganising the classification of French industry. The Rü and V Betriebe (short for Rüstungs and Verpflegungsbetriebe, Armament and Food Industries) were reclassified 'S' betriebe. Agriculture and timber industries (termed E und Fo Betriebe) were placed on a priority level with 'S' industries. OT's priority within the 'S' group was on a level with that of the Salvage and Repair and Clothing industries. All industries outside of the 'S' group were considered unessential as far as tapping their sources of manpower were concerned.

(2) By combing out all but an irreducible minimum of male personnel from non-essential industries and all superfluous male personnel out of essential industries, for possible deportation to Germany. In this manner Frenchmen were to replace German workers called up for the Wehrmacht, and Frenchwomen were to fill the essential jobs vacated by Frenchmen.

Aktion Frankreich

Aktion Frankreich was that part of Aktion 44, the last great German manpower recruitment drive in Europe, which applied to France. It set up a quota of one million Frenchmen between the ages of eighteen to sixty to be deported to Germany, less 100,000 who were to be allotted to the OT in France. The rest of

Aktion 44 called for the following quotas: one million men from Italy; 600,000 men from the Baltic countries; 250,000 men each from Belgium and Holland; 100,000 men from the rest of occupied Europe; one million German women up to the age of fifty. The entire programme thus totalled 3,700,000 men and half a million women. In addition it called for the replacement by women of jobs vacated by foreign workers who were deported to Germany. Aktion 44 was to start official operations on 1 January 1944, but directives for its organisation go back at least as far as June 1943. Gigantic as the operation was in conception, it was still to be carried out ruthlessly. (Actually, however, only a minor fraction of the entire scheme was realised.)

At the head of it stood Fritz Sauckel whose full title is Beauftragter Göring für den Vierjahresplan, Generalbevollmächtigter für den Arbeitseinsatz im Reichsabeitsministerium, (Göring's Deputy for the 4 Year Plan, Plenipotentiary General for Manpower Allocation in the Reich Labour Ministry) abbreviated GBA. His offices are situated in the Reichsarbeitsministerium (Reich Labour Ministry) but are not part of the Ministry. His henchman for France was Dr Ritter whose title was GBA in Frankreich, abbreviated GBAF. The man responsible for the execution of Aktion 44 was Dr Oberregierungsrat Hötzel. Dr Fritz Schmelter, OT's manpower administrator, was appointed to the GBA's labour staff and was empowered to direct recruitment of labour for the OT within the European, area. Actually Schmelter's functions in this respect were routine administration, EG chiefs such as Weiss in EGW exercising such executive authority as was allotted to the OT under Aktion 44. In fact, as far as the EGW was concerned, the recruitment plans were to be submitted to Weiss for approval and such further directives as were issued by him were to be incorporated into the plans.

Allotments to Germany of French manpower thus obtained under Action Frankreich were effected by defining forty-two French zones, each of which acted as a manpower pool termed Patengau for a corresponding Gauarbeitsamt in Germany. Any manpower left available in a Patengau after the corresponding Gauarbeitsamt quota had been filled was to be transported to a central manpower pool in Germany. The rate of transfer was to be approximately 100,000 a month.

As far as the Franco-German political background in relation to manpower was concerned, the Sauckel-Laval Agreement, providing for a stabilisation of French Labour in Germany and a temporary halting of manpower transfers, expired on 1 January 1944. (This short-lived agreement had suited the Germans as much as it had the French, insofar as it gave them the time to re-appraise the situation on the basis of the projected Aktion Frankreich requirements, and to study the French reaction to the compulsory labour calling-up now that all Frenchman had been promised exemption from deportation to Germany.)

Negotiations between Laval and GABF for a resumption of transfers dragged on until some time in March 1944 and culminated in Propaganda Minister Henriot's efforts to recruit manpower for Germany by the power of persuasion. The results were negligible. In the meanwhile a new decree was published on 2 February 1944 which extended the labour service obligations of men from sixteen to sixty and that of women from eighteen to forty-five.

Henriot's commentary on the new measure left little doubt that it was intended to extend considerably the manpower draft for Germany. The class of 1944 which was called up in mid-February was not exempted from foreign labour service obligations as had been the class of 1943. Death sentences were imposed for offences of a serious nature on the part of employees who violated labour service regulations, with imprisonment and heavy fines as penalties in lesser cases.

The only conciliatory gesture was the extension from 1 January to 1 April 1944 of the amnesty granted to workmen who had failed to register for labour service or to appear for work in an essential industry such as the OT. Included in the amnesty were the 50,000 Frenchmen who had failed to return to work in Germany after their furlough in France had expired. Administering the above disciplinary regulation was the head of the French police, Joseph Darnand, in co-operation with the GBAF's counter-intelligence organisations (see below).

Methods and procedure of Action Frankreich were as follows:

Hauptabteilung Arbeit of Militärverwaltung Paris worked out a formula of French manpower requirements needed by the various industries and the OT, both in France and in Germany. The formula was called Aktion Frankreich. Inasmuch as it was based on manpower statistics of the year 1936, a Prüfungskommission (Examining Commission) was created to investigate the practicability of the Aktion and to make recommendations for workable modifications. Next the Auskämmungskommission (Commission for Weeding out and Requisitioning of Superfluous Manpower for French Trade, Industry and Agriculture) was established followed by the establishment of the Zuweisungskommission (Classification and Assignment Commission) which separated the fit from the unfit and designated who was to be deported to Germany and who was to be assigned to the OT and other essential industries in France. Those assigned to the OT were required to sign a Verpflichtungsbescheid (Certificate of Obligation, GBAF Compulsory Labour Decree Form of 8 October 1943, 2/5230 a) which made the conscripts' obligatory term of service of indefinite duration. Refusal to sign was to be noted on the form but did not invalidate the obligation. The work of the latter two commissions was performed by the French under German control, and with final decision in the hands of the German members of the commissions including the medical examiners. Orders had come through to class everyone destined for Germany 'physically fit' unless the contrary was undeniably obvious.

In that case the labour conscript was to be assigned to an essential industry in France if that was at all possible.

The GBAF took labour recruitment out of the Army's hands in France in August 1943 by the simple process of moving a GBAF staff into the offices of the Abteilung Arbeit in the various echelons of Army Administrative HQ and employing the existing Wehrmacht personnel as a clerical staff for matters which required going through military channels. The arrangement proved both uneconomical and productive of friction; consequently the former Wehrmacht staffs in the Abteilung Arbeit were reinstated in their functions in January 1944, but remained subordinated to a GBAF deputy left in executive control. To all intents and purposes they formed the GBAF staffs in the Feldkommandanturen.

The French Department was the basic political district for manpower quotas, which were communicated to the departmental prefecture by the Kommandant of the corresponding Feldkommandanturen on the basis of instructions from above. The prefect accordingly communicated instructions to the mayors of towns and rural communities in his department. From there on the requisitions were handled on the German side by the local GBAF personnel in the Feldkomnandanturen. The mayors sent part of their quota as they could assemble to the departmental depot (Sammellager). There the men were grouped into trade categories including those allotted to the OT. The allotment for the OT was convoyed by French police who in turn were watched by the Sicherheitsdienst (German Security Service). Those destined for Germany were sent by the various departments to a central depot where they were regrouped and transported to Germany. An agreement between the Vichy and Belgian collaborationist governments not to transport Belgian residents in France to Germany was not recognised by German Occupation authorities.

Below is a summary of the contents of an official Vichy document illustrating procedure used in forcible manpower levies for the OT.

The 'Secretariat Général à Main d'Oeuvre, Direction de la Main d'Oeuvre Encadree, Bureau des Mutations' issued an order dated 8 December 1943, ordering the forcible requisitioning for OBL Cherbourg of foreign workers residing in the south of France. The order was addressed to the Regional Directors of Manpower in Marseilles, Toulouse, Clermont-Ferrand, Montpellier and Limoges. Results falling short of expectations, a secret order went through, originating in the office of Colonel Thomas, Regional Chief of Group No. 1 of Manpower Formations. It fixed H hour of J day as the time for a concerted raid on foreign workers residing in Southern France, (No. 1169, 19 April 1944). The signal was to be an official routine telegram with the code word 'operate'. The mode of procedure was to be as outlined by Circular 8/T/4 of 24 Mar 1944. The order affected foreign workers aged eighteen to forty-five of the following nationalities: Armenians, Italians, Poles,

Russians and those Spaniards who were not covered by an acknowledgement of protection by their consulate, dated before 25 February 1944. The appointment was based on the relative importance of the industries to be raided, Spaniards seized in the raid were to be sent not to OT Cherbourg but to Germany.

Results of Aktion Frankreich were negligible; a total of some 50,000 men had been raised by 4 April 1944 despite frantic efforts of the GBAF organisation. In a confidential speech on that day, Sauckel berated the organisation for being ineffectual, and claimed that as a result he had been forced to requisition German women over forty-five years of age for labour service, against the Führer's express wishes.

German Counter-Intelligence Organisation of the GBAF

The negligible results produced by the GBAF organisation led to the establishment of a counter-intelligence network created specifically to assist forcible impressment. This constituted the following organisations:

(1) Schutzkorps (SE)

(The 'Schutzkorps' here mentioned is not to be confused with Schutzkorps comprising the Sohutzkommando units in OT). Created 13 April 1944, the GBAF Schutzkorps formed the counter-intelligence corps proper. It consisted of a body of 600 men dressed in civilian clothes. It was administratively subordinated to the SD or Sicherhetsdienst (Security Service) in Paris. The men were distributed among the Feldkommandanturen where they were controlled lay the local GBAF leader who received daily reports from the local SD office on the labour situation in the area. The men acted both as agents-provocateurs or as labour propagandists, where the situation warranted.

(2) Liga für Soziale Ordnung und Gerechtigkeit (League for Social Order and Justice)

Created in May 1944, the Liga was the code name for a body of 3,000 collaborationist 'recruiting agents' prepared to use effective methods in dealing with obstinate cases. They were allotted to the Feldkommandanturen in detachments of fifty men.

(3) Komitee für Sozialen Frieden (Committee for Social Peace)

Created in May 1944, the Komitee für Sozialen Frieden was the code name for a collaborationist auxiliary police corps of 5,000 men placed under administrative command of the Allgemeine SS. Its functions were: to make French authorities who had been carrying on a covert campaign of sabotage 'see the light'; to help carry through measures for the transfer of workers to Germany, especially in

In newly liberated Cherbourg, American soldiers assist the locals in removing another emblem of the German occupation at the OT offices. The sign reads, 'Organisation Todt, Einsatzgruppe West, OBL Cherbourg'. *(NARA)*

respect to tracking down those absent without leave from German factories, etc, and service dodgers; to report on popular sentiment and the influence of enemy propaganda. In connection with the second of their functions they had received Sauckel's written instructions to permit convoys on their way to Germany to sing the 'Marseillaise' or the 'Internationale' or for that matter any anti-Nazi song until they arrived in Germany, at which time 'they would be taught to sing a different song very quickly'.

The authorities of the latter two bodies were co-ordinated by Oberregierungsrat Meinckle. In fact they were commonly regarded as forming one organisation, called Komitee und Liga. An initial appropriation of 3 million RM was set aside as an expense fund. Out of it, among other expenses, premiums were paid for every prospect brought in: 10 RM for unskilled workers and 20 RM for skilled workers.

Conclusion

Aside from the fact that Germany was losing the war and as a consequence, resistance in occupied Europe was stiffening in proportion to Germany's need for collaboration the two key factors which caused labour conscription for Germany's benefit to bog down in France at the time of her greatest need were the French prefects of the Departments and the British radio propaganda. The German Feldkommandanturen who were the military channels for dealing with the French prefects and through them with the French population were, for the most part, veterans of the First World War, and were no match for the Frenchmen, practically all astute politicians. If the Feldkommandanturen did not have their way, at least they were provided with excellent reasons for partial or total failure, reasons which in reports to higher echelons read at least as well as those or the adjoining Feldkommandanturen.

(c) Belgian and Dutch Manpower

Age Groups and Emphasis on Racial Kinship

The Belgian and Dutch labour problem as handled by the German authorities can, for the purpose of this study, be assumed to be an extension of the French labour problem. The fact that the emphasis on German exploitation in France was industrial, while in Belgium and Holland it was political , makes it unsafe, however, to draw too close a comparison. For example, all but approximately 50,000 Belgian prisoners of war were released from PoW camps by the Germans. The Belgian age group of twenty-five to forty in the OT is therefore comparatively much larger than that of French for example. Another point is the relative deference which the Germans paid to the Nederlandsch Verbond van Vakverenigingen (Dutch Trade Union Association) comprising over 600,000 members. While it had been the German policy in France to keep collaborationist groups divided, and to play one off against the other, German policy in Holland was not to antagonise the Dutch Labour Unions, in the hope of obtaining co-operation on the basis of racial kinship. A third point is that there was a greater proportion of Belgian and Dutch OT personnel in responsible positions than French.

(d) Englishmen in OT

Guernsey, Jersey and Alderney Islands

The English in the OT are confined to the Channel Isles. Indications are that their number is small and that they are under at least some measure of compulsion.

(e) Norwegian and Danish Manpower

Proportion of Norwegians and Danes in the OT and Their Assignments
The Norwegians and Danes have been so unwilling to enrol in the OT that the Germans were compelled to import manpower consisting of Russians, Polish, Czech, Greek and Serb PoWs and Croat, Belgium Dutch, Italian and French volunteers. Calling up of the age classes twenty-one to twenty-three for Compulsory National Labour Service in May 1944, brought a response estimated at approximately 10%. Norwegians are found in comparatively large proportion in OT-NSKK and Legion Speer units, and, to a somewhat lesser extent, in SK units in Norway. Recruiting for the SS amongst Norwegian OT workers has been carried on, on an intense scale for the last two years.

(f) Italian Manpower

Fascists and Anti-Fascists
Available sources of information indicate that Italians form a smaller group in OT field personnel than might be assumed from the fact that Italy and Germany were in close co-operation over a period of years. There were several reasons for this. One was the basic jealousy of an independent government of its prerogatives over its own nationals and in controlling strategic defense work within its own domain. Another reason was the fact that recruitment for war production work in Germany was considered more imperative than recruitment for the OT.

(One qualification which should be made to the above statement is the fact that it appears that at the present time there are a number of Italians in Germany working for the OT in industrial plants. Their number may amount to 100,000.) When the Badoglio government withdrew from the Axis and declared war on Germany, non-fascist Italians were impressed locally by the Army for erecting defence work as prisoners or hostages of war rather than as compulsory OT labour. Fascist Italians in German controlled Italy on the other hand were in a position to volunteer for the OT as one way of complying with the Fascio government's Labour Service Regulations. This they did all the more readily in as much as OT pay scales were by far higher than anything offered by Italian concerns and individual employers. Next to the concentrations in Italy, notably in the Alps, Italian personnel was most numerous along the French Mediterranean coast and in the Cherbourg and Calais area. Except for personnel of the Italian divisions at one time stationed in the French Riviera, and enrolled in the OT, the preponderant age groups of Italians in the OT are below twenty-one and over forty. It is possible that some volunteer Italians in the OT in France are still in such beleaguered garrisons as La Rochelle and Lorient: more probably however, the larger number has been evacuated into Germany.

(g) Spaniards in the OT

'Insurgents' and 'Republicans'

The Spaniards in OT were in a somewhat similar political position to the Italians. There were two basic Spanish groups: Republican Spaniards ranging in political conviction from mild Republicanism to Anarchism and grouped by the Germans under the headings of Rotspanier (Red Spaniards), pro-Franco Spaniards who joined the OT for personal and economic reasons. The first group consisted of three subgroups; Republican Civil War soldiers interned in France and fallen in the German hands; those who had escaped from the internment camps and had taken up residence in France; and finally those who had accepted deportation from Spanish jails to feed Germany's industrial manpower needs, as the lesser of two evils. As far as the political status of Spaniards residing in France was concerned, subjects of neutral nations obviously were not liable for compulsory labour. A Spanish resident in France might, however, be forcibly inducted through lack of proper papers which he had been unable to obtain from the Spanish consulates in France. Convoys of Spanish workers arrived at OT centres continuously during 1943 and the first half of 1944. Subsequently a large number of them deserted.

When the French authorities in the spring of 1944 combed southern France for manpower for German essential industries, including the OT, they had specific orders to earmark for transport to Germany Spaniards who had no adequate papers in their possession. OT's needs were, however, not ignored; part of the shortage of tunnelling specialists including 'sand-hogs' was met by allotting Asturians and other Spanish miners to the organisation. Some of these Zwangsarbeiter are still on Alderney Isle at present. Similarly 'Rotspanier' (Loyalist Spaniards) were allotted to the OT-NSKK as motor vehicle drivers. Inasmuch as regulations did not permit the employment of Zwangsarbeiter SK in the NSKK and Rotspanier were of Zwangsarbeiter status, the term of Rotspanier for this type of personnel was replaced by Transportspanier. Next to the Belgians, Dutch, and Danes, the Spanish personnel had probably the highest proportion of military age groups. It is a practical certainty that the Germans did not succeed in evacuating more than a minor fraction of Spaniards out of France after D-Day.

(h) Baltic Manpower

Proportion and Status

Esthonians, Lithuanians, Latvians, as a racial group, were considered superior to Rumanians, Croats, etc., even though their political standing was lower. They do not form a considerable element in the OT and are composed of volunteers and the residue of those who were left at German disposal after the selection of men for SS Baltic Legions and for war production in Germany.

(i) Russian Volunteers

'Vlasov' Russian Units
The following is a quotation from secondary sources, dated April 1945:

> The German authorities have announced that from this week all Russians in Germany will receive most-favoured-nation treatment, with food and wages on a scale that has hitherto applied only to the best paid foreign workers.
>
> They have stated also that they will no longer deduct 15% of all wages, as they have done up to the present, and Himmler has proclaimed that anybody who allows any injustice to Russian workers employed in Germany will be severely punished. These orders complete the promotion by stages of Russian workers since last year from the lowest to the highest grade.
>
> What is even more significant, an agreement between the renegade Russian General Vlasov and the chief of the SS seems to show that the Germans have decided to abandon the idea of sending large units of armed Russians to the front. According to this agreement Russians organised as military units and commanded by renegade Russian officers will henceforth be placed under the Todt organisation for non-combatant tasks instead of directly 'fighting Bolshevism and liberating the homeland', as formerly advertised.
>
> These Russians of Vlasov's 'army' will receive from this week even better financial treatment than the labourers of the otherwise most favoured nations. An agreement says explicitly – apparently to avoid any disappointment among the men at being switched over from sword to shovel – that 'besides military pay soldiers of this auxiliary army will receive also payment for their labour according to the Todt Organisation's rates. Food will also be plentiful and its quality good. Their spiritual requirement will be satisfied by the chief of the propaganda department of the Committee for Liberating the Peoples of Russia. Vlasov has appointed a special general staff for the Todt service with an engineer named Popov as its chief.

(k) Balkan Manpower

Collaborationist
Hungarians, Bulgarians, Rumanians, Croats and Slovaks are not found in large numbers in the OT inasmuch as they remain under immediate control of their government even though the policy pursued was dictated from Berlin. Those who were in a position to volunteer for the OT were at the same time able to

choose the location of their employment. The West, because of the higher wages paid there, was first choice; Norway was second choice. The group in France contained in addition Hungarians, etc., who had been residents there for some time. Men of military age are in the minority among these groups.

Enemy

The Balkan nationals of enemy countries: Greeks, Serbs, Albanians, were put on a level with the Ostarbeiter (see below) as far as treatment was concerned. The military age groups in this category were small. These Balkan nationals were employed locally on road construction, exploitation of mines, etc. This type of labour proved notably undependable and irresponsible. Small groups of Greek, Serbian and Albanian volunteers were to be found in France, especially in the south, and probably there are some equally small groups In Norway at present.

(1) Ostbarbeiter
Hilfswillige and Others

The next lower category in accordance with Nazi racial doctrine comprised the Ostarbeiter (Ukrainians, white Ruthenians and people from regions eastward, as well as regions east of Latvia and Esthonia whose inhabitants had been moved out and whose land had been resettled by Germans) and the Turkomans. The proportion of military age in this category is greater than in the case of the Russian and Balkan natives. Volunteers of military age were, however, apt to find themselves in the Ost Legion before the OT got to them. Apparently they were transported west in large groups. They were scheduled for evacuation after D-Day. It must be assumed that the Germans succeeded in evacuating at least half of the original contingent.

The term Hilfswillige (volunteer assistant labourers) specially refers to Ostarbeiter volunteers for the OT.

Indo-Chinese and North Africans

Colonials from the Far East such as Indo-Chinese (Annamites, Siamese, etc.) were employed, it is believed, exclusively in Southern France. On the other hand North Africans (Moroccans, Senegalese, etc.) were scattered fairly evenly throughout the French Atlantic Coast with a heavy contingent probably running into the thousands on the Channel Isles.

(n) Zwangsarbeiter (Forced Labour)
Communists, Partisans, Jews, Special Convict Units

Russians and Spanish communists, Polish and Czech conscripts, partisans, convicts (German soldiers and foreign civilians), miscellaneous politically hostile elements (foreign), workers considered untractable, homosexuals, Jews,

Above: Photograph from the 1943 book celebrating Fritz Todt's life and work, featuring a large 'schiffsbunker', literally a protective bunker for ships, located in an unnamed harbour on the western coast of France.

Battered by the British Tall Boy and Grand Slam bombs, the impressive blockhaus at Watten – located a few miles to the north-east of Omer on the Pas de Calais – was built as an assembly and launch facility for the V-2 rockets. Construction had commenced in March 1943, and two workers' camps were built near the site to house PoWs from Eastern Europe and Russia. Its 18-foot thick flat concrete roof was designed to withstand the biggest bombs. *(CMcC)*

part-Jews and state-less individuals comprised the lowest category, that of Zwangsarbeiter. Ages in this category are as unlimited as they are in the highest category, that of the Germans themselves. Russian boys of twelve have been mentioned in captured OT documents, while those of fourteen are taken for granted. The Germans did not manage to any considerable extent to put their hands on Russian youths approaching the age of military usefulness outside of those which were seized in the early stages of the war and have since matured by three years. This limitation does not however apply to the Poles, Czechs, etc.

Russians, Poles, and, to a lesser extent, Czechs formed, strategic reserves of manpower pools which were shifted to priority locations. Thus tens of thousands were transferred to the West, particularly the Atlantic coast in France, in the winter of 1943, presumably to assist in the constriction of V-sites and equally urgent tasks. The same holds true for fortifications and construction in Norway and Jutland.

A mass levy of 150,000 Hungarian Jews was made in August 1944. This levy had probably been proceeded by similar forcible levies, mainly recruited from Central Europe and the Balkans.

There were two special formations of convict labour in France whose only connection to the OT is that that were detailed to it. The first is the SS Baubrigade of which there are known to exist at present: SS Baubrigaden 1, 3 and 5. These are formations of German political and other convicts from German concentration camps formed into convict labour details and loaned to the Army, Air Force and OT authorities.

The brigade personnel is composed of inmates of various concentration camps but for reasons of expediency is, as a unit, under the administrative authority of one camp. The brigades come under the central administrative authority of the SS Wirtschafts- und Verwaltung Hauptamt. They are convoyed to their assignment by the concentration camp SS personnel, where they are taken over by the OT, Army etc. guards, as the case may be. It is assumed that while there have been some escapes, the greater number of such personnel in France, Belgium and Holland have been successfully evacuated. The second formation comprised two distinct subgroups; the first consisted of political internees from French concentration camps; the second consisted of French convicts who were serving two-year, or shorter, sentences. The latter were farmed out to the OT by the Vichy Government to whom the OT paid 35 francs per day per convict.

All Jews in France between the ages of twenty to thirty-one (July 1943) and all Jews of 1924 Class (June 1944) were assigned to the OT.

The OT is known to have used and is still using prisoners of war, particularly Russians. This type of labour is, however, outside the range of this handbook.

On trial at Nuremburg

Fritz Sauckel, fourth from the left on the top row, in the dock at Nuremburg. Albert Speer is out of shot to the right. Their fellow defendants shown in this photograph are, from left to right on the top row: Karl Dönitz, leader of the Kriegsmarine and, following Hitler's death, the temporary President of Germany; Erich Raeder, the former head of the Kriegsmarine; Baldur von Schirach, head of the Hitler-Jugend, the Hitler Youth; Fritz Sauckel, General Plenipotentiary for Labour Deployment. In the front row is Hermann Göring, head of the Lufwaffe and Hitler's designated successor at one time; then there is an empty space for Rudolf Hess, Hitler's former deputy; next comes Joachim von Ribbentrop, the racial theory ideologist who became Minister of the Eastern Occupied Territories; Wilhelm Keitel, the Oberkommando der Wehrmacht (Supreme Commander of the Armed Forces) who was, in effect, the war minister under Adolf Hitler. To the far right of the dock are Alfred Jodl and Alfred Rosenberg. *(US Army Signal Corps)*

Postscript

At the end of the war only two individuals directly concerned with the running of the Organisation Todt actually appeared in the dock at the International War Tribunal held at Nuremburg between 20 November 1945 and 1 October 1947. The main tribunal was tasked with trying twenty-three of the most important political leaders of the Third Reich; or at least the surviving leaders, as by this time Hitler, Himmler and Goebbels had all commited suicide, and one of the defendants, Martin Bormann, was tried *in absentia*. Another defendant, Robert Ley, who had been the head of the Deutsche Arbeitsfront (DAF) – the German Labour Front – committed suicide in October 1945 before the trial commenced.

Fritz Sauckel, the Gauleiter of Thuringia 1927–45, and Plenipotentiary of the Nazi slave labour programme between 1942 and 1945, was found guilty of War Crimes and of Crimes Against Humanity and sentenced to death. He was hanged on 16 October 1946.

Albert Speer, the Nazi architect who succeeded Fritz Todt as head of the OT in 1942 and also became the Minister of Armaments and War Production, was also accused of War Crimes and Crimes Against Humanity; the charges in particular relating to the use of slave laborours from the occupied territories. Found guilty on both counts he escaped execution as he had been, in the judge's words, 'one of the few men who had the courage to tell Hitler that the war was lost and to take steps to prevent the senseless destruction of production facilities both in occupied territories and in Germany. He carried out his opposition to Hitler's scorched earth programme ... by deliberately sabotaging it at considerable personal risk.'

During the trial Speer made no attempt to shirk his responsibility or his guilt, and he later became known as 'the Nazi who said sorry'. He was sentenced to twenty years imprisonment at Spandau Prison in Berlin. Speer served his full sentence and was released on 1 October 1966. A controversial figure to the end, he died of natural causes while on a visit to London in 1981.

Charts

The following selection of charts is reproduced from the 1945 Handbook. Note that the original publications does contain several more but these have not been omitted as they were not suitable for clear reproduction. For reference, here is the full list of charts:

1. General Organisation of the OT – shown opposite.
2. OT HQ Structure on Various Levels – shown on page 250.
3. Table of Mobile OT Units as Acitivated for the 7th Army, 18 May 1944.
4a. Organisation Todt – Zentrale (OTZ) Berlin (as of June 1944).
4b. Current Organisation of AMT Bau-OTZ.
5a. Organisation of an Einsatzgruppe HQ.
5b. Organisation of an Einsatzgruppe (Area Control Staff, Army Group Level) HQ.
5c. Current Organisation of an Einsatz HQ in Germany.
6a. Organisation of an Oberbauleitung HQ in German Occupied West (June 1944).
6b. Current Organisation of an Oberbauleitung (Basic OT Construction Sector and Administrative HQ) in Germany.
7. Organisation of a Frontführung (Front Area Personnel Section) on OBL Level in German Occupied West (June 1944).
8. Status of the German Building Industry in the Reich Economic System.
9. Personnel Administration of a Construction Firm or Combine – shown on page 252.
10. 1-6 Insiginia – see colour section.
11. Organisation of an OT-Firm HQ – shown on page 253.

The map showing OT Einsatzgruppen, Autumn 1944, is reproduced on page 172.

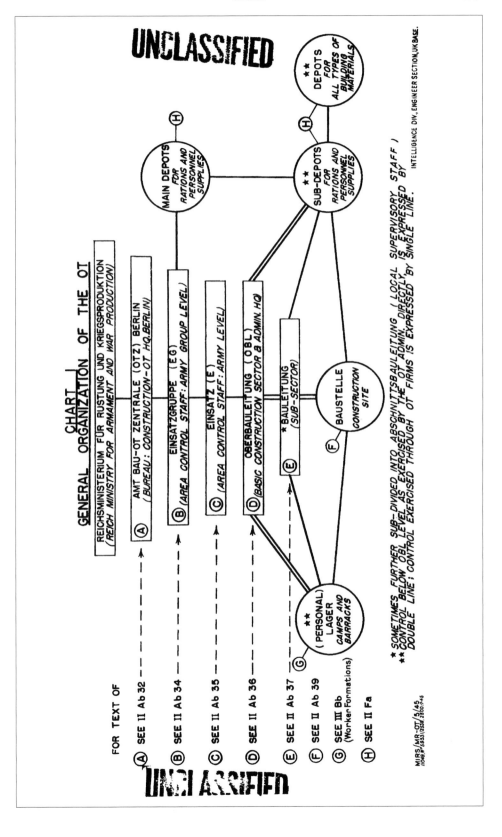

UNCLASSIFIED

CHART I
GENERAL ORGANIZATION OF THE OT

REICHSMINISTERIUM FÜR RÜSTUNG UND KRIEGSPRODUKTION
(REICH MINISTRY FOR ARMAMENT AND WAR PRODUCTION)

Ⓐ AMT BAU-OT ZENTRALE (OTZ) BERLIN
(BUREAU: CONSTRUCTION-OT HQ.BERLIN)

Ⓑ EINSATZGRUPPE (EG)
(AREA CONTROL STAFF: ARMY GROUP LEVEL)

Ⓒ EINSATZ (E)
(AREA CONTROL STAFF: ARMY LEVEL)

Ⓓ OBERBAULEITUNG (OBL)
(BASIC CONSTRUCTION SECTOR & ADMIN. HQ)

Ⓔ * BAULEITUNG
(SUB-SECTOR)

Ⓕ BAUSTELLE
CONSTRUCTION SITE

Ⓖ ** (PERSONAL)
LAGER
CAMPS AND
BARRACKS

Ⓗ MAIN DEPOTS FOR RATIONS AND PERSONNEL SUPPLIES

Ⓗ ** SUB-DEPOTS FOR RATIONS AND PERSONNEL SUPPLIES

** DEPOTS FOR ALL TYPES OF BUILDING MATERIALS.

FOR TEXT OF

Ⓐ SEE II Ab 32
Ⓑ SEE II Ab 34
Ⓒ SEE II Ab 35
Ⓓ SEE II Ab 36
Ⓔ SEE II Ab 37
Ⓕ SEE II Ab 39
Ⓖ SEE III Bb (Worker Formations)
Ⓗ SEE II Fa

* SOMETIMES FURTHER SUB-DIVIDED INTO ABSCHNITTSBAULEITUNG (LOCAL SUPERVISORY STAFF)
** CONTROL BELOW OBL LEVEL AS EXERCISED BY THE OT ADMIN. DIRECTLY IS EXPRESSED BY
DOUBLE LINE; CONTROL EXERCISED THROUGH OT FIRMS IS EXPRESSED BY SINGLE LINE.

INTELLIGENCE DIV, ENGINEER SECTION, UK BASE.

MIRS/MR-OT/5/45.
11048.Nᵒ6933/17234 23000-7-45

UNCLASSIFIED

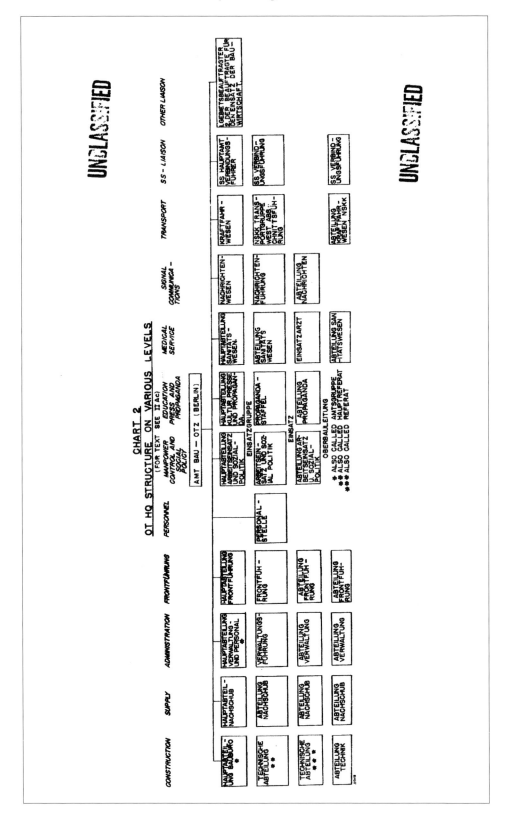

UNCLASSIFIED

CHART 2

OT HQ STRUCTURE ON VARIOUS LEVELS

(FOR TEXT SEE II Ac)

AMT BAU — OTZ (BERLIN)

EINSATZGRUPPE

EINSATZ

OBERBAULEITUNG

* ALSO CALLED AMTSGRUPPE
** ALSO CALLED HAUPTREFERAT
*** ALSO CALLED REFERAT

CONSTRUCTION — SUPPLY — ADMINISTRATION — FRONTFÜHRUNG — PERSONNEL — MANPOWER CONTROL AND SOCIAL POLICY — EDUCATION PRESS AND PROPAGANDA — MEDICAL SERVICE — SIGNAL COMMUNICATIONS — TRANSPORT — SS-LIAISON — OTHER LIAISON

HAUPTABTEILUNG BAUBÜRO *
HAUPTABTEIL-NACHSCHUB
HAUPTABTEILUNG VERWALTUNG UND PERSONAL *
HAUPTABTEILUNG FRONTFÜHRUNG
PERSONAL-STELLE
HAUPTABTEILUNG ARBEITSEINSATZ UND SOZIAL POLITIK
HAUPTABTEILUNG KULTUR PRESSE UND PROPAGANDA.
HAUPTABTEILUNG SANITÄTS-WESEN.
NACHRICHTEN-WESEN
KRAFTFAHR-WESEN
SS HAUPTAMT VERBINDUNGS-FÜHRER
GEBIETSBEAUFTRAGTER BEI LUFTRAGTE FÜR DEN EINSATZ DER BAU-WIRTSCHAFT.

TECHNISCHE ABTEILUNG **
ABTEILUNG NACHSCHUB
VERWALTUNGS-FÜHRUNG
FRONTFÜH-RUNG
ARBEITSEIN-SATZ UND SOZIAL POLITIK
PROPAGANDA-STAFFEL
ABTEILUNG SANITÄTS WESEN
NACHRICHTEN-FÜHRUNG
NSKK TRANS-PORTGRUPPE WEST ABSCHNITTSFÜH-RUNG
SS VERBIND-UNGSFÜHRUNG

TECHNISCHE ABTEILUNG ***
ABTEILUNG NACHSCHUB
ABTEILUNG VERWALTUNG
ABTEILUNG FRONTFÜH-RUNG
ABTEILUNG ARBEITSEINSATZ U. SOZIAL POLITIK
ABTEILUNG PROPAGANDA
EINSATZ ARZT
ABTEILUNG NACHRICHTEN

ABTEILUNG TECHNIK
ABTEILUNG NACHSCHUB
ABTEILUNG VERWALTUNG
ABTEILUNG FRONTFÜH-RUNG
ABTEILUNG SANITÄTSWESEN
ABTEILUNG KRAFTFAHR-WESEN NSKK
SS VERBIND-UNGSFÜHRUNG

UNCLASSIFIED

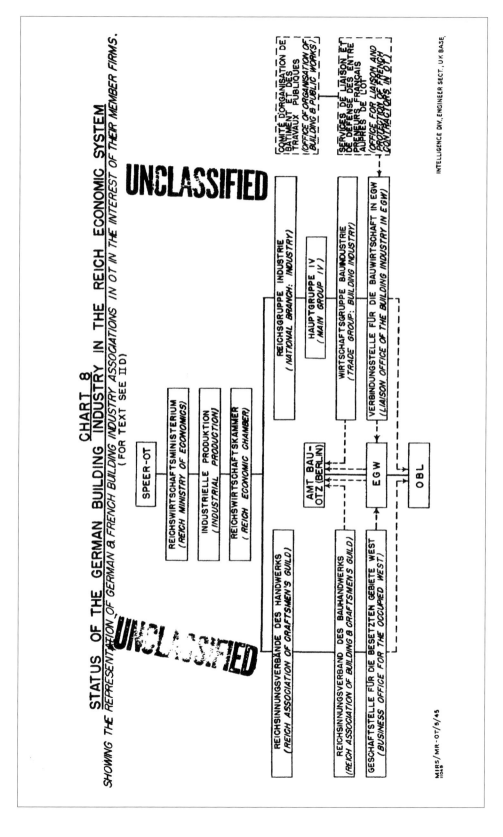

CHART 8
STATUS OF THE GERMAN BUILDING INDUSTRY IN THE REICH ECONOMIC SYSTEM
SHOWING THE REPRESENTATION OF GERMAN & FRENCH BUILDING INDUSTRY ASSOCIATIONS IN OT IN THE INTEREST OF THEIR MEMBER FIRMS.
(FOR TEXT SEE II D)

SPEER-OT

REICHSWIRTSCHAFTSMINISTERIUM
(REICH MINISTRY OF ECONOMICS)

INDUSTRIELLE PRODUKTION
(INDUSTRIAL PRODUCTION)

REICHSWIRTSCHAFTSKAMMER
(REICH ECONOMIC CHAMBER)

REICHSGRUPPE INDUSTRIE
(NATIONAL BRANCH: INDUSTRY)

HAUPTGRUPPE IV
(MAIN GROUP IV)

WIRTSCHAFTSGRUPPE BAUINDUSTRIE
(TRADE GROUP: BUILDING INDUSTRY)

VERBINDUNGSTELLE FÜR DIE BAUWIRTSCHAFT IN EGW
(LIAISON OFFICE OF THE BUILDING INDUSTRY IN EGW)

COMITÉ D'ORGANISATION DE
BATIMENT ET DES
TRAVAUX PUBLIQUES
(OFFICE OF ORGANISATION OF
BUILDING & PUBLIC WORKS)

SERVICES DE LIAISON ET
DE DEFENSE DES ENTRE
PRENEURS FRANÇAIS
AUTRES DE L'OT.
(OFFICE FOR LIAISON AND
PROTECTION OF FRENCH
CONTRACTORS IN OT)

UNCLASSIFIED

AMT BAU-
OTZ (BERLIN)

EGW

OBL

REICHSINNUNGSVERBÄNDE DES HANDWERKS
(REICH ASSOCIATION OF CRAFTSMEN'S GUILD)

REICHSINNUNGSVERBAND DES BAUHANDWERKS
(REICH ASSOCIATION OF BUILDING & CRAFTSMEN'S GUILD)

GESCHÄFTSTELLE FÜR DIE BESETZTEN GEBIETE WEST
(BUSINESS OFFICE FOR THE OCCUPIED WEST)

UNCLASSIFIED

INTELLIGENCE DIV., ENGINEER SECT., UK BASE.

MIRS/MR-OT/5/45
1104b

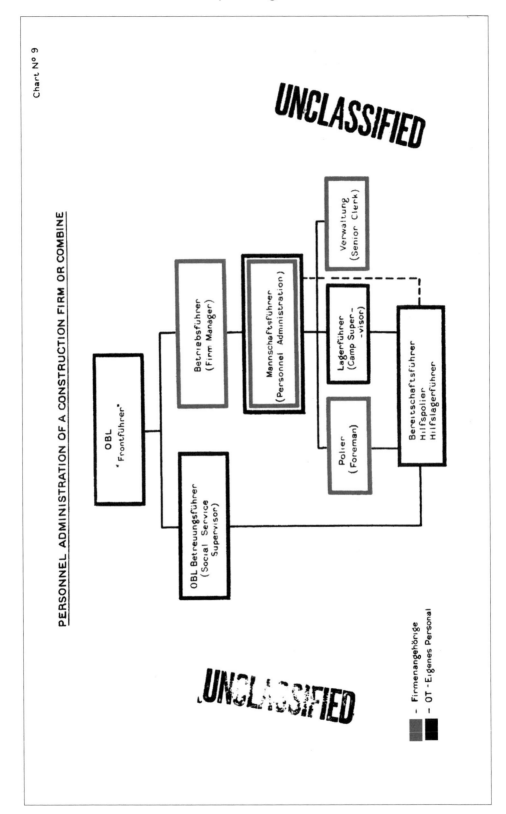

UNCLASSIFIED

PERSONNEL ADMINISTRATION OF A CONSTRUCTION FIRM OR COMBINE

OBL
"Frontführer"

Betriebsführer
(Firm Manager)

Mannschaftsführer
(Personnel Administration)

Verwaltung
(Senior Clerk)

Lagerführer
(Camp Super-
-visor)

Polier
(Foreman)

Bereitschaftsführer
Hilfspolier
Hilfslagerführer

OBL Betreuungsführer
(Social Service
Supervisor)

UNCLASSIFIED

– Firmenangehörige

– OT - Eigenes Personal

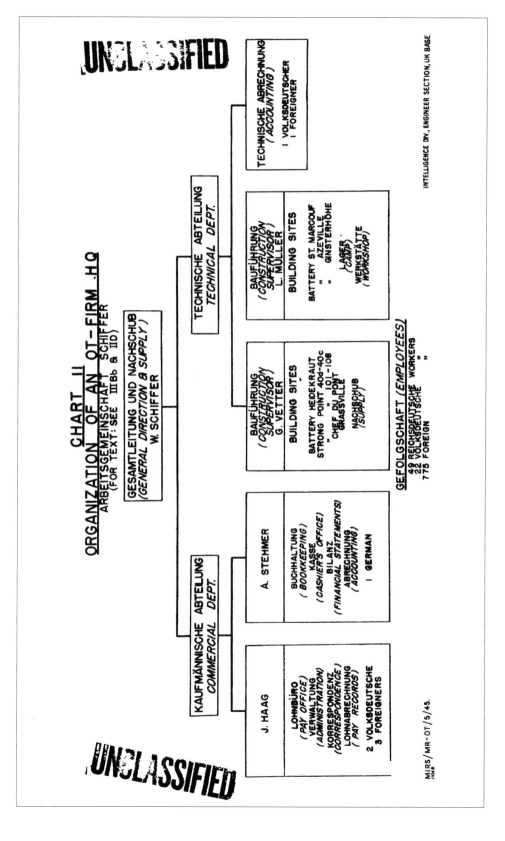

CHART II
ORGANIZATION OF AN OT-FIRM HQ
ARBEITSGEMEINSCHAFT SCHIFFER
(FOR TEXT: SEE IIBb & IID)

GESAMTLEITUNG UND NACHSCHUB
(GENERAL DIRECTION & SUPPLY)
W. SCHIFFER

KAUFMÄNNISCHE ABTEILUNG
COMMERCIAL DEPT.

TECHNISCHE ABTEILUNG
TECHNICAL DEPT.

J. HAAG

LOHNBÜRO
(PAY OFFICE)
VERWALTUNG
(ADMINISTRATION)
KORRESPONDENZ
(CORRESPONDENCE)
LOHNABRECHNUNG
(PAY RECORDS)
2 VOLKSDEUTSCHE
3 FOREIGNERS

A. STEHMER

BUCHHALTUNG
(BOOKKEEPING)
KASSE
(CASHIER'S OFFICE)
BILANZ
(FINANCIAL STATEMENTS)
ABRECHNUNG
(ACCOUNTING)
1 GERMAN

BAUFÜHRUNG
(CONSTRUCTION
SUPERVISOR)
G. VETTER
BUILDING SITES
BATTERY HEDEKRAUT
STRONG POINT 40d-40c
"   "   101-108
CHEF DU PONT
GRASSVILLE
NACHSCHUB
(SUPPLY)

BAUFÜHRUNG
(CONSTRUCTION
SUPERVISOR)
L. MÜLLER
BUILDING SITES
BATTERY ST. MARCOUF
"   AZEVILLE
"   GINSTERHÖHE
LAGER
(CAMP)
WERKSTÄTTE
(WORKSHOP)

TECHNISCHE ABRECHNUNG
(ACCOUNTING)
1 VOLKSDEUTSCHER
1 FOREIGNER

GEFOLGSCHAFT (EMPLOYEES)
48 REICHSDEUTSCHE WORKERS
22 VOLKSDEUTSCHE   "
775 FOREIGN

INTELLIGENCE DIV., ENGINEER SECTION, UK BASE.

MIRS/MR-OT/5/45.
1048

Bibliography

English-language books:

Very little has been published on the Organisation Todt in English. However, there are a number of books on the end products of its construction activities. The following are of interest:

Hitler's Engineers – Fritz Todt and Albert Speer – Master Builders of the Third Reich, by Blaine Taylor, Casement, 2010.
Driving Germany: The Landscape of the Autobahn, 1930–1970, by Thomas Zeller, Berghahn Books, 2007.
Wehrmacht Auxiliary Forces, by N. Thomas & C. Caballero, Osprey Publishing, 2005.
Hitler's Siegfried Line, by Neil Short, Sutton Publishing, 2002.
Hitler's Atlantic Wall, by Anthony Saunders, Sutton Publishing, 2001.
Hitler's V-Weapons Sites, by Philip Henshall, Sutton Publishing, 2002.
Fortress Europe – Hitler's Atlantic Wall, by George Forty, Ian Allan, 2002.

German-language books include:

Die Organisation Todt: Bauen für Staat und Wehrmacht, 1938–1945, by Franz W.
    Seidler, Bernard & Graefe, 1987.
Phantom Alpenfestung? Die geheimen Bauplane der Organisation Todt, by Franz
    W. Seidler.
Fritz Todt: Baumeister des Dritten Reichs, by Franz Seidler, Bublies Siegfried, 2000.

A number of books on the building of the Reichsautobahn and the Organisation
Todt were published by the Nazis in the 1930s. The following have been
consulted in the production of this book:

Fritz Todt – der Mensch, der Ingenieur, der Nationalsozialist, Verlag Gerhard
    Stalling, Oldenburg 1943.
Bauen und Kampfen – Gedichte und Bilder vom Einsatz der Frontarbeiter, Verlag
    Georg D. W. Callwey.
Arbeit an den Strassen Adolf Hitlers – a series of photographic year books.
Reichsautobahnen vom Ersten Spatenstich – zur Fertigen Fahrbahn, Edited by
    Dr Otto Reismann.

Journals and magazines:

Signal, Der Frontarbeiter and *Der Wehrmacht*.

Acknowledgements

The images used in this book have come from a number of sources in addition to the editor's collection. These include the US National Archives (NARA) and the US Army Signal Corps, the Wolfsonian – Florida International University Miami Beach, Florida, The Mitchell Wolfson Jr. Collection, Sjam2004, C-Mezzo-1, Sorin Lingureanu, Man vyi, Pawl 'pbm' Szubert, DSMD and Campbell McCutcheon (CMcC).

Other images are from John Christopher's collection. New photography of the Éperlecques blockhaus at Watten and of the Betterie Todt is also by the editor.